Balzac and the Human Comedy

Balzac *and*

The Human Comedy

By *PHILIPPE BERTAULT*

English version by Richard Monges

NEW YORK UNIVERSITY PRESS   1963

© 1963 BY NEW YORK UNIVERSITY
LIBRARY OF CONGRESS CATALOG CARD NUMBER: 63–19362
MANUFACTURED IN THE UNITED STATES OF AMERICA

*The original French edition of this book appeared under
the title* Balzac *and was published by Hatier, Paris.*

CONTENTS

v

Biographical Sketch

BALZAC'S work is so closely related to his life that in the course of this study it will be necessary to stress certain biographical facts in order to cast light on the genesis and the composition of *La Comédie Humaine*.[1] This brief sketch recalls certain events that are usefully kept in mind in order to understand thoroughly the character of the author and to follow the unfolding of his destiny.

Honoré de Balzac was born at Tours on May 20, 1799. Together with his sister Laure, he was brought up by a nurse in Saint-Cyr, a suburb of Tours. Before he was five years old, he was attending the Leguay day school at Tours. From June 22, 1807, until April 22, 1813, he was enrolled at the Oratorian school in Vendôme, run at that time by two former monks who had become secularized during the Revolution. During these six years he did not once return to his home, and he received only one visit from his mother. He underwent a crisis of mystical exaltation at the time of his first communion (see *Louis Lambert*).

1814. His parents moved the family to Paris. Honoré continued his studies there, at first at the boarding school of the royalist Lepître and later at the Sganzer and Beuzelin Institute.

1816–1819. He pursed his law studies and simultaneously

---

1 English translations of Balzac's titles appear in the Chronological Table at the back of this book. [Trans.]

had a period of training in the office of an attorney, Guyonnet de Merville, the Derville of *La Comédie Humaine*. Balzac later continued this training in a notary's office. Meanwhile, he was studying literature at the Sorbonne.

1819. While living alone in a garret in the rue Lesdiguières, he tried his hand at literary work, using up a good deal of paper and ink without much success. (See *Louis Lambert, La Peau de Chagrin, Le Lys dans La Vallée*.)

1820. Balzac resumed his place in the family circle, now located in Villeparisis. He stayed there only intermittently, however, for the Balzacs had also rented a pied-à-terre in Paris. In 1822, he developed a passionate love for Madame de Berny, born Louise Antoinette Laure Hinner, the daughter of a harpist in the service of her godmother, Queen Marie Antoinette. The de Berny family spent their summers at Villeparisis. Twenty-two years older than Honoré, Laure became an incomparable friend: she was deeply devoted to him; she had a profound influence on his moral and literary development; and she continued to give proof of her boundless love until her death on July 27, 1836. She enveloped her friend with warm tenderness. One may well wonder what the undisciplined temperament of Balzac would have brought forth without the counsels of *La Dilecta*.

1821–1824. Under various pseudonyms he collaborated on several novels, collected and published with the title *Oeuvres complètes d'Horace de Saint-Aubain* (Souverain, 1836–40). By 1819, he had already formed a noble friendship with Zulma Tourangin, who had been in boarding school with his sister Laure; and was now the wife of Artillery Commandant Carraud. This modest and virtuous woman had her share of influence over the writer, who was a frequent visitor at the Poudrerie (Powder Mill) of Angoulême and later at Frapesles, near Issoudun, as a guest of the Carraud family.

1825–1828. Balzac attempted to capture riches by engaging in business as an editor and then as a printer and typefounder, but he was forced into liquidation by a court order. This brought financial ruin on his family and was to weigh heavily on him for the rest of his life. He turned once more to literature; and, becoming intimate with the Duchess of Abrantès, he collaborated closely on her *Memoirs*.

1829. Balzac's father died. *Les Chouans,* composed in part on the spot at Fougères, earned Balzac a certain notoriety. He broke with Latouche. *Physiologie du Mariage* was a success attended by further notoriety.

1830. Balzac collaborated on various newspapers. He began to be seen in several salons (for example, those of Princess Bagration, Countess Merlin, Baron Gérard, Sophie Gay, and Madame Récamier), as well as at the home of Olympe Pélissier, a demimondaine. The *Scènes de la Vie Privée* brought him some celebrity. From June to September, he stayed with *La Dilecta* at the estate of La Grenadière in Saint-Cyr near Tours. Together they took a steamer down the Loire to Saint-Nazaire, going on to Le Croisic later.

1831. *La Peau de Chagrin,* which appeared in August, was a great success. Balzac indulged in a spell of dandyism, which was to reach a high point in 1832. A mania for luxury took possession of him; the decoration and furnishings of the apartment in the rue Cassini were magnificently renewed and the apartment was enlarged. He incurred enormous expenses of every sort, acquiring, among other things, two horses, a tilbury, livery for his domestic personnel, and a loge at the Opéra. He became known for his sartorial elegance, thanks to the skill of the celebrated tailor Buisson, who was later to appear in *La Comédie Humaine.* Balzac did most of his work at night, wearing a hooded monk's gown of white cashmere, a custom that he continued thereafter.

1832. Balzac's political ambitions took shape, but his candidacy for the office of *député* proved abortive. Abortive also were certain marriage projects. He acquired formal membership in the neolegitimist party directed by the Duke of Fitz-James and Laurentie. *La Bella Imperia* appeared in the first *dixain* (book) of the *Contes Drolatiques,* exciting the mirth of some readers, scandalizing others. For several months, he had been smitten with the beautiful Marquise de Castries, niece of the Duke of Fitz-James. In August he joined her at Aix-les-Bains and then followed her to Geneva, but he was rudely awakened from his dream at the beginning of October. *La Duchesse de Langeais* (1833–1834) was intended to be his revenge as a lover thrown over by a flirt; *Le Médecin de Campagne* (1833) was a quest for consolation. On February 28, the first anonymous letter from the Polish Stranger arrived, the unknown Princess.

1833. This Stranger continued to write missives, vibrant with admiration, to the novelist, who answered at length, exulting in the idea of this new, fine love. Balzac began to frequent a number of aristocratic salons. *Eugénie Grandet*, Balzac's supremely classical work, appeared. On September 25, the meeting of Balzac and his Stranger, Countess Eveline Hanska, took place at Neufchatel in Switzerland; there he spent five days with her and her husband. Another meeting of the two lovers followed at Geneva from Christmas of 1833 to February 8, 1834.

1834. This was a year of "mad" and "exorbitant" work, from which, however, neither social events nor worldly ostentation was excluded. On March 23, Balzac was admitted to the presence of Countess Apponyi, the wife of the Austrian ambassador, to pay his respects. On May 8, he was present at one of her receptions, and a few days later she introduced him to Countess Guidoboni-Visconti, "a blond bacchante," born Sarah Lovell. A close intimacy was to develop from this encounter. *Le Médecin de Campagne* failed to win the Prix Monthyon, which was awarded by the Academy to a young lady, the author of *Le Petit Bossu* and *La Famille du Sabotier*, which were preferred to the *Médecin*. In August, 1834 came the ordering of the famous cane, its gold head inlaid with turquoises. Balzac gave a splendid dinner for Rossini, in honor of Olympe Pélissier, Rossini's current mistress; Nodier, Sandeau, and others were invited. Sandeau, deserted by George Sand, was taken on as a collaborator by Balzac at the rue Cassini address. Balzac also engaged Werdet as editor, although he already had six others. From the end of September to mid-October, he stayed at Saché with M. de Margonne to work on *Séraphîta* and *Le Père Goriot*. He was active in social events and attended performances at the Opéra and the Théâtre des Italiens. *La Recherche de l'Absolu* appeared, as did *Le Père Goriot*. The latter novel, the masterpiece of his genius, is the first in which the systematic reappearance of characters was adopted.

1835. In the spring, Balzac took up residence in the rue des Batailles at Chaillot in an apartment secretly rented under the name of "Widow Durand." He wanted a refuge from his creditors and a way to avoid spending days of imprisonment in the Hôtel des Haricots. ("The Beanery" was a prison for undisciplined National Guardsmen, who were fed "haricot beans" as a staple diet.) The threat of imprisonment resulted from his absences from National Guard meetings. In any case, this retreat enabled him to receive Countess Guidoboni-Visconti at his ease. Here he would no longer have to fear importunate visitors and could work in peace. He had a sumptuous boudoir fitted out, whose decorations were later described in *La Fille aux Yeux d'Or*. To come into his presence, the few persons admitted had to know such passwords as "The season of plums has come." He worked day and night, sometimes for sixteen hours at a stretch. On the door of the apartment in the rue Cassini was hung a sign, "Apartment for rent," although his cook and Sandeau remained in it. On May 9, Balzac left for Vienna, where he again met Madame Hanska and her husband. On May 20, he had an audience with Metternich. He returned to Paris at the beginning of June. His brother Henri, returning from Mauritius with his wife, was a cause of some worry to Balzac. Then followed a stay at La Bouleaunière with *La Dilecta*, who was suffering from aneurism of the heart. In November and December, *Le Lys dans la Vallée* was published serially in *La Revue de Paris*. Balzac invited his two secretaries, De Belloy and De Gramont, with Nettement, to a luncheon. Two main dishes, one of cutlets, the other of oysters, were brought in four times for extra helpings.

1836. Balzac repurchased *La Cronique de Paris*, which caused him many financial worries and embarrassments. In July came his first eventful trip to Italy to defend the rights of the Guidoboni-Viscontis in an inheritance case. Balzac departed accompanied by a little page, "Marcel," a young woman dressed as an elegant gallant; in reality she was Madame Caroline Marbouty. The couple stayed in Turin for a month, and he was entertained by the high society of the city.

On his return, Balzac learned of the death of Madame de Berny, *La Dilecta*. A correspondence sprang up between Balzac and an unknown woman he was destined never to see, Louise. The painter Louis Boulanger painted a portrait of Balzac attired in his white monk's robe; Balzac sent the painting to the

Hanski family at the château of Wierzchovnia in 1837. At the end of November, he spent ten days at Saché with M. de Margonne, after which he made a visit to Talleyrand at the château of Rochecotte, home of the Duchess of Dino.

1837. Balzac made a trip to Milan, again in the interests of the Visconti family. Arriving on February 13, he was entertained by the Milanese aristocracy during his stay. He paid a visit to Manzoni. He started for Venice, went on board a ship at Genoa on April 8, and then proceeded overland from Leghorn to Florence. He returned to Paris on May 3. Sought by process-servers in the matter of a debt to 'Werdet, he hid, on June 17, in the Guidoboni-Visconti mansion on the Champs Elysées. A loan from Madame Guidoboni-Visconti was all that saved him from court action. In August he was again at Saché. Then he purchased a little house and some grounds, Les Jardies, between Sèvres, and Ville-d'Avray. Little by little the property was increased, and later a villa was built. All this was to be the cause of innumerable disappointments and catastrophic financial disasters. *L'Histoire de la Grandeur et de la Décadence de César Birotteau* was published.

1838. He stayed at Frapesles with the Carraud family. From there he went to Nohant to visit George Sand, staying from February 24 to March 2. Between March 20 and June 6 he traveled to Sardinia to explore ancient silver mines, exploited long before by the Romans. A Genoese merchant had told him about them the preceding year. Balzac dreamed of starting a company to reopen them and so make his fortune. His itinerary was Marseilles-Toulon-Ajaccio, then Alghiero, and then a visit to the mining sites at Argenteria and Nurra. Actually, this was not a chimerical project, for today these mines are being worked and paying substantial dividends; they have made their owners rich. Balzac returned to Paris by way of Milan. A first letter arrived from Hélène de Valette, then living at Guérande; there is reason to believe that during this year Balzac and she visited Guérande, Le Croisic, and the town of Batz, where he had previously vacationed with Madame de Berny in 1830. This is the place he chose as the setting for the plot of *Béatrix* (1839). He gave up his two apartments, one in the rue Cassini and the other in the rues des Batailles, and settled at Les Jardies with the Guidoboni-Visconti family.

1839. This year was especially noteworthy for the Peytel case: The notary Peytel, accused of having murdered, with premeditation, his wife and his manservant, had been judged at Bourg and condemned to death. Balzac had known Peytel in 1831, when he collaborated on *Le Voleur*, a paper of which Peytel was part-owner. The case was appealed; Balzac came to Bourg with Gavarni to confer with the condemned man. Wishing to prove his innocence, Balzac published a *Mémoire sur le Procès Peytel*, but in vain: Peytel was executed on October 28, 1839. In July, Victor Hugo lunched at Les Jardies with Gozlan; Balzac was thinking of becoming a candidate for a seat in the French Academy.

1840. *Vautrin*, a play by Balzac, was staged at the Théâtre de la Porte Saint-Martin on March 14. It was a failure. On March 16, the play was banned by the Minister of the Interior: the actor Frédéric Lemaître was so costumed and made up that, with his wig, he resembled King Louis Philippe.

Balzac launched *La Revue Parisienne* with himself as sole editor. Three numbers appeared: July 25, August 25, and September 25, 1840. Two of its articles are still talked about: the one, *L'Histoire de Port-Royal* by Sainte-Beuve, and the other in enthusiastic praise of Stendhal's *La Chartreuse de Parme*. Balzac left Les Jardies and in the autumn took lodgings in the rue Basse at Passy. His impoverished mother came to live with him for a few months, but they separated, mutually irratated. Meanwhile, Les Jardies was sold; for his property, which had cost him some 90,000 francs, Balzac received only 17,500.

1841. By the end of May Balzac was seriously ill and barely able to work. In October, he concluded an agreement for the publication of *La Comédie Humaine* by an association of book dealers, Furne & Co., Dubochet, Hetzel and Paulin.

1842. In January, Balzac received important news: Count Hanski had died on November 10. On March 19 came the failure of his drama *Les Ressources de Quinola* at the Odéon. On April 16 the *Bibliographie de la France* announced that the first part of *La Comédie Humaine* was on sale. In July, the

"Avant-Propos" (Preface) was published in the last installment of the first volume.

1843. The period between July 29 and November 3 was occupied by a trip to Saint Petersburg, where he met Madame Hanska. The return trip to Paris was broken by stops at Berlin, Potsdam, Leipzig, Dresden, Liége, and Brussels; he visited museums and cities. He was suffering from arachnitis, an inflammation of one of the three membranes that compose the meninges, and was treated by Dr. Nacquart. On December 3, David d'Angers finished his bust of Balzac. Balzac was now yielding more and more to his mania for collecting curios and bric-à-brac.

1844. He worked hard despite alarming symptoms, which betrayed extreme exhaustion. Lirette Borel, the Swiss teacher of Madame Hanska's daughter Anna, stayed at Balzac's apartment in Passy before entering upon her novitiate at the Visitation, where she took her vows under the name of Sister Dominique on December 2, 1845. Balzac had arranged for her admission to the Convent with Father Eglée, a vicar general, and he was present at the ceremony. He continued his ardent correspondence with the Stranger.

1845–1846. On May 1, Balzac rejoined Madame Hanska in Dresden, where she was living with her daughter Anna and the latter's fiancé, Count Mniszech. They all took nicknames: Bilboquet for Balzac, Atala for Eveline, Zephirine for Anna, and Gringalet for George. They assumed the group name of *La Joyeuse Troupe des Saltimbanques* (The Joyous Troupe of Tumblers). Balzac left for Italy with Madame Hanska and her daughter. Later Eveline and Anna spent a month at the rue Basse address in Paris. The trio made a tour through France, Holland, and Belgium. Balzac had a servant-mistress who had assumed the name of Madame de Brugnol. (Her real name was Louise Breugnot; he had nicknamed her *La Chouette*—the screech owl.) Her jealousy aroused, she stole some letters written by Madame Hanska to Balzac. On September 28, 1846, Balzac purchased a house in the rue Fortunée, La Chartreuse Beaujon. On October 13, Balzac attended the wedding of George Mniszech and Anna Hanska. An illegitimate daughter, instead of the expected boy who had already been named Victor-Honoré, was stillborn to Eveline Hanska in Dresden; Balzac was in Paris.

1847. From February to April, Madame Hanska lived in a furnished apartment in the rue Neuve-de-Berry in Paris. Greatly worried by both health and money, Balzac spent huge sums on furnishings for his apartment in the rue Fortunée, where he hoped to reside after his marriage to Eveline. He was blackmailed by La Chouette, Madame Brugnol, who threatened to make public the letters from Madame Hanska to Balzac. He felt physically and morally exhausted. On the night of June 28, he drew up his will. He broke with Emile de Girardin. In September, 1847 occurred his first stay with Countess Hanska at Wierzchownia. He left Paris on September 5, 1847, and after a nine-day trip he arrived almost dead with fatigue. He visited Kiev in November and returned to Paris on Febraury 16, 1848.

1848. Balzac was disheartened by the riots of February 21 and 22, and by the sack of the royal apartments in the Louvre. On April 29, his candidacy for election to the Constituent Assembly met defeat. On May 25, his drama, *La Marâtre* was a success at the Théâtre Historique. From May 28 to July 7, Balzac stayed for the last time at M. de Margonne's house at Saché. On July 8, he attended the funeral of Chateaubriand, whose seat in the Academy he was hoping to win. The hypertrophy of the heart that had caused him such suffering at Saché grew worse. In mid-September of 1848 Balzac left Paris for what turned out to be his last stay at Wierzchownia.

1849. During the winter 1848–49, which he spent in the Ukraine, Balzac suffered a new crisis in the hypertrophy of his heart. On January 11, he failed to win the seat in the Academy vacated by Chateaubriand. M. de Noailles was elected by twenty-one votes; Balzac's two votes were cast by Victor Hugo and Lamartine. On January 18, his bid for the seat of Vatout failed when M. de Saint-Priest was elected. On the third ballot Balzac received no votes.

1850. The state of Balzac's health grew still worse in January. Nevertheless, at the cost of extreme fatigue, he accompanied Madame Hanska and the Mniszech couple to Kiev. While Balzac was in the Ukraine, his mother occupied the apartment in the rue Fortunée in Paris, looking after the final

preparations there. On March 14, Balzac and Countess Eveline
Hanska were united in holy matrimony in the Church of
Sainte-Barbe in Berditcheff by Father Victor Ozarowski, a
family friend, who had been delegated by the Bishop of Git-
omir. This priest was a confessor of the faith, and the new
husband and wife had confessed to him and participated in the
communion service. Balzac's illness showed no signs of lessening. In the month of May, the couple set off for Paris; the condition of the roads and Balzac's attacks of near-suffocation made
this last voyage an agonizing one. When they arrived at the house
in the rue Fortunée on May 21, they were unable to gain ad-
mittance, although there was a light inside. The manservant
who had been awaiting their arrival had suddenly gone mad.
A locksmith was necessary in order to enter the home so lovingly prepared by Balzac for his Fairy of the North. Balzac
immediately took to his bed, completely exhausted. There was
a consultation of several doctors on May 31. On July 11, the
diagnosis was peritonitis; the patient was suffering terrible pain.
On August 12, dreadful swelling set in; Balzac was breathing
with great difficulty and was parched with thirst. On August
18, a Sunday, at the point of death, Balzac received extreme
unction. Victor Hugo came to see him at nine in the evening;
in *Choses Vues* he relates his interview with the dying man.
At half past eleven Balzac breathed his last. On August 21,
funeral services were held in the church of Saint-Philippe-du-
Roule. An admirable address was delivered by Victor Hugo at
the cemetery of Père-La-Chaise.

Balzac and the Human Comedy

Part One • Preparations

1 · Origins and Atavism

THERE IS a certain pleasure in looking closely at the vestiges of an atavism. Despite the necessary inconsistencies, one always hopes to discover in them the hidden influences that shaped a destiny. To be the only one of eleven brothers and sisters to know how to read and write—to start as a minor clerk to the scrivener of the neighboring town after having been the shepherd of his parents' flocks—then to leave his family abruptly in obedience to an ambition as burning as the sun of the Albigensian countryside—to leave home before his seventeenth birthday, on foot, with a staff in his hand and heavy hobnailed shoes on his feet, his pack on his back, as he traveled the King's Highway in the direction of Paris—there and still only twenty years old, to become the clerk of the royal prosecutor and then to win the post of secretary of the King's Council—such was the Odyssey of Bernard-François Balzac, the father of Honoré de Balzac.[1] He was born in 1746 in the village of La Nougayrié

1 It is hard not to believe that Balzac had his father in mind when, with these colorful touches, he limned the silhouette of César Birotteau as he left his native Touraine behind him. "He was the last child of the family. . . . When at the age of fourteen César had learned to read, write and do sums, he left the town and came to Paris with a louis in his pocket, seeking his fortune. . . . At that time César possessed a pair of hobnailed shoes, blue breeches and stockings, a flowered vest, a peasant's jacket, three heavy shirts of good linen, and his traveler's cudgel. Although his hair was cut in the fashion of the choirboys, he had the strong back of the peasant of Touraine; if sometimes he was guilty of the laziness customary in the countryside, he made up for it by his desire to make a fortune. . . ." It is worth noting that Bernard François Balzac owed his

3

in the Parish of Canezac, a commune of Montirat in the department of the Tarn (and he was to die in Paris in 1829 at the age of eighty-two). In the extraordinary success of such a father —who never let it be forgotten—was there not something to stimulate the ambition that set the son's blood afire?

In Honoré, this ambition was to be dissipated in projects aiming at honors and at riches, in fluency of speech, and most especially in "the ravishing language of those inspired exaggerations and that Gascon poetry so akin to love." This intoxication with words, this self-deception, this seething of wonderful hopes, this liveliness of imagination that beautifies and gilds the future in spite of all past failures, all these derive from the paternal ancestry. In this family environment, parents and children prided themselves on their search for understanding; they had a passion for talk and for discussions; "they lived in the most eager profusion of ideas that can be imagined," prolonging until midnight the evenings when Honoré read and declaimed the great authors, both ancient and modern. The mother, Madame Balzac, the sister, Laure, Honoré himself, have written about this period in their letters. The father strongly influenced the moral nature of his son, between the ages of sixteen and twenty-eight, by conversations on sociology, politics, history, ethnology, law, religion, and physiology in which each member of the family warmly defended his or her personal opinion. Early in life, Honoré had become aware of his father's eccentricity and had noted the conclusions that he drew from his experiences and his reading. In his first youthful novels (*Argow-le-Pirate*) and throughout the whole *Comédie Humaine*, we find the physical silhouette as well as the theories, mannerisms, hobbies, and foibles of the older man. His personality casts light upon that of the son and explains several of his philosophical tendencies. From his father comes "the

---

education and some smattering of Latin to the parish priest of Canezac, M. Vialar, whose choirboy he was. He had become acquainted with the language of legal deeds while working for Maître Albar, the notary of Monestiès. It may be that before his arrival in Paris he had done some work for certain public officials along the way, in order to pay his keep and to improve his juridical knowledge. He was considered an expert on common law.

religion" that Honoré professes in his youth for Rabelais, Sterne, Rousseau, Voltaire, and the philosophers of the eighteenth century. From him, the taste for research into physiological influences, eugenics, heredity, generation, education, and longevity. And, above all else, that physical strength that defied all accumulated physical fatigues—"a force of nature" the son was to be called—and the moral energy that overcame all obstacles. Honoré would not have attempted such ambitious projects "had he not possessed such confidence in himself," like his father.

Many of these characteristics common to both Balzacs are found, in varying degrees, in the types of men from the southern provinces whose challenging successes, flashy good luck, that "sprightliness of temper which makes them move straight against any difficulty, in order to overcome it," the resounding laughter, the beneficent exploits, put a thrill into many a page of *La Comédie Humaine*: Rastignac, the petty nobleman from Ruffec (*Le Père Goriot*), Bénassis, the son of a commoner (*Le Médecin de Campagne*), the soldier from Provence (*Une Passion dans le Désert*), Théodore de la Peyrade (*Les Petits Bourgeois*), Paul de Mannerville (*Le Contrat de Mariage*), Gazonal (*Les Comédiens sans le Savoir*), the Lestrades, the Maucombes (*Mémoires de Deux Jeunes Mariées*), for example. According to Balzac, "the constitution of this race deserves a careful examination by medical science from the viewpoint of philosophical physiology." When Honoré was twenty years old, the case of his uncle Louis Balssa (the true spelling of the family name), guillotined in 1819 for a murder caused by jealousy, gave rise to much exchange of opinion in the family circle: there was a matter for physiological inquiry. In Honoré's view, physiology was *the* great science for explaining reality. His father had been the first to teach and demonstrate this principle to him. There is no doubt that Balzac, in the earliest version of the *Physiologie du Mariage* (1826), made use of many remarks and reflections that he had heard from his father.

According to Balzac, the miracle of chance to which we owe the existence of great men remains "of all the mysteries of generation the one most inaccessible to our ambitious modern analysis." In any case, it was Bernard-François Balzac who broke open the rock vein in which genius lay sleeping. We think of Renan, of Veuillot, of Péguy, who spoke with emotion of their unknown ancestors. There are no such echoes in Balzac. He hastened to disown the nickname *The Albigeois*, the man of Albi, which he had inherited. Never did he feel any need to breathe the odor of that soil where his forefathers had worked out their lives, to pay them any homage for his great success. He chose the great, the powerful, the rich. He struggled to penetrate their sphere, and he let himself be won over to their self-conceit, their complacency. And he usurped the coat of arms of the Balzac d'Entragues family. He became the portrayer of the aristocracy, from which in great part his creatures and their models come. And he came to consider the peasants only in terms of the lord of the manor and of entailed property. Romantic exaggeration was to warp his views: peasants, both male and female, he looked upon as primitive beings whose earthbound instincts remain, with few exceptions, those of the "savage" and the brute and the lowly. This realism, brutal, severe, partial, and unjust, darkens certain pages of *Le Médecin de Campagne*, *Le Curé de Village*, and *Les Paysans*. In the eyes of some readers, other shapes stand silhouetted against other horizons, bent over their unproductive fields. We think of the Maréchal de Montcornet in *Les Paysans*: he "willfully forgot" that he was the son of a workman of the Faubourg Saint-Antoine. Balzac himself felt this reaction of disdainful vanity in regard to his grandparents, uncles, and cousins still in the village of La Nougayrié.

Balzac's mother, Anne Charlotte Laure Sallambier, belonged to the Parisian middle class. Her father was an important figure in the grocery business; and a cousin, a dealer in embroideries, trimmings, and drygoods, was established in the Marais section of Paris at the Sign of the Golden Fleece. She was eighteen years old when Bernard François Balzac, aged fifty and a fanatic on eugenics, married her. She was beautiful, elegant, and richly dowered. The new household, in which four children were born and raised (Honoré, the eldest, and Henri, and the two daughters, Laure and Laurence), was not a model of family virtue, as might well be expected of so ill-assorted a union.

"Wealth—great wealth—is everything today," was the mother's favorite remark. The golden future, eagerness for money, a taste for luxurious fancies filled the dreams of Honoré at an early age. If we are to believe his confessions, as well as those of Fessart, a friend of the family, Madame Balzac was not a very affectionate mother to her elder son, "the child of duty and of chance," whereas she showered "extravagant caresses" on the younger, "the love child," the illegitimate, the favorite. Rebuffed by "maternal coldness," Honoré soon enough divined its cause. He judged his mother severely in his harsh confidences to his three dearest friends, Madame Zulma Carraud, Madame de Berny, and Madame Hanska (see *Lettres à l'Etrangère*, 1842–48, especially for June 19, 1848). Like an old wound, the sharpness of this secret pain often rankled. His bitterness is clearly alluded to in *Le Centenaire, Jane la Pâle, La Femme de Trente Ans*, and *Le Lys dans la Vallée*. When the reader is able to grasp these references, he experiences a shock; the fictional tale becomes all the more moving. Indeed, the friction between Madame Balzac and her son never ceased its destructive work. It had other causes, too: the mother's nervous irritability and her touchiness—excessive eccentricities that her son also possessed in no small measure. "We are a precious lot of eccentrics in our family," he once wrote. And then there was the question of money, which riveted them together. Deeply in debt to his mother, he had, in fact, more or less ruined her by his bankruptcy as a printer. This debt doomed them both to unending mutual recriminations: her, "to receive a crust of bread"; him, to renew his promises of repayment and to give plausibility to his dilatory subterfuges.

It has been said that all this wretchedness was the origin of certain maternal figures in *La Comédie Humaine*. There are some admirable ones, such as Madame Birotteau, Lady Brandon, Madame Hochon, Madame Sauviat. Some are frankly odious, such as the Marquise d'Aiglemont. But is not diversity a happy effect of art and of life? Nevertheless, in the maternal portraits of Balzac we do find some false and clumsy touches: J. de Maistre, Victor Hugo, Lamartine are not guilty of such maladroitness.

The *Mémoires de deux Jeunes Mariées* (1846) presents to the public a sort of lyrical poem praising to the skies the "great art of maternity." Encased in traditional dogmatics, happiness reaches its high point in this book. It is the fruit of philosophical reflection—entirely cerebral and not preceded by an outpouring of the heart. This novel was written under the stress of an inward reaction: the author was striving to free himself of the gloomy memories in which his mother was all too present. And a blemish results, that is, the calculating prudence of the bourgeois selfishness that the young wife professes, to the detriment of conjugal and Christian honor. Just reread the *Lettres à l'Etrangère* of the same date: you will be enlightened.

The Balzac's home atmosphere was definitely anti-Christian, although religion was much discussed from rational points of view. Madame Balzac was interested in ideas and liked to discuss them, as her correspondence attests. She fully satisfied her beliefs through the esoteric teachings of the sects that abounded at the time—Swedenborgians, Martinists, Mesmerists—and devoted herself wholeheartedly to magnetism and occult practices. Her library was well stocked with Illuminist authors. Swedenborg and Saint-Martin, "the Unknown Philosopher," were always nearby on the shelf. She early put them in the hands of Honoré, whose curiosity was just awakening. His imagination stirred, the adolescent delighted in the paradisiacal representations of splendor and of sensual pleasure, and this initiation was destined to have repercussions throughout his work. When he was only seventeen, responding to a kind of mystic appeal, he composed a poem in rhythmic prose, *Falthurne*, about which he later said to Madame Hanska that it was "mere stammering," "the manuscript of a child," a "sketch" for the great painting that was to become *Séraphîta*. Each new essay, the second *Falthurne* (1820), *Le Centenaire* (1822), and the *Traité de la Prière* (1824) attest the progressive development of a religious ideal based on Martinist Illuminism. Indeed, the personality of Madame Balzac casts much light on the genesis of several characters and situations in *La Comédie Humaine*, and it is useful to know a great deal about her. She had the sorrow of outliving her son and died at Les Andelys, April 1, 1854, at the age of seventy-five.

Extraordinary affinities between Paris and Balzac are evident. Must one bow, here, before the maternal atavism? From 1814 until his death in 1850, the writer left the city only for fleeting trips. Let us point out, very concisely, the immense role that Paris plays in *La Comédie Humaine*—Paris, which he studied in its minutest details, its houses and its monuments, "with the analytic attention of a connoisseur," Paris whose pavements he trod night and day, "nose to the scent!" He regarded Paris as a living being, "a creature" whose "cellular tissues" he subjected to physiological examinations. He was one of those "who taste, who sip, their Paris, who know its face so well that they see each wart, pimple, blotch." He enthroned Paris as queen and mistress of his whole gigantic work. Paris formed its vast heart. As schoolboy, student, attorney's clerk, beginner in literature, dweller in Bohemia, lover, dandy, famous author, the fabulous city of legendary skies, the city "of a hundred thousand romances," aroused, saw, and crowned all his ardors. It is necessary to read the *Scènes de la Vie Parisienne* and more particularly the descriptions of Paris in *Ferragus*, *La Fille aux Yeux d'Or*, and *Le Père Goriot* to admire their high relief. Balzac succeeded in extracting all the juices, the substance, the contrasts, from this habitat so congenial to his creative genius. *La Peau de Chagrin*, *Z. Marcas*, *Les Martyrs Ignorés*, the confession of *Le Médecin de Campagne*, the little pictures in the *Oeuvres Diverses* evoke his ardent and ambitious youth.

But, after all, Balzac was born in Tours, May 20, 1799. The transfer of an official—his father—resulted in the child's being born a native of Touraine. As a boy of eight, in 1807, he left his native city, carrying away with him to school in Vendôme "amid the first remembrances of my life," he says in *Le Lys*, "a feeling for the beauty that pervades the landscape of Tours, with which I had become familiar." This impression is very distinct in one quality of his future work.

Until he was four years old, he and his sister Laure had been brought up by a wet nurse living in Saint-Cyr. This is a suburb of Tours and one of the most beautiful spots in Touraine. The houses of the village, all white, stood along an embankment "edged with magnificent poplars whose rustling we heard."

The town lies along the Loire, whose waters, looking like moiré silk, slowly flow between the copper-colored sandbanks, past the pale gold shorelines, the islets verdant and leafy with their osier beds. On the river, ceaselessly, majestically, passed the groups of big boats, their whitish sails billowing in the breeze, and the echoes brought back the shouts and cries of the boatmen. The child opened his eyes on life under that wide pearly sky, bathed in its quiet, enchanting atmosphere "where reigns, not boldness, not grandiosity, but the ingenuous goodness of nature," he says in his recollections of that time. The velvety, bluish hillsides rose in the distance, marked with the white that indicated the castles and the villas surrounded by woods, gardens, and vineyards. "It was under your pure sky that my childish eyes first saw the clouds drifting away." This marveling, this astonishment, had marked the beginning of his precocious sensibility; "these fragments floating in his memory," which from his early childhood astonished all his relatives, reconstructed the pictures with which the schoolboy of Vendôme charmed his melancholy.

These first sensations had etched themselves deeply into his being; they revealed their authenticity, their sharpness, their charm in the budding author's first essay, *Sténie* (1819). Its scenes unfold at Tours, at Saint-Cyr. Its landscapes, described lovingly and minutely, play a role closely tied to the action by the sentiments that they inspire in the principal characters, Job and Sténie.

In April, 1813, the adolescent returned to Tours after an uninterrupted six years at school. For a year, 1813–14, he was enrolled in the fourth form of the lycée. But he also rambled around the city, and his eyes never tired of admiring its monuments. He enjoyed the picturesque old houses and the districts where the narrow, winding streets had kept their archaic appearance; more than one of the *Contes Drolatiques* was to be impregnated with their atmosphere. Oftener than any other monument the cathedral of St. Gatien drew him into its shadows. He came frequently to wander about in the "desert of stone" that surrounds its nave, seeking religious and romantic sensations in the quiet streets reached by the muted waves of the sacred chants and the swell of the great organs. Even the *choucas*, the jackdaws, set aflutter by the vibrations of the bells, were immortalized; their flights animated some of his descriptions. "The very name of Saint-Gatien reawakened whole worlds of recollection in him," according to his sister Laure. He himself repeatedly said that he had come under the magic of the liturgical ceremonies. How many novels show traces of those impressions—*Sténie* and *Jane la Pâle*, *L'Excommunié*, *Maître Cornélius*, *La Femme de Trente Ans*, *Le Curé de Tours*, and an unfinished novel, *Le Prêtre catholique*. Always drawn by the majesty of the river, he kept returning to the embankments where "the Loire, extremely wide, flowed past the city as if in a canal cut by an architect." A real son of Tours, he was proud of having been born in one of those noble dwellings, all built on the same architectural plan, that, before the rue Royale was destroyed in the war, made it a street of classic form, and he celebrated it in "L'Apostrophe," one of the *Contes Drolatiques*, with a descriptive, lyrical hymn. It would be possible to point out many other imprints of the spell that Touraine cast upon his temperament and his work.

When at the end of 1814 the Balzac family left Tours for good, they had been living there for thirteen years. They had developed many ties and had made many precious friendships in the best society. The atmosphere of Touraine would not be dissipated for a long time: the conversations in the family circle often revived the pleasant memory of a province where every success had been visited upon the Balzac household. In addition, they kept a financial interest in the region: the farm of Saint-Lazare, some forty acres just outside Tours, remained a family property until 1830. Throughout his lifetime, Honoré returned to Touraine, to Saché, to restore his mental equilibrium or to seek the solitude and the silence so favorable to his work. Saché was the home of Monsieur de Margonne, one of his mother's intimate friends. There he lived the happiest, the most productive moments of his life; there he wrote some of his greatest masterpieces: *Louis Lambert*, *La Recherche de l'Absolu*, *Les Illusions Perdues*, *Séraphîta*, *Le Père Goriot*, *César Birotteau*, and *Le Lys dans la Vallée*, the action of which takes place at Saché. In the midst of this harmonious natural setting, which he repeopled with beloved phantoms, the sensibility of the writer grasped and translated, one by one, the splendors of his native province, its nature, and its art; the softness of its skies, the mildness of its climate, the special quality of its light make the outlines of objects stand out in extraordinarily clear relief. With what enthusiasm he loved the valleys of the Loire, the Cher, the Indre, and the Cisse, the alluring undulation of hills and dells! "Ask me not why I love Touraine; I do not love it as one loves his birthplace, nor as one loves an oasis in the desert; I love it as an artist loves art! Were it not for Touraine, perhaps I would no longer be alive!"

Have you ever wandered through the regions of Saché and Vouvray, forevermore famous, with the novels that have made them illustrious in your hand? Have you ever gazed alternately at Nature's landscape and at its artistic reproduction on the printed page? If so, you will not be one of those who reproach Balzac for the inferiority of his visual gifts. On the contrary, you will verify the firmness of line in his sketches, the shimmer of his coloring. He is precise; he fixes points of reference in the perspective. To him, they were signs of exactitude and of reconnaissance, and they still are, for the face of the enchantress enjoys eternal grace and has not grown old. These descriptions "are real, with an inner and profound reality: they reveal the most secret charm of lines and light," said one competent judge, André Hallays. The lyricism of the poet demonstrates the tenderness of the words, the vivacity of the sensations, reborn and vibrant with life when he summoned up the unforgettable images: he is fond of repeating that his soul has inscribed them forever. Between them and his sentimental life, a very close relationship exists. By letting his characters commune with the harmonious peacefulness that the misty enchantment of delightful Nature brings to the feelings, as in *La Grenadière* (the name of a country house), he was entrusting us with the secrets and the enchantments of his own heart. That poetic home, that retreat of Love—had it not enfolded in its seclusion, during the summer of 1830, the young writer, inebriated with his new glory, and *La Dilecta*, whose pride took the form of redoubled tenderness? This same rapport he establishes between these places and the fictional characters he leads into them, with the result that his descriptions of the landscapes of Touraine escape the reproach leveled at others, that is, having no psychological connection with the action.[2] *Le Lys dans la Vallée* refutes the accusation superbly.

This novel belongs to that group of works commonly called the Touraine Cycle. To the list already cited, let us add *La Grenadière, Madame Firmiani, Eugénie Grandet, L'Illustre Gaudissart,* the unfinished *Deux Amis,* not to mention several of the *Contes Drolatiques* and some articles and letters. *Le Lys* is both a hymn and a memorial. What descriptions, full of scent and sound, colored by their contact with this smiling Nature, this opulent land, these ever-changing places with their tidy prettiness! Who better than Balzac among the painters of Touraine, recent and contemporary—Maurice Bedel, Henri Guerlin, André Hallays, Jacques Marie Rougé, André Theuriet —has been able to render the enchanting grace of "his beloved valley," which, as he said, puts sorrow to sleep and awakens the passions? "This vale of love" was running over with mysterious poetry that pervaded the heart of the pilgrim to Saché; it raised the voice of inspiration, nourished his most secret desires, maintained his dreams of sensual delights, cured a hopeless passion. By his artistry, the river Indre remains an ancient Naiad fleeting through the meadows, twining itself serpentlike between the undulating rows of reeds and willows, hiding from our sight, capricious or nonchalant according to the hour or to the season, leaping from the eddies when the river is churned by the mill wheels, reappearing behind a clump of rushes, crowned with waterlilies and nenuphars, as if to lead the watcher to some trim manor house mirrored in the crystal of a quiet bend, framed in the pale gold of the poplars.

And should we pass on to geography—economic, gastronomic, or enologic—we could demonstrate that he had explored all these domains and that he appreciated all the flavors and savors of his province. We could prove the same of its history and its famous monuments, chateaux, churches, and homes: he found among them the subject or the setting for many tales. Nor could he forget its inhabitants, and in *L'Illustre Gaudissart,* he

2 Cf. a discussion on this talent as landscape artist, in Maurice Bardèche, *Balzac romancier* (Plon, 1940), pp. 551–53.

devoted a long paragraph to them, remarking that their character is the exact reflection of their environment. His theory of environmental influence led him to attribute a wonderful influence to Touraine. In this land of Rabelais, it is natural to find a reign of banter and epigram, an artful spirit of storytelling!

But Touraine is also the land of marvelous castles, the land of delights that Renaissance kings and queens could not do without, any more than could royal mistresses, courtesans, or artists. In that atmosphere float delicacy and politeness, taste for the fine arts, ardent poetry, and perfume to charm the senses. All these the child new-born in Touraine inhales with his first breath. But to develop these seeds, to make good the promises they bear, the Tourangeau, the native of Touraine, must, one fine day, be transplanted elsewhere. If he remains at home, the softness of the air, the beauty of the climate, the ease of existence will in time corrode his will. Here I suspect Balzac of composing his own encomium, so many contrary arguments could be brought against him. Why, for instance, did he return so often to renew his strength in that life-giving air? In his antithesis there is more literature than reality. The victory that the novelist gives the townsfolk of Vouvray over the illustrious Gaudissart, the king of traveling salesmen, a Norman by birth, moreover, and a Parisian by adoption—as the mystifying power of his glib tongue attests—this victory is proof of the high esteem in which Balzac held his compatriots, whose qualities and defects (mostly likable) he shares. How often he repeated that he would like to end his days in that beloved country! For example, he wrote to Ratier, the director of *La Silhouette*, on July 21, 1830: "Oh, if only you knew what Touraine is like. . . . I have reached the point of looking on glory, the Chamber of Deputies, politics, the future, literature, as so many bullets good for killing stray dogs, and I say: 'Virtue, happiness, life itself—all this to be had with six hundred francs income on the banks of the Loire.'"

Many other provinces contributed to his inspiration: Ile de France, Berry, Burgundy, Champagne, Flanders, Auvergne, Bresse, Gascony, Provence, Savoy, Comtat, Angoumois, Périgord, Dauphiné—one would have to name them all. But none of them was ever celebrated more lovingly by a son proud of his origin. It is only just to conclude that without the influence of his native soil Balzac would not have acquired the sense of unity, measure, and harmony that counterbalanced in part the presumptuousness and the fire of his southern atavism.[3]

He knew how to convey the feeling of provincial life, how to show the spirit peculiar to each province. He excels in depicting little towns drowsing in their melancholy past—melancholy, because their glory is forever dead. He loves to put new life into their historic annals: Provins (*Pierrette*), Issoudun (*La Rabouilleuse*), Saumur (*Eugénie Grandet*), Alençon (*La Vieille Fille, Le Cabinet des Antiques*), Nemours (*Ursule Mirouët*), Angoulême (*Illusions Perdues*), Sancerre (*La Muse du Département*), Besançon (*Albert Savarus*), and so on. A monument, a house, a piece of furniture, a picturesque feature, any one is sufficent to symbolize the provincial environment, to reveal the seamy side of its suffocated existence.

But do not be deceived by the calm atmosphere. It enfolds, it masks, passions, conflicts, and emotions overheated by all sorts of rivalries and hatreds. Immediately there comes to mind La Bruyère's vignette of the small city: "There is one thing that has never been seen under the sky and that there is every reason to believe never will be seen: that is, a small city in which there are no divisions, in which families are united and cousins regard each other with equanimity, where a marriage does not engender a civil war, . . . whence all gossip has been banned, along with lies and slander. . . ." Balzac was the first writer to carry this probing of the environment into the most minute details of morals and manners; no one before him had unveiled the tragic mysteries hidden by the seeming monotony of provincial existence, an existence in which selfish motives and constant reflection "attribute enormous significance to the most inconsequential acts."

And, finally, he brought out the profound changes created by the Revolution, changes in the appraisal of all social values

3 Albert Arrault, in his handsome work illustrated by Picart Le Doux, *La Touraine de Balzac* (Tours, 1943), has been able to restore this influence to Touraine, showing the literary flowering and blooming of the storyteller as the result of his birth and long sojourn in the province.

and in the relationships between social classes. The lower-middle class takes possession of the political position that the nobility had dominated (*Les Paysans*). Rivalries excite angers: "systems become men, and men of incessant passions, always face to face, watching each other like duelists, busy with their hatreds like players without pity." Political opinions create private enmities, which are passed on to the next generation. At this point, as at so many others, Balzac is a historian: he recounts not only what he sees, but also what his conversations with relatives and friends have taught him.

It has often been remarked that Balzac is more interested in social realities than in pictures of Nature. Nature assumes her deepest character only when she is a player in the spiritual drama that overwhelms the souls of the human characters: it is with their eyes and through their thoughts that the novelist perceives the circumstances of landscape and feelings. In this connection, *Le Médecin de Campagne* and *Le Curé de Village* are always quoted. Dr. Bénassis, whose heart is ravaged by disillusionment and troubled by remembrance of his weaknesses, utters this remark: "Love of Nature is the only love that does not deceive human hopes. No disappointments here." He experiences "delights" in smelling "the perfumes exhaled by the resin of poplars and the exudations of larches," the kinds of "emotions of whose very existence city folk are unaware." In the delightful avenue, "a gallery of verdure where the hoofs of their horses resound as if they were beneath the arches of a cathedral," "there is most certainly something religious about this spot," said Bénassis to Commandant Génestas, "and the consciousness of our pettiness brings us inevitably into God's presence." Véronique Graslin reaches the same conclusion in her rides through the forest of Montégnac. Her despairing, remorseful soul communes with "the profound sadness expressed by this haunt of wild, ruined nature, deserted and barren," which "responded to her inner feelings." At last the austere calm and the serenity of the wooded hilltops turn her thoughts and her musings toward levels higher than her customary ones: it is necessary to submit to the law of expiation.

The consciences of Bénassis and Véronique Graslin struggled in moral crises that required the spectacles of Nature to direct their repentant thoughts toward religious heights. The same thing is true of Camille Maupin (in *Béatrix*), disappointed in her love for Calyste du Guénic: the immensity of the ocean throws her into the arms of God. *La Bourse, La Peau de Chagrin, La Femme de Trente Ans,* and *Le Lys dans la Vallée* all depict the twilight hour as it calls up gentle reveries in which the heart finds balm soothing to the sufferings of love or rapture conducive to the soft yielding to caresses or to disturbing confessions. *Les Chouans* portrays perfectly the relationships between Nature and the human being, and we shall examine it presently.

Descriptions of Nature abound in *La Comédie Humaine*. A wide assortment could be cited: the sea, the mountains, the valleys—described, in fact, with a certain wordiness. Sometimes these passages are rather colorless. The region of the Monts Dore and the Pic de Sancy appears in *La Peau de Chagrin* in a topographical description. The author is endeavoring to multiply contrasts and we become aware of his effort, which becomes painful in its search for strange expressions. Reread in *Le Curé de Village* the account of the celebration of the newly built dam that is to transform the valley of the Gabou, assure it of marvelous fertility, and turn the new park of Montégnac into an enchanted place. It must be confessed that this picture falls flat. Banal epithets abound: "perfect elegance," "charming effect," "superior design," "pretty spots," "lovely furniture" in a small Carthusian monastery; "limpid brooks," "elegant masses or indentations delightful to behold," "an air of solitude pleasing to the soul," "superb day," "melodious cascades." These words and phrases do not create a procession of visual or auditory images.

Let us pause with these samples, let us be convinced by them that the palette of Balzac is sometimes heavy with lusterless colors, that verbal imagery can be lacking. Such a palette is not always equal to the powerful emotions aroused by scenes of Nature. And how many repetitions in how few lines! On the other hand, not many pages later, the same novel conveys an impression of evening in a village and a haying scene in unhackneyed descriptions that give wings to poetry. Their truthfulness and genuine sensibility need no indulgence on the part of the admiring reader. In short, without rising to the splendor of Chateaubriand and Victor Hugo, Balzac was endowed with visual gifts, even though his claims as landscape artist are perhaps excessive. When he describes, his paintings—sometimes, but not always—enchant us more by the accuracy of the brush strokes than by the originality of the expression.

2 · Beginnings and Success

THE LITERARY vocation of Balzac—"The Poet," as his school-mates in Vendôme nicknamed him—revealed itself in the third form at school. And the "rhymester" persisted in his quest of the Muse. By 1818, the beginner's experiments, still poetic, were "romantic" in the style of Lamartine, then pseudoclassic in the manner of Voltaire; he experimented with the epic in the style of *La Henriade* and *La Pucelle* and worked on a tragedy, *Cromwell*, which he finished in that year. This play was a failure, which decided him to turn his literary ambitions in another direction.

Philosophy had already attracted him. At the Sorbonne, between 1817 and 1819, he studied with Victor Cousin: this teacher "seemed a sort of hierophant, coming from a world invisible to announce things unknown," says Philippe Damiron. If one compares the theorics that Louis Lambert professes in his letters from Paris dated 1818, while he was studying at the Sorbonne, with those that Victor Cousin dealt with in the same year, one cannot but notice the precise similarities between them. Cousin inquired into the forms that religious feeling had assumed, over the course of centuries, in its most exalted aspects, in beings endowed with unusual gifts, in mystagogues. He sought the explanation for these phenomena in the laws of psychology, putting on the same plane the manifestations of fanaticism and of authentic Christian saintliness, visions, and ecstacies. Later this topic was to be Balzac's theme in *Le Livre Mystique*, including *Les Proscrits, Louis Lambert,* and *Séraphita*

19

(1831–35). There he showed the formation and the evolution of beliefs under ethnic and geographical influences, an idea that would persist in his thinking to the end of his life. Two problems troubled him most: the existence, and the spirituality and the immortality of the soul. Such concern in a youth of eighteen merits the esteem that Pascal bestowed on those who do not remain indifferent to the problems.[1] Balzac accepted the materialist solution offered by the psychophysiological theory of Cabanis, which was in keeping with the rationalistic philosophy of the eighteenth century. He concluded in favor of atheism—or a deism so vague that it has no effect on moral consciousness—and entrusted these opinions to *Notes sur l'Immortalité de l'Ame, sur la Philosophie et la Religion.*

What purpose would be served by describing once again, after so many biographers, the difficult lot of the apprentice during the year 1819, in that wretched attic room in the rue Lesdiguières? It would be more profitable to mention what he did first: he immediately made use of those notes in his first two romantic experiments—in *Falthurne* and more particularly in *Sténie, ou Les Erreurs philosophiques* (1819).[2] The latter is a novel in epistolary form and shows slight traces of the influence of Rousseau's *La Nouvelle Héloïse.* Each letter is the equivalent of a learned dissertation (composed by philosophy-student Balzac), and the arguments demonstrate the absurdity of Catholic dogmas (particularly that concerning the existence of God and the soul) and the beauty and clarity of rational verities, so superior to those of stupid revelation. The love letters are suffused with metaphysical perfume. These pages reflect the moral physiognomy of their author. In them, he analyzes himself, he takes his bearings in philosophic navigation; he judges his position— moral, religious, sentimental—in relation to the end of his voyage, that is, the harbor of pleasures that heathen love will provide when he has destroyed every principle of Christian belief and morality in the soul of his beloved, in order the more easily to lead her into adultery. *Sténie* is above all a first-rate psychological and philosophical document. It sends out a beam of light

1 *Pensées,* ed. L. Brunschvicg, p. 416.
2 This unpublished text was established by A. Prioult (Paris: Courville, 1936).

that will shine through *La Comédie Humaine* to the end (for example, in *Séraphîta*).

In an entirely different but necessary direction lie the periods that Balzac spent in a lawyer's office in 1817 and in a notary's in 1818. Their atmosphere was recreated in several novels, in particular, *Le Colonel Chabert* and *Un Début dans la Vie*. The author made use of the faces of the clients, in which he read downfall and wretchedness; the morals and manners of the clerks; the aspects of legal procedure; the mechanisms of justice; the hearings in the courts; and so on.

The great works of Balzac, at least as regards the means of art and expression, were already germinal in these very beginnings. Filling a total of 32 volumes, they were issued between 1821 and 1824 under various pseudonyms—Lord R'Hoone, Horace de Saint-Aubin, Viellerglé—from a kind of workshop managed by a broker of sorts, Le Poitevin de l'Egreville. They have since been published under the collective title *Oeuvres complètes d'Horace de Saint-Aubin* (Souverain, 1836–40), but individually they are: *L'Héritière de Birague* (The Heiress of Birague); *Jean-Louis* (*La Fille trouveée*) (Jean-Louis—The Foundling Girl); *Clotilde de Lusignan* (*Le Beau Juif*), (Clotilde de Lusignan—The Handsome Jew); *Le Centenaire* (*Les Deux Peringhelds*) (The Centenarian—The Two Peringhelds); *Le Vicaire des Ardennes* (The Vicar of the Ardennes); *La Dernière Fée* (*La Nouvelle Lampe merveilleuse*) (The Last Fairy—The Wonderful New Lamp); *Annette et le Criminel* (Annette and the Criminal), sequel to *Vicaire des Ardennes*, reprinted in 1836 under the better-known title of *Argow-le-Pirate*; *Wann-Chlore*, reprinted under the title *Jane la Pâle* (Jane the Pale). This group is also often designated by the general title *Oeuvres de Jeunesse* (Youthful Works). Balzac's companions, young writers who for the most part had to content themselves with aspirations to glory, were destined to be characterized in *La Comédie Humaine*: Finot in *César Birotteau*, Lousteau in *La Muse de Département*, Lucien de Rubempré in *Illusions Perdues* among others.

A remark supposedly made in confidence to Champfleury no longer appears to be retrospective boastfulness on Balzac's part: "I wrote seven novels merely as studies: one to learn

dialogue, one to learn description, one to group characters, one
for composition. . . ." This remark permits the critic to consider these attempts as experiments and to seek out the model
on which the student based his efforts to perfect some particular
technical procedure, as has been done by Albert Prioult in
Balzac avant la Comédie Humaine and by Maurice Bardèche
in *Balzac romancier.* The former has noted minutely all the
successive authors imitated by the young apprentice; the latter,
all the tricks of treatment that he methodically borrowed from
them in order to acquire the secrets of the trade. Balzac took his
courses in novel writing, and he profited by them. Until
quite recently, the *Oeuvres de Jeunesse* received little attention
beyond being consigned to the ranks of the flattest and most
contemptible productions, completely devoid of interest and
literary merit. This position is permissible no longer. First, the
apprentice chose his masters, as he himself later averred through
his mouthpiece, Joseph Bridau, in *La Rabouilleuse* (literally,
The Woman Who Fishes in Muddy Waters). In addition, "he
read a great deal; he gave himself that profound and thorough
instruction which one gets only from one's own self, and to
which all talented people have devoted themselves in their
twenties." Here are some of the principal figures on his list:
Byron, Fenimore Cooper, Anne Radcliffe, Maturin, Walter
Scott (whose influence was to be deep and decisive), Rabelais,
Molière, Diderot, Montesquieu, Locke, J. J. Rousseau, Ber-
nardin de Saint-Pierre, Beaumarchais, Chateaubriand, Ducray-
Diminel, and Pigaut-Lebrun. Furthermore, his reading included
a great many authors who are forgotten today. He endeavored
to reproduce these different styles: the novel of plot, the historical novel, the novel of adventure, the sentimental novel, the
"black" novel, fantastic, terrifying, picaresque. One or another
of them furnished him with an outline of exercises, of subjects
for imitation: parody, comic or dramatic dialogue, description,
and so on. *Argow-le-Pirate* (1824) is an attempt at the psychological novel. It is important as a proof of progress in the construction of characters and plot by recourse to the passions
rather than, as previously, to coincidental and faked catastrophes.
        About 1824 another broker of literature, Horace Raisson,

started the fashion of literary "Codes." He engaged Balzac, who had already achieved some notoriety, to put out in 1825 his *Code des Gens Honnêtes*. This satirical style inspired and animated him. He enounces, in short articles like the sections of a code of laws, the usages and prescriptions of society life. His power of observation sharpens; he paints with all the care of a psychophysiologist; he interprets the outer details of the person, the attitude, the garment, the furniture, as the signs, the positive documents, of moral temperament. Since 1822 he had been familiar with Lavater's work, *L'Art de Reconnaître les Hommes par la Physionomie*,[3] and he applied its principles with such conviction that he had no hesitation in detecting in each gesture, each attitude, each play of expression, the realistic and somewhat pessimistic explanation of social life—actuated mainly by money. So much for the gist of the thought. As for form, those rapid sketches, those silhouettes of genre, were the forerunners of many a character in *La Comédie Humaine*.

After money—love. *Physiologie du Mariage*, conceived in 1824 and half-written by 1826, did not appear in its definitive form until 1829. It is a satire on contemporary mores, the eternal drama with the cast of three, played since the appearance of the serpent to the couple in Eden. In spite of many borrowings, this work is somewhat remarkable for its strength of observation and analysis, uncommon in a young author. What total skepticism with regard to marriage! But the irony overshot its mark; it was too satisfied with ribald remarks and musk-scented trivialities. By heaping excessive ridicule on a solemn and sacred institution, the work failed to achieve the moralizing purpose that its author ascribed to it. Considered as literature, it was an anomalous work. Certain of its elements were not wasted, however, for when Balzac later dealt with conjugal psychology, he made use of several situations that he had worked on in *Physiologie du Mariage*.

It is now clear when one should make use of the *Oeuvres de*

3 Later he wrote *L'Art de payer des dettes . . . sans débourser un sou* (The Art of Debt-Paying . . . without Spending a Penny); *Etude de moeurs par les gants* (A Study of Morals by Means of the Gloves); *Théorie de le Démarche* (A Theory of Gait) and all the *Physiologies* of dress, cigars, gastronomy, and so on.

Jeunesse and the *Code des Gens Honnêtes.* To start with them would be a disappointing, even fatal, experience. But suppose one wants to examine the development of Balzac's art and thought; it would be impossible to do so without going back into that period of exercises, of gropings, of repeated experiments. It would be necessary to stay out of the bright zone of *La Comédie Humaine* and to plunge into the chiaroscuro of the beginnings, where there will be found many a page rich with promise.

From 1825 to 1828, Balzac deserted literature for publishing and printing. He wanted to become wealthy, and he came out of this adventure, which was a dramatic one, condemned in the present to poverty and in the future—what is worse—to an existence of financial contrivance and expedients. Some of his work gives the reader an opportunity to observe how the novelist skillfully recreated the environment and infuses it and his fictional adventures with real pathos.

The detailed account of this financial failure and the anguish it caused the imprudent industrialist, victim of his own lack of professional skill and his own flightiness, has been written by René Bouvier and Edouard Maynial in *Les Comptes Dramatiques de Balzac.* This history brings out clearly the defect of a character that had an extraordinary propensity to luxury and prodigality, and the book is of particular interest to his biographers.

Let us look at the repercussions of this commercial catastrophe as they appear in *L'Histoire de la Grandeur et de la Décadence de César Birotteau.* The author's experience in a notary's office served him here, but still more helpful was the memory of his own tribulations and anguish when his personal honor and that of the family were under discussion between the claimants and Balzac's cousin Dédillot, charged with the liquidation of the printing shop. It is no surprise that he is exact in the use of legal terms, informed about the phases of this legal operation, and so penetrating in his psychological analysis of a bankrupt. The conscience here had been his own before it belonged to Birotteau; it had been wrenched in opposite directions, tormented beyond measure by fear for the future, tortured by those birds of prey, the shady financiers, lawyers, and creditors. Like Birotteau, he had "felt, more than once, the spurs of that harsh rider, necessity, struck into his heart!" "But just as many people have mistaken for energy the confidence given by illusion," he persisted tenaciously "in making a novel of hope out of a series of reasonings." All these remarks throw light on the depths of his character; his own personal character becomes that of his literary creature. At the very time that he was kneading its clay, in 1837, he was able to philosophize at length about his own case; he had risen from the abyss into which he plunges the victim of his imagination: "the business accidents that strong characters surmount turn into irreparable catastrophes for petty spirits. Events are never absolute; their results depend entirely upon individuals; misfortune is a step-ladder for the genius, a piscina for the Christian, a treasure for the clever man, an abyss for the weak." He considered himself a man of genius, a strong clever character. Moreover, he had discovered "the great secret of strong creative existences," which is "to forget": "to forget, like nature, which recognizes no past, which at any time recommences the mysteries of its untiring creativeness." His experiences as a printer and a bankrupt supplied him with documents to utilize once more for *L'Interdiction, Le Cabinet des Antiques, Illusions Perdues.* His musings took on an accent of truth; his psychological analyses were conducted with a sure touch that he would not have had had he not himself passed that way. As a result, when he fashions stories, it is not always a demon of invention that guides and inspires him. He relives his own past, and we with him; we have become his confidants. The pleasure of our reading becomes tinged with gravity, enriched with sensations, as the sound of his groans reechoes from his soul to ours.

Autobiographical verity is thus mingled with fiction in many novels; Balzac's sensibility gives warmth to the plots and animates their settings with the joys and sufferings of all the ages of his life. Dream creatures, under pseudonyms, appear with known faces, loved or hated. We do not try to materialize them out of an enigma or a mystery in order to satisfy an erudite curiosity, but to experience the full enjoyment of witnessing that artistic miracle—literary metamorphosis. Of these transfigurations, Madame de Berny, *La Dilecta,* offers an example of the highest interest: she became the heroine of *Les Chouans*.

In 1828, with the threat of bankruptcy temporarily disposed of, Balzac was faced with the problem of earning a living. He turned once again to literature, and henceforward until death, there would be no turning away. Historical revivals were back in favor at the time. His first experiments in the medium had not been satisfactory, and he had judged them severely. Now he plunged passionately into the reading of memoirs relating to the Revolution and the wars of Vendée, and his imagination caught fire. *Le Dernier Chouan, ou La Bretagne en 1799*, later entitled *Les Chouans*, was the first novel that he considered worthy of acknowledgment, and he signed it.

Now historical information from books no longer satisfied him. By going to Fougères to saturate himself with the atmosphere in which the plot of the novel he was writing actually took place, he developed the documentary method that he was to use from that time on. He felt the need of contemplating with his own eyes the sites he wished to describe, of hearing with his own ears the people talking in their native surroundings. He put questions to them, made them talk, collected the vocabulary and the expressions of the soil, and observed local customs. Then he could reenact the drama in its natural environment. Nature, for him, became a fabulous actor from whom the other actors receive impulses, with whom they commune in the excitement of their passions. In short, he came to understand that, to be true, nothing takes the place of letting one's entire being be permeated by the physical reality before proceeding to poetize it. From all creation, living or inanimate, from the environment, visible or invisible, he extracted all the secrets, all the significance. He caught the mysterious muttering by which material things communicate with the spirit of man; he was not far removed from believing in the physical existence of this spiritual interpreter. At every turn of the road, the genius of Brittany loomed, attentive as an accomplice favoring the progress of the lovers, Montauran and Marie de Verneuil, or crouched behind each shrub, patient as a spy who thwarts their plans. There is no doubt but what "all" Fenimore Cooper "is there"; the wiles of the Chouans duplicate those of the Mohicans. "All Walter Scott" also: Balzac declared it and demon-

strated it, obeying to the letter the precept of his master. Instead of "reproducing a great personage or a tremendous historical happening," the novelist must "explain their causes in
general by depicting the mores of the characters and the spirit
of a whole epoch."

He brushed in his background with broad strokes, but sharply
enough for his political preferences to be recognizable: he is
on the side of the Blues, of the Republic, of dogmatic liberalism.
This fact has been denied, on the basis of his indifference to
religion at that time. Nevertheless, the unbeliever's jousts with
his pious hostess at the chateau of Fougères, where he was a
guest of the Pommereul family while writing this novel, are
unquestionable indications of his Voltairianism. The good Commandant Hulot, Captain Merle, Sergeant-Major Gérard, "those
truly republican souls," "with their nobly obscure self-sacrific-
ing devotion to duty," unselfish and energetic, proclaim the
object of their double mission: "to save the doctrines and the
country," the idea of liberty and the conquests of "human reason revealed by our assemblies." The convictions of the peasants
facing martyrdom in the defense of their Catholicism are low-
ered to the level of idolatry, "obscure fanaticism," and super-
stition. The "Jesuit" and rector, Gudin, is portrayed as a greedy,
ambitious, fanatical soul, prodigal of the grossest deceptions.
The caricature is pushed to the extreme and stands out the more
strongly in contrast to the wan, colorless sketch representing the
priest faithfully upholding the ancient, pious usages in spite of
dangers.

The Marquis of Montauran, *le Gâs* ("the Lad"), is brave
and generous, but the fluctuations of his mad passion and the
victory of his love end by bringing about the defeat of the very
cause that he is defending; as a leader, he is a worthy puppet.
The character of Commandant Hulot, that great patriot, presents a prouder, more likable portrait. As for the other par-
tisans, noblemen of no great intelligence, they are portrayed as
paltry defenders of throne and altar. "Harassing" their leader
to commend them to the King, they are concerned with little
except rank, gain, decorations, and favors. The erotic jests uttered by the Count of Beauvan before the altar, during the
marriage ceremony *in extremis* which joins Montauran and

Marie de Verneuil, are odious, improbable sacrilege at such a grave moment. One of the most evocative, most significant scenes of the novel is the mass of the Chouans, celebrated at night in a glade. Balzac likens these peasants, kneeling armed before the host, to savages, to Hurons before their fetishes ("all Fenimore Cooper"). For him, they were "only a fact and not a system; it was a prayer and not a religion." His interpretation makes a comedy of this sacred ceremony, destined by those who "had prostituted the priesthood to political interests" to excite the passions of rude spirits. "The peaceful cross of Jesus became an instrument of war." The historical surroundings are supposed to explain the event. Here, the novelist distorts it by magnifying blemishes. His personal opinion makes it a travesty by restricting to earth the heavenly scope of the supernatural drama: he admires only its setting. Because of lack of sympathy, he has not credited the Chouan uprising with the sublime and fierce heroism of an unconquerable faith. A contemporary novel, *Sous la Hache* by Elémir Bourges, deals with the very same plot, situations, vicissitudes, and themes as *Les Chouans*. In Bourges' novel the study of political passions is fuller and the characters of the Republicans are aroused by more violent convictions. Although the reader of that book will notice some concern with impartiality, he will conclude that a historical novel is always swayed by the opinions of its author.

Many years later Balzac reread *Les Chouans*. He mentioned his impressions to Madame Hanska: "Decidedly it is a magnificent poem. . . . The passion in it is sublime. . . . The countryside and the war are depicted with a perfection and a success which surprised me. . . ." The country, the war—these are the externals of the drama. "The sublime passion," the secret mainspring, is that of Balzac himself, first for Madame de Berny in the original edition, later for Madame Hanska in the edition of 1834, much altered to fit changed conditions. Charms, attractiveness, glamor—the heroine Marie de Verneuil has all these in abundance and even "virginal graces" besides. This transformation, too daring for a woman who had lost her social status, an infamous creature, a venal spy, and a sublime lover, betrays the first transports of a young author in quest of wild happiness, in the surging swells of his first loves. He clothed his creatures in all the seductiveness that he saw or dreamed of in the radiance of *La Dilecta* and later in the Stranger: it was "the poem" of his inner enthusiasms. It was also the successful union of all his literary endeavors. The historical material that had come to his etcher's burin in this Brittany and this peasant uprising had allowed him the use of contrasts in his descriptions, his characters, and his ideas. Then each character stood as a "type," a symbolic figure representative of his social class: Montauran, young, elegant, valiant, a "gracious image of the French nobility"; Commandant Hulot, the stern-faced old soldier, "presented a living image of that Republic"; Gudin, the fanatical priest, "the image of the clergy of those countries." The Chouans, whose nicknames reveal their popular origin—Galope-Chopine (something like "Rush-the-Mug"); Pille-Miche (Bread Snatcher), and especially Marche-à-Terre (Walk-on-the-Ground)—were the symbols of a fanatical peasantry. This technique became a constant method, as did the enlivening of nature. All together, everything sparkled with youthfulness: the flowing style, the colorful vocabulary, the overpolished picturesqueness, the sometimes ingenuous declarations, the pretentiously philosophic or erudite opinions.

At the same time, this work was the beginning of the *roman policier* or detective novel: a plot started by Fouché, who had set one of his agents, the cunning, wary Corentin, to follow the spy Marie, was to culminate in the arrest of "the Lad," the leader of the Chouans. Balzac was writing the prelude to episodes that were to follow in *L'Auberge Rouge, Le Requisitionnaire, Une Ténébreuse Affaire, Splendeurs et Misères des Courtisanes, L'Envers de l'Histoire Contemporaine*, and still others.

Les Chouans was dedicated to Théodore Dablin in terms indicative of great pride: "To my first friend, my first book." It would be more correct to say *the last of his youthful works.* Each of the others, so to speak, had stripped itself of a gift received in the cradle, to cooperate in the success and the riches of the first masterpiece, the masterpiece of proficiency. In its multiple beauties, it bore witness to a talent sure of its strength and its resources.

3 · The Method of Observation
and Documentation

WHEN *Les Chouans* appeared in January, 1829, the novel itself was only a partial success, but it did open the door to renown. In December that renown was very clamorously increased by *Physiologie du Mariage*, whose spicy anecdotes and scabrous observations brought Balzac a *succès à scandale* in fashionable circles. In April, 1830, appeared the two volumes of *Scènes de la Vie privée*, a series of moralizing novelettes of touching delicacy and refinement, intended for "young souls," unmarried girls as well as mothers, to help them avoid shedding "tears of blood." These volumes definitely won the feminine public over to his side. The *Physiologie* had already excited their curiosity. All at once the author was generally deemed by that segment of the population to possess sterling qualities and merit. In 1831, *La Peau de Chagrin*, an "occasional" piece, a vast and scourging satire of contemporary morals and manners, touched off a new scandal crowned by a real literary triumph.

In 1832, Balzac was that famous writer whom the mistress of the house delights in receiving in her drawing room, whom the editors of reviews and newspapers are happy to list among their contributors. He professed to be "bewildered with subjects and requests." He had become the lover of the Duchess of Abrantès and a frequent visitor in the salons of Madame Récamier, Princess Bagration, Countess Merlin, Madame de Girardin, Madame Hamelin, Countess Guidoboni-Visconti, Countess d'Agoult, and the Marquise of Fitz-James, among others. The aureole of aristocracy was always, for Balzac, an irresistible feminine seduction. This came to general notice very soon, when it was perceived that he was paying assiduous court to the Marquise of Castries. She was very beautiful, very heedful of literary merit, haloed by a legend of melancholy love from which she had taken refuge in intellectual pleasures. An enticing hope took form and stirred the proud heart of the writer. A few months later the illusion was shattered. The jilted suitor sought revenge for his ulcerated heart: *La Duchesse de Langeais* (1833) gave expression to the sly, calculated coquetries, the hypocritical wiles and stratagems in which a noble lady indulged in the Faubourg Saint-Germain. And it was for her sake that the slave of the pen had turned himself into a dandy, exhausting himself to maintain a grand scale of living. It was for her sake that, heedless of the cruel reproaches of his two best friends, Madame de Berny and Madame Zulma Carraud, he had joined the party of the neolegitimists—"those people!"

It is well to remember also that he considered conversation the supreme pleasure of social living, the most refined diversion. He thought of it as a literary genre, as is demonstrated by *Autre Etude de Femme, Echantillon de Causeries françaises*, and *Conversation entre onze heures et minuit*. His frenzied animation, "the magnetic sparkle, the richly golden highlights of his eyes," said Théophile Gautier, his mimicry and his eloquent gestures, his powers of imagination, made him one of the most dazzling of talkers. But he was a good listener as well.

Etudes de Moeurs was the generic title under which Balzac in 1834 published his early novels, grouped in categories: *Scènes de la Vie privée, Scènes de la Vie de Province, Scènes de la Vie Parisienne, Scènes de la Vie Politique, Scènes de la Vie Militaire, Scènes de la Vie de Campagne*. Félix Davin provided the introduction to this edition, but Balzac confessed to having inspired, documented, "drummed the data" into his friend. He endorsed all the opinions of this manifesto, which he had revised and "recorrected" down to the smallest detail. In it he assumes the pose of a "deep, sagacious observer" who "constantly spied upon Nature," "examined her with infinite precautions." "To see all and forget nothing" is his motto. He challenged any one to find any flaws in his "exactitude" in this "examination of details and small facts."

By supporting his assertions with proof taken from his novels, he refuted the objection that critics were already bringing against him: "But would it not be a false idea to believe that such a young man could have had such wide experience? He would not have had time. . . . No, M. de Balzac must be proceeding by intuition." The two viewpoints still remain opposed. Some critics, like Champfleury and, succeeding him, all the realists of the school of Zola, those who have been called "the tail of Balzac," considered him a hunter of documents, a tireless investigator, and ever unsatisfied ferreter, a confessor. There is no end to the anecdotes about his methods of garnering material. He filled little notebooks that he carried with him. His work was continually fed and enriched with all the observations collected with such burning curiosity. Those holding the opposing view, like Philarète Chasles, Desnoiresterres, consider Balzac a diviner, a man of intuition, an instinctive perceiver—one who sees.

Whoever would have defended the thesis of the realists in the presence of Sainte-Beuve, as Théophile Gautier and Edmond de Goncourt did at the dinner at Magny's in 1863, would have drawn this retort upon his head, for Sainte-Beuve cried tartly: "It is pure imagination, sheer invention!" Listen to one of the more recent exegetes, Léon Emery. "Some people hold Balzac to have been a great observer. When would he have found the time for it? Where are his notes? Did he ever plume himself on reproducing what he had seen? Does he not always speak of his books as a world issuing from his head?" After the peremptory affirmation of Max Nordau—"His work owes absolutely nothing to observation. . . . Reality was nonexistent for him"—the opinion of André Bellesort is more conciliatory: "Did he observe everything he relates? You would not want to believe that. . . . Balzac has much more intuition than observation." That is the proper formula, in my opinion, because it admits that there are proportions; it is incomplete, however, because it does not distinguish any chronological periods. The day was to come when the artist, freed from all bondage, would rely entirely upon the fecundity of his genius. "I carry a whole society in my head."

This thesis puts too low a price on Balzac's affirmations to the contrary. It is not necessary to go through many random pages of any novel in *La Comédie Humaine* to find the word and the deed, the action and the habit, stand revealed. "Ample material for the reflections of those who wish to observe or portray the different social zones . . ." (*Autre Etude de Femme*). "The events of human life, either public or private, are so intimately bound to architecture that the majority of observers can reconstruct nations or individuals in all the verity of their customs, from the remains of their public monuments or by *examination* of their domestic relics" (*Recherche de l'Absolu*). "To keep the critics from accusing us of puerilities, it is perhaps necessary to call their attention here. . . ." "At all stages of society the observer finds the same absurdities. . . . So it is that by comparing the elements of jokes, of jesting, by echelons from the street urchin of Paris to the peer of the realm, the observer understands. . . ." These phrases are taken from a single paragraph in *La Duchesse de Langeais*. In *Madame Firmiani*, he brings upon the stage "an old man belonging to the genus of observers." This sort of appraisal is possible in a score of places in *La Comédie Humaine* and demonstrates that Balzac himself belongs to the same genus.

Let us go back two years, to 1830, to the beginning of his career as an author, and run through the collection of his *Oeuvres Diverses*. After long, consecutive hours spent at his work table, does he seek a little relaxation? "I give myself up," then, "to the diversion that external Nature offers," "my gaze darts right and left upon my fellow men. I observe. . . ." Thus begins *L'Oisif et le Travailleur*. Justifying a remark of Félix Davin before he made it, Balzac puts "life in the remarks of Lavater by applying them." A rereading of the *Physiologie Gastronomique* is convincing in this respect. He begins the story with some thoughts on that science, so profound, so useful, and so agreeable, "discovered by Lavater and Gall." At the instant of putting into practice their methods of discerning different genera within the species "eater," Balzac, adding ten years to his age, declares: "For forty years I have been observant at the dining table." He provides further demonstration of this method in *L'Auberge Rouge*: he observes everywhere—in the streets, in the stagecoach, in the thatched cottage, in the drawing rooms, and in the churches, by day and by night. He wants "to spy the mysteries hidden behind the curtains of the apartments." He enumerates, he discloses all his secrets to us, calling attention to everything that careless or inept eyes have missed. The results of these researches are exposed in *L'Epicier, Madame Toutendieu, Le Bois de Boulogne et le Luxembourg, De la Vie de Château, La Consultation, La Grisette, La Cour des Messageries Royales, Le Dimanche, Une Vie du Grande Monde, Un Conciliabule Carliste, Les Horloges vivantes*. These titles are in themselves quite evocative. They lead us through all the spheres of the society of 1830. They are, all of them, *things seen*.

Balzac attributed to them an importance equal to the consequences that he claimed to draw from them. In *Le Contrat de Mariage*, he reproaches Paul de Mannerville for being unable "to discover in the attitude or in the features, in the speech or in the gestures" of his betrothed "the signs that would have revealed the tribute of imperfections comprised in her character, as in that of any human creature." To that end, "Paul should have possessed not only the sciences of Lavater and of Gall, but also a science for which there exists no corpus of doctrine, *the individual science of the observer, which demands almost universal knowledge*." After this remark, he discloses what "a man skilled in wielding the scalpel of analysis [i.e., Balzac himself] would have discerned in Nathalie." But Nathalie is an imaginary character and, like a great number of others, owes her descriptive features to the customary inquiry of the author, who claimed to detect the invisible psyche, its almost physical reflection on the facial features, in the lines and structure of the silhouette. Let us find proof of it in the evidence that "the most practiced observers alone could then divine." Where others saw nothing out of the ordinary, he detected signs of great importance. *Sarrasine* and *L'Auberge Rouge* contain similar remarks.

Is it admissible that so many reiterated declarations, of which we have here given only a few picked at random, are due to nothing but a wish to trick the reader? Balzac is obsessed with one concern: to see everything, record everything, in order to describe Nature, things, people, for the purpose of revealing the mysteries of a more secret life.

Now, let us watch him live. His faculty of observation was, he claimed, innate, a disposition strengthened by being put to the test: "Only misunderstood, unappreciated souls and the poor know how to observe, for everything wounds their feelings, and observation is a result of suffering. Only the sorrowful is well remembered." This confidential opinion, revealed to Madame Hanska in 1833, concerned his worldly beginnings, his start in life; he had been mortified in those days by snubs and disdain. He did not hesitate to see in "the constant wretchedness of my life" the primary cause "of what has so incorrectly been called my talent." He complained of his moral abandonment by his mother in his childhood. But he blessed her indifference: it had accustomed him early in life to find pleasure in solitude, in the rear of the garden, "watching the insects," "gazing at a star" with an "odd passion" that he attributed to his "precocious melancholy" (*Le Lys dans la Vallée*). Are we not, then, justified in taking this series of childish remembrances literally?

Who has not once in his life watched the marches and countermarches of an ant, poked straws into the single aperture through which a slug breathes, studied the whimsical flight of a slender dragonfly, admired the thousand veins colored like the rose window of a Gothic cathedral, which contrast with the reddish background of a young oak's leaves? Who has not gazed at length with delight at the effects of rain and sun on a brown-tiled roof, or contemplated the dewdrops, the petals of flowers, the varied serrations of their chalices? (*La Peau de Chagrin.*)

Like Raphaël de Valentin, like Félix de Vandenesse, the Accursèd Child became familiar from his earliest years with the phenomena of nature and the vicissitudes of the sky; he spied out everything "from the blade of grass to shooting stars" (*L'Enfant Maudit*, literally, The Accursèd Child, published in English as *The Father's Curse*). In each of these fictional characters Balzac expressed a profound aspect of his personal character, "the life of childhood, the lazy life." With the addition of "the life of the savage" it can be assumed that he was mindful of his adolescent readings in the *Lettres Edifiantes*, which caused him to dream so much. He very probably rediscovered the atmosphere of the "primeval forest" in Cooper's *Last of the Mohicans*.

Balzac led the kind of existence most suited to enriching the storehouse of his memory with observations. It is wrong to think of him seated always at his worktable, sleeping by day in order to write at night; his monkish garb is only an intermittent symbol. He did have periods of frenzied labor and crises of absolute solitude, when he cut himself off from the world of the living so as to know only the phantoms of his imagination and to incorporate them in his work. Except for these periods, he used to go out, happy to meet his friends, relaxing before a copious meal, letting himself go in conversation. He also enjoyed traveling. Remember his endless walks through Paris with Léon Gozlan, seeking on shop signs the name that would fit the character he had created, a predestined name—Z. Marcas. He commented constantly on the appearance and type of this or that passerby whom his scrutinizing eye had picked out on street or boulevard. Recall the multitude of motley social groups through which he passed going from Paris to Rome, to Turin, Venice, St. Petersburg, Vienna, Berlin, and elsewhere. The foreigners, men and women, whom we meet as characters in *La Comédie Humaine* were painted from life. It should not be forgotten, either, that he was often a visitor at one or another of the embassies in Paris and was acquainted with a number of the foreign colonies in the city.

Thus, the method begun with *Les Chouans* became a rule of composition. Before describing the places where he wished to set the plot of a novel, Balzac would visit them, unless he had previously paid them an attentive visit. So it was for Alençon in *La Vieille Fille* and *Le Cabinet des Antiques*, for Bayeux in *Une Double Famille*, *La Femme abandonnée*, Guérande in *Béatrix*, Le Croisic in *Un Drame au Bord de la Mer*, Tours and Touraine in *Le Lys dans la Vallée*, *La Grenadière*, *Le Curé de Tours*, *La Femme de Trente Ans*, *L'Illustre Gaudissart*, Saumur in *Eugénie Grandet*, Angoulême in *Illusions Perdues*, Issoudun in *La Rabouilleuse*, Limoges in *Le Curé de Village*, Sancerre in *La Muse du Département*, Nemours in *Ursule Mirouët*, Besançon in *Albert Savarus*, Voreppe in *Le Médecin de Campagne*, and many another town or region in many another novel. Numerous scholars and archeologists (for example,

De Contades, Alençon; Etienne Aubrée, Fougères; Maurice Serval, Albert Arrault, M. E. Weelen, Tours and Touraine; Fray-Fournier, Limoges) have verified the exactness of the descriptions of sites, monuments, houses, and streets. This exactness is very often complete, always expressive; if it sometimes strays from reality, it always gives the sensation of truth. Balzac's work is an album of widely extended sketches, wherein are gathered the landscapes that held some shreds of his heart, the sensations of his quivering being. Not content with noting what he saw and its effects upon his sensibility, he would question passersby for the explanation of some detail. He was providing himself with a map, with a plan.

Not only did Balzac study the sites; he gathered information about historic epochs and scientific questions that he wanted to write about. He questioned people who had lived under the *ancien régime*, like his friend Monsieur de Villers, former *Abbé de Cour* and *Maître de l'Oratoire* of the Count of Artois; or the mother of Madame de Berny, lady-in-waiting to Marie Antoinette; or those who had lived under the Empire, like the Duchess of Abrantès, and so on. And if he wanted to write of musical theories, as in *Massimilla Doni?* Although he was a great lover of music, he realized his technical deficiencies. He had an old German musician play the *Mosè* of Rossini for him, over and over, and he plied the man with questions. Thereafter he was able to give a long and very exact analysis of this opera in his novel.

And what if he needed to reconstitute the atmosphere of a jail, to depict the morals of criminals and policemen, to reproduce their speech? He was no longer satisfied to read the *Mémoires* of Vidocq, a former convict who became chief of the *Sûreté*. He had to have direct contacts, to hold conversations with Vidocq in person. And what impressions, what information he extracted from him! All this would be used for *Le Père Goriot*, in which Jacques Colin, called Vautrin, assumes the strong and singular individuality of his model, as Léon Gozlan describes it for us in *Balzac chez lui*. Balzac contrived to have some interviews with the former prison inhabitant and invited him to dine at Les Jardies. There he listened to advice about stressing reality strongly. And so Vautrin tells his yarns and narrates the horrible facts of convict life. In his turn, Farrabesche did the same in *Le Curé de Village*. The *bagne* or convict prison, and other types of prisons, the criminal investigations, the interrogation of prisoners, make up the dark, heinous, baleful surroundings of "La Dernière Incarnation de Vautrin," the fourth part of *Splendeurs et Misères des Courtisanes*. The slang of mob, murderers, and thieves offers us all its flavor and its terrible, clever, brutal images. Bibi Lupin, chief of the detective division (Criminal Investgation Department), and officers Louchard, Contenson, Peyrade, and Corentin were more or less modeled on the pattern of Vidocq.

The same method of eliciting information permitted him to describe military episodes, either singly as in *El Verdugo* and *Adieu*, or inserted into a novel as in *Les Marana, Le Médecin de Campagne*, and *Une Ténébreuse Affaire*. At the home of the Carraud family, where the husband was an instructor at the French military school of Saint-Cyr, Balzac became acquainted with such former officers of the imperial armies as Commandant Périolas, who recounted their adventures. He was likewise in debt to General de Pommereul for a large number of anecdotes. He stored all that away and made note of the most striking particulars. Traces are to be found in his album *Pensées, Sujets, Fragments*.

And there is still more proof of how Balzac succeeded in making up for what he did not see with his own eyes. In 1832 the Carrauds were residing at the Poudrerie of Angoulême, where their friends came to see and hear the already famous author. One of them, ship purser Grand-Besançon, had traveled widely, especially in the Indies and Malaya. Balzac questioned him eagerly and was able to elicit enough details for a very long article, which appeared in *Revue de Paris*, entitled "Voyage de Paris à Java." It is very witty and full of verve, but the descriptions of the places and the accounts of the mores of the natives are couched in terms so authentic that it is possible, when the opportunity offers, to evoke the romantic exotism and the ideas about those distant and marvelous isles that the men of 1830 entertained. Nor is that all. Balzac had never seen the fjords; yet in *Séraphîta* he described them in such appropriate terms that the Norwegians themselves declared them highly satisfactory. Might one perhaps believe that as early as 1830 he was thinking of setting a plot in a Nordic landscape when he gave this advice to Countess d'Oultremont, in an article "De la Mode en Littérature:" "I could tell you to study the local color of Lapland, and you would build for us an admirable Spitzbergen with quite natural ice, and aurora borealis that you had never seen, and reindeer, fish bones, whale oil, a snowy horizon, white Polar bears, and lichens. . . ."

There is no end to quoting proofs of the care with which this documentation is done, even to its minor details. Whether it concerns chemistry in *La Recherche de l'Absolu*, Swedenborgian theories in *Séraphîta*, theories of magnetism or mesmerism in *Ursule Mirouët*, Balzac, before letting a topic come up or be discussed by his characters, must impregnate himself with it to such an extent that very often he cannot refrain from intruding his own opinion. He obtained his information from specialists or at least from competent men. He endeavored to assimilate the scientific substance.

A problem insistently posed by literary criticism concerns the historical value of *La Comédie Humaine*. Nobody denies that this work is a live, animated, and picturesque portrayal. But certain exegetes wonder if it is an exact likeness, if, as Balzac claimed, his work is "a history of Society painted in action," "a complete history" of the France of the nineteenth century," "the tableau of Society modeled from life, in a manner of speaking, with all its good and all its evil." Brunetière did not hesitate to answer in the affirmative. Taine and Albert Sorel had a high opinion of Balzac as the historian of his century. *La Comédie Humaine* reproduces all the movements of political and social life from 1789 to 1848: peasant uprising, revolutionary agitation, imperial splendors, the blindness and unyielding stubbornness of the aristocracy under the Restoration. The rise of financial powers, the ascension of the middle classes, the frenzied, unscrupulous ambition of several politicians, the increasing importance of businessmen, the downfall of a nobility fixed in its sterile regrets, the triumph of democratic aspirations, the impetus of the social clergy carried away by the eloquence of Lamennais, the daring and generous projects of Saint-Simonism, all the jars and jolts that so profoundly stirred all classes of society and changed their aspect, at the time of the July Revolution and under the reign of Louis Philippe, are observed, related, described in *La Comédie Humaine,* studied for both causes and effects, both public and private.

And in their men also. A large number of those who emerged, as a result of their political roles, or thanks to their understanding of current needs, or because of their scientific, philosophic, literary, or artistic influence, are designated by name.[1] Others are submerged in fictional characters, very often composites. Let us not call the research undertaken to identify them "useless games." Such research makes it possible to put a firm base under the judgments made elsewhere by Balzac on the social categories represented by these individuals.

Let us pause to look at Balzac's portrayal of the aristocracy of Faubourg Saint-Germain. Even today there is lively argument concerning its veracity.[2] Sainte-Beuve, who had his own reasons for not caring for Balzac, lashed him pitilessly: "He has inventiveness and some degree of genius in the observation of morals —of some morals." He does not deny Balzac's ability "to paint and to describe"—but only shady, dubious persons. The people of polite society, and especially the women, he disguises with false elegance. Gustave Lanson, discussing the debate on these ladies, reproached the painter of history for the inexactness of their portraits. Has not Balzac been rated as "one of the foremost slanderers of the ruling classes" in Thureau-Danginin's reception speech at the French Academy in 1893? This gentleman, moreover, declared Balzac to be "just about incapable of creating a pure type of girl or woman," a statement which Jules Claretie treated with the severity that justice demands.

It would be possible to widen the debate on aristocratic society, to follow it up by a comparison with contemporary novelists (Bourget, Marcel Proust, Emile Baumann, Madame Claude

---

1 A remark of the Duchess of Dino, Talleyrand's niece, who had insisted that Balzac remain for dinner, in 1836, on the occasion of a visit he made to the Prince, then stopping at the chateau of Rochecotte, in Touraine, catches the novelist in a significant attitude: "He examined and observed us all most minutely, especially Monsieur de Talleyrand."

2 Cf. Ramon Fernandez, *Balzac,* p. 13.

Silve, and other writers not suspected of defamation because they belong by right of birth to that stratum of society) or by a comparison with professional historians and chroniclers of the early twentieth century. Opposite the *Cabinet des Antiques*, *Béatrix*, *La Duchesse de Langeais*, and *Le Lys dans la Vallée* would be set *L'Emigré*, *L'Etape*, and *L'Ecuyère* of Paul Bourget; and the conclusion would be that, in spite of the disintegration of the aristocratic class, it was possible—at least prior to 1940—to encounter in several districts of Paris and in the provinces, islets of society whose members preserved a body of manners, morals, and habits, an integral part of their temperament that continued to act on things and on people, just as Balzac had depicted them at the time of the Restoration and the reign of Louis-Philippe. It is "an antiquated atmosphere that has not been disturbed by the strong winds of our time," said Albéric Cahuet, referring to *L'Ecuyère* in 1920. The old mansions of the Faubourg Saint-Germain, which were still under the rule of unchanging principles and out-of-date customs, were filled with the nostalgic and stagnant majesty of that atmosphere. The walls, the furnishings, the ceremonious pomp still shaped minds that nevertheless retained a certain insolent ease of manner,[3] a boldness of musk- scented gallantries. The conclusion of such a comparison would be that Balzac's successors discerned in the mores and the characters of the descendants exactly the same marks and the same failings that he himself had so well observed. It was purposely that the sketch of the already famous author introduced into Parisian high society appears at the beginning of this chapter. Here is proof that he was speaking of men and women he had clearly seen and clearly heard, that his portraits and his pictures had been

---

3 Let us recall a still observable trait. With what disdain the Duchess of Langeais takes pleasure in mispronouncing the name of the father, Goriot, a former manufacturer of food pastes (vermicelli), whose daughter has regilded the coat of arms of the Count of Restaud. "This father Goriot . . . Doriot . . . Moriot. . . ." It is not a "famous name," so it is all right to mangle it. This passing remark fits in with the general truth expressed by La Bruyère: "If a person pretends sometimes not to remember certain names that he thinks are obscure, and he affects to corrupt them by his pronunciation, it is because of the good opinion he has of his own" (*Les Caractères*, in the chapter "Concerning Society and Conversation").

painted from living models and not from imagination. It might be said that his detractors are satisfying the vengeance of their ancestors; it is a sort of legacy of tradition.

But how far was his initiation carried? Some historians, critics, and specialists have begun to verify the historical value of *La Comédie Humaine*. Let us mention, among others, Le Nôtre in *La Chouannerie Normande au Temps de l'Empire* with regard to the ordeals suffered by Madame de la Chanterie and her daughter (*L'Envers de l'Histoire Contemporaine*); and Marc Blanchard in *La Campagne et ses Habitants dans l'Oeuvre de Balzac* concerning social, economic, and agricultural theories expressed in *Le Lys dans la Vallée, Le Médecin de Campagne, Le Curé de Village, Les Paysans,* and so on. Numerous studies, innumerable articles are concerned with the world of the judiciary, the police and policemen, medicine and doctors, religion and priests, music and musicians, the arts and artists, finance and bankers, and more besides. Taken as a whole, their conclusions concede his exactness in depicting types, in making composite portraits, in reconstructing atmosphere. Technical documentation is found to be carried out more or less thoroughly depending on the matter under examination; sometimes it is incomplete and superficial. In *Balzac, les Médecins, le Médecine et la Science* (1945), Dr. Bonnet-Roy notes certain reservations concerning the competence of the great author. He finds that in large measure Balzac absorbed the theories and the learned doctrinal ideologies of his time, professed by numerous doctors whom he had known and associated with. Bonnet-Roy finds a double current of realistic information and imaginative distortion in certain diagnoses: "fictionalized pathology," based on peremptory assertions and often on excessive generalization. Although an inspired intuition sometimes takes the place of positive clinical and biological knowledge, Balzac nevertheless methodically gathered enough information to describe with certainty the ills from which his characters were suffering.

He had merely to avail himself of his own experiences and observations when he decided to describe and pass judgment on the press of his time, to depict the situation among the journalists of Paris. Such was his object in *Un Grand Homme*

de Province à Paris (Part II of *Les Illusions Perdues*; 1839).
These portraits shout their truthfulness. They are "of a frighten-
ing exactitude," he wrote Madame Hanska. And again, on June
2, 1839: "It is not merely a book but a fine brave action; above
all, the howls of the press are still continuing." Balzac knew
well what he was talking about: as we have said, he had collaborated on a number of journals from 1830 on; and he had
tried to found several. He had suffered attacks, often venomous
and unjust, dictated by the jealousy of the literary fraternity, and
he took his revenge by remaining faithful to truth. In *Illusions
Perdues*, we are confronted by a violent satire, as we are in
"Une Chronique de la Presse," which appeared in the *Revue
Parisienne* of August 25, 1840, and then in the *Monographie
de la Presse Parisienne*. Meanwhile, competent historians have
found in the characters and episodes of the novel authentic
features of the journalistic habits of the period, and they have
been able to identify particular persons and their characteristics.
The protagonist, Lucien Chardon de Rubempré, represents some
of the methods and some of the behavior of Sainte-Beuve and
Jules Janin and certain adventures of Albéric Second. By Balzac's
own admission, Lousteau, the serial writer, is Sandeau. There is
something of Du Gozlan in Nathan, of Girardin in Finot; there
is something of Roqueplan in La Palférine (*Un Prince de la
Bohême*). These more or less pronounced resemblances give
solidity to the historical base. Others can be found for Blondet
and Vignon, critics on *Les Débats*, or for Félicien Vernon, the
spiteful anticlerical chronicler, or Hector Merlin, the chief of
the Royalist press, the caricaturist Bixiou, and so on. A shameful, seamy side, secret machinations, bargaining, blackmail, personal vengeance, the spirt of anger, and a total lack of conviction—all these characterize the press of the Restoration and
the Bourgeois Royalty; it was a sorry business. The newspaper
office, the editorial room, the publisher's den, the bookseller's
shop have their dark corners where behind the scenes, deals,
dishonest and sometimes infamous, are arranged. Blondet states
it for us: "The press no longer exists to enlighten but to flatter
opinions. It is a shop where words are sold to the public in any
color it desires them." Corruption reigns and spreads afar; it
affects the least of the journalists as well as the directors; the

offices of a newspaper are "evil places of thought where all forms of literature are prostituted."

But what is to be said of criticism? Here, praise and blame are weighed on precision scales. Reputations are made and unmade with the aid of banknotes and bidding. "But we are dealers in words and we live on the proceeds of our commerce . . . articles read today, forgotten tomorrow: in my view, all that is worth only what you can get for it." So speaks Félicien Vernon, one of the most cynical of the group, who has it in for everyone because of the sordid existence to which his marriage to a fat cook confines him. Here, as Blondet instructed Lucien de Rubempré, is the principle that justifies this venal conduct: "Everything is bilateral in the domain of thought. Ideas are binary: Janus is the myth of Criticism and the symbol of Genius." Stated in other terms, it is proof of a critic's talent to oppose tomorrow the judgment he expressed yesterday, or even to write two contradictory articles one after the other.

Balzac had a lofty idea of journalism; he wanted it to be "a priesthood, respectable and respected." So, facing this troop of profligates and puppets, he created the coterie of Michel Chrestien, Joseph Bridau, Léon d'Arthez, and their friends. These men are virtuous and incorruptible; they profess that work and integrity are the only roads to success and true glory: their stoicism supposes a will of iron, a scorn for money and hypocrisy. Never has the art of Balzac succeeded in imparting a sensation of such profound truth. In scourging so cruelly the base writers who prostitute their talent (like Lousteau), he has nonetheless underlined the sharp, subtle mind, that keen-edged instrument that the French temperament handles so alertly. *Les Illusions Perdues* is another page of literary history where the fashion and the genres, the ideas in vogue under the Restoration, are studied. On that page there are striking formulations that bring together judgments passed with firmness and expressed with banter. This study of journalism is as good as a page from someone's memoirs, written with conscience, emotion, energy, and color— the qualities of Balzac as historian.

Furthermore, he divined and predicted the immense role of the press and the influence it was to exercise in every domain:

"Journalism will be the madness of the nineteenth century." Everyone is privileged to verify the accuracy of the expression by comparing the present state of the press with the unfettered passions, hatreds, and rivalries which Balzac has described to us; let every one form his independent judgment.

Observation, intuition—these are the two poles at which the magnetic force of his creative power is concentrated. He had stored in his brain an infinite multitude of images and remembrances. When he dipped into this harvest of art, a sort of delirium took possession of him. Then the miracle of true invention occurred. He described it himself in the Preface to the first edition of *La Peau de Chagrin*:

There takes place in poets or in really philosophical writers a moral, inexplicable and extraordinary phenomenon, which science can hardly understand. It is a sort of second sight that allows them to divine the truth of any possible situation; or better yet, a kind of power that carries them wherever they ought or wish to be. They invent the true, by analogy, or they *see* the object to be described, whether the object comes to them or they go toward the object. . . . Have men the power to bring the universe into their brain, or is their brain a talisman with which they abolish the laws of time and space?

Many other statements make it easy to believe that Balzac was endowed by the fairies with special psychic faculties that gave him *intuitive sight*, and he believed himself to be clairvoyant. Diderot had already described this "particular, secret, indefinable quality of soul, without which one achieves nothing very great nor very beautiful." It is the mark of genius, in poets, philosophers, orators. He does not know to what mental or physical state it is to be attributed. To it must be added "the observant spirit," which "acts without effort, without restraint; it does not look, it sees. . . . There is no phenomenon present, but they have all had an effect on it, and what remains of them in it is a kind of sense which others do not have . . . a sort of prophetic spirit" (Quoted from Curtius, *Balzac*, p. 322).

"In me, observation had become intuition; it penetrated the soul without neglecting the body; or, rather, it gave me the faculty of living the life of the individual on which it was acting, allowing me to substitute myself for him . . ."(the opening of *Facino Cane*).

Trained as a soothsayer in the interpretation of signs, Balzac plumbed the depths of the apparitions that assailed him. He probed their hearts and their loins. For were they not as alive as he? He grasped the entire being, now become human; he uncovered secret actions, past and future, shameful thoughts and hidden passions. He outdistanced the contrivings of a destiny too slow to catch up with him. He scudded ahead of his powers of observation, urged on by his "monstrous" and "necessary fecundity." The moment had come: his intuitive genius, of itself, sufficed to put in motion, *vita in motu*, all the earthly and spiritual realities, now enslaved for his art. Cherished companions of his vigils, the shadows trooped around him, swarming before his hallucinated eyes. He watched them move about, dance, live, mingle, join in pairs: it was the great nocturnal witches' sabbath. It is not this or that particular mortal who can be recognized in the magic mirror; it is this or that actor in the Human Comedy: it is old Goriot, it is old Grandet, it is Monsieur Balthasar Claës, it is old Madame Cibot, it is Véronique Graslin, it is Diane de Maufrigneuse, and the De Marsays, the Du Tillets, the De Trailles, and it is the Girl with the Golden Eyes, a collection of humanity that makes one wonder on what planet they were born. The reader contemplates these samples of a strange species and repeats to himself with astonishment the words of Balzac the demigod: "Would art then be kept from being stronger than Nature?" Such is the Balzacian miracle.

Underneath the transparency of the individual, we come in contact with the universal man; thus, Balzac continues the line of the great classics. However, the enchantment evaporates suddenly at the ironic outburst: "My concierge? Why she's old Mrs. Cibot." And from another: "Last night, when she arrived at the ball so beautifully gowned, I thought I was seeing Diane de Maufrigneuse. What a vamp!" That is why, every day, so many people relating some occurrence misuse the expression: "But it was absolutely Balzacian!"

It is in vain, it is quite wrong, to set the novelist Balzac against Balzac the historian, to confront the idealist with the realist. They are inextricably intertwined; the one complements the other. We have remarked on this, and we shall demonstrate it when considering the structure of the characters. As for Balzac, the one side could not exist without the other. If his most famous creations are types raised to a very high power, whether in vice or in virtue, it is nonetheless certain that they are exact in every detail. I am considering only the vicious ones: Gobseck, Grandet, Vautrin, Hulot, Marsay, who, fortunately for humanity, are exceptional types. No longer does anyone deny Balzac his title of historian of the mores of the France of the nineteenth century. He has, indeed, bequeathed us "that book which we all regret that Rome, Athens, Tyre, Memphis, Persia, India, unfortunately, did not leave to tell us about their civilizations" (Preface). Said George Sand: "He has written, for the archives of the history of mores, the memoirs of the half-century just past." Even in his first novels, he carefully noted the old-fashioned forms of dress and accessories of adornment, the customs, objects, and relics "of the past century," which, in a changed world, give a strange or comic touch to the old or eccentric people who have remained faithful to former fashions and manners.

He remained ever interested in these living anachronisms, as attentive to these details as an archivist, an archeologist, or an annalist. Is not that in the highest degree the attitude of the historian and the chronicler? Flaubert's opinion remains indisputable: "No one, later, will be able to write the history of the reign of Louis Philippe without consulting Balzac." The same can be said of the reigns of Louis XVIII and Charles X. The abundance of documents in *La Comédie Humaine* give this work "the value of a book of annals." Brunetière, in his *Balzac*, asserts that the *Comédie* is equal in value to *Memoirs for the History of the Society of His Time*. To conclude: I am one of those who do not consider the judgment of Anatole France to be exaggerated: "I consider him to be the greatest historian of modern France, which fills his immense work with its living presence."

4 · The Determinant Role of Description

NOW THAT we are acquainted with the turn of mind characteristic of Balzac, we shall not be surprised to find that he allots
a very important place in the economy of his novels to descriptions and, indeed, assigns them a role of capital importance.
This is a proceeding significant for its components: a precise
sketch, a full palette of colors, details reproduced minutely. In
addition, the lines and the colors put into very strong relief and
highlight certain objects, "some singularities," where the observer rightly perceives "more than one problem to be resolved."
Scènes de la Vie privée is something rather like a picture gallery where the artist's technique reveals his intention: he not
only satisfies his desire to master Nature by capturing her on his
canvas; he also introduces her as an actress who plays her role
aside, intervening in the vicissitudes and the movements of the
drama. When this characteristic is understood, it condemns the
disparagement with which some critics treat these descriptions
because of their abundance and their "interminable" length.
We should like to make it clear by means of some examples
taken from *Scènes de la Vie Privée* (1830–32), and others from
the novels composed toward the end of Balzac's career (1846).

Walking in the rue Saint-Denis, let us stop to contemplate the
old house of the wool merchant Guillaume, with its gro-
tesque façade bearing the sign of a cat playing with a racket
(*La Maison du Chat-qui-pelote*); in the Faubourg Saint-Germain, the "ancient and sumptuous" mansion of the Duchess
of Langeais; in the rue du Tournquet-Saint-Jean, the somber

48

dwelling where Caroline Crochard lives with her mother; at the
corner of the Vieille-Rue-du-Temple and the rue Neuve-Saint-
François, the town house where the austere and icy bigotry of
Madame Granville runs rife; in the rue Taitbout, the new house
where the latter's husband conceals his illicit love affair with
Caroline (*Une Double Famille*). Then we go up the stairs, to
the woolen shop, and into the drawing rooms, the boudoirs,
the bedrooms.

Before any of the inhabitants appear, their passions and the
secrets of their souls have been revealed to us by the exterior
and interior appearance of the dwellings where an evil fate has
forced them to seek domicile, unless perhaps their desires and
their whims have chosen deliberately. When Balzac imagines
a stage setting, three words often emerge from his pen: he always supposes that an *observer* interprets the *particularities* of
things and persons and discovers in them the *harmony* that he
has himself preestablished between these details and the souls
of the people whom he has pushed onto the stage of the drama.
He has no difficulty in seeing these relationships. Is he not both
the observer and the creator? "Everything here is in harmony"
because he has so willed it and because he aims to demonstrate
this principle: "the science of the setting," which includes the
knowledge of the archaeologist and the antiquary, is infallible
in expressing the physical and mental complex of the occupant.
He is the arranger who marks the harmony of the parts and the
unity of attention. At the same time he is "one of those tapestry
makers who guide the artists"; today we would say one of those
clever decorators who do applied psychophysiology, interpreting
or anticipating the preferences of their clients. Today's decorators can claim Balzac as an illustrious predecessor. The boudoir
of the Duchess of Carigliano, the salon of Madame de Granville, the bedroom of Caroline Crochard (alias Caroline de
Bellefeuille) might be reproduced in colored illustrations, together with the text of their description, in an expensively styl-
ish magazine; they would make an alluring advertisement for
some furniture manufacturer. Each piece—each bed, writing
table, chest of drawers, drape, mirror, curtain—reveals the spirit
of the woman who lives among them, whose beauty they accentu-
ate and whose charms they reinforce. Only Madame de Gran-

ville, on the contrary, "inscribes her own character in a world of things" where everything is "discord"; the niggardliness, the meanness, narrowness, and coldness of heart, the rigidity of her essentially formalistic piety are divined in these arrangements.

Balzac was undertaking a task that twelve years later he would be able to contemplate with a certain complacency as he gave himself the title of "narrator of the dramas of intimate life, archaeologist of social furniture." A determinant principle suddenly became clear, from which he was to draw all possible consequences. The individuals who deviate from it habitually go to their ruin—habitually, not inevitably, "for the social state affords chances that Nature does not permit." Monuments shape the souls and inculcate observance of the laws proper to the development of the species. And if these souls change their habitat, what then? Then they are in danger. Moral situations go hand in hand with material modifications or, perhaps one might say, local changes.

Let us use *La Maison du Chat-qui-pelote* to demonstrate the grounds of these Balzacian truths. This is the first novel to use the various techniques that Balzac was soon to develop into a system. Here, three descriptions precede three decisive situations; by their contrasts they announce the series of vicissitudes in which the fate of the heroine will be played; they mark its turnings. First the business house stands before us, its hoary appearance, a miracle of archaeology, perpetuating a way of life that must adopt itself to the dwellers in a century-old building. Its interior had trained Augustine Guillaume in the modest virtues and practical ideals of the housewife, in good business sense, commonplace to be sure, but scrupulous in its probity; the house held the promise of the happiness of family life, the joys that recompense a laborious existence, and above all the pleasure of husbanding the money earned by unremitting work. "In the silence of the dark counters" the girl flourished "like a violet in the depths of a wood," protected against the storms of passion. How could whim, humor, poetical enthusiasm, mirages of the imagination, capriciousness, even the delirium of impetuous inspiration, associate with the regulated ordering, the punctual timetable, the monotonous tasks, whose tangible rewards were at last entered in the big accounting ledger that

Augustine, when she became the bride of the shop assistant who would be her father's successor, would continue to keep up, as her mother now did. That unlikely, incongruous possibility appears, however, in the person of an artist, a painter, the scion of a noble family, Théodore de Sommervieux, who is charmed by the girl's prettiness. Misfortune is foreordained in this rupture of immemorial tradition, symbolized and protected up to that time by the venerable house; Augustine yields to the attractions of her love. Her parents' counsels fall on deaf ears; Augustine marries her artist.

Here is the second description and the second contrast. After they have savored the delights of a year's honeymoon, a lack of understanding creeps insensibly between the young husband and his wife. Augustine's home training had not prepared her for life in artistic circles; she is incapable of adapting to it, unable to respond to the whims and fancies that Théodore's enthusiasm for his art provokes. Too prudish, too rigid in the applications of the principles that she had learned from her mother, Augustine inspires in her husband a coolness that increases as time passes; he turns away from her. Her native wit is not sufficient to help her overcome her prejudices. Although she endeavors to win back her husband's heart, her happiness is over. Théodore de Sommervieux frequently deserts the conjugal apartment although a baby has now come into it. He becomes attached to the Duchess of Carigliano, a "famous coquette of the Imperial court." In despair, "weeping tears of blood," Augustine decides to have recourse to the counsels and consolations of her family.

Now a small middle-class mansion in the rue du Vieux-Colombier opens its doors to us. Here the Guillaume household is living a life of complete boredom, having turned their business over to their eldest daughter, Virginie, the well-behaved, prudent, and sensible girl who married her father's first assistant, Joseph Lebas. The cold, gilded, and silvered luxury, lacking in taste, has turned this dwelling into a "bazaar" and each room in it into a "chapel." In the eyes of Augustine, who by now has developed into a more mature young woman, all this seems to be the image of an artificial, backward world, empty of feeling and of "life-giving ideas." The crisis grows more complex. How can she hope for enlightenment, constructive ideas, or help in her misfortune from such petty people, for whom the allegorical Land of Love (of Mademoiselle de Scudéry) and its sentimental pathways are sheer nonsense? The same impression and the same contrast result when Augustine takes her sorrowing heart to Joseph and Virginie Lebas. In the old shop, their household continues the ponderous, mechanical existence that insures the ancient honor of the Cat-Who-Plays-with-a-Racket. In these two people the sorrow of Augustine's soul hears no echo. They answer her appeal with commonplaces concerning the morality of the rue Saint-Denis; such morality is sufficient for their simple conduct. Augustine, by breaking away, had long ago repudiated those precepts, and now the rupture is total and complete. The wretched girl flees with relief from these dull-minded people and their horrible house. These two visits were, in effect, but a single visit: the depressing mansion of her parents, lacking any elegance, is similar to the Lebas rear-shop living quarters, only more ornate. Augustine goes out heartsick, feeling that her life is ruined, blaming her misfortune on the people confined inside those walls, which exclude the outer world. It was within those walls, it was their fault, that her imprisoned heart had been overburdened with lessons in narrow, vulgar requirements and any impulses toward the heights of sentiment had been repressed. Who then would have initiated her into the exalting secrets of the kind of love that subdues and masters men? Now it was too late.

The third description, by a violent and more complex contrast, reveals to the young woman the abyss that separates her from her husband, the abyss in which her happiness is already engulfed. Summoning a "supernatural" courage, timid little Augustine resolves to confront the Duchess of Carigliano, the haughty great lady, who has been revealed to her as her triumphant rival. How does the modest violet bear the suffocating heat of the ancient and sumptuous mansions of the Faubourg Saint-Germain? She had never before set foot in one.

When she walked through those majestic halls, up those grandiose stairways to those immense drawing rooms decorated with flowers despite the rigors of winter and furnished with that taste characteristic of women born into opulence or the distinguished customs of the aristocracy, Augustine felt a sharp pang in her heart. She envied the secrets of this elegance, of whose existence she had never even dreamed; she breathed an air of grandeur which revealed to her the attraction which this house held for her husband.

Having come with the intention of learning from the duchess the artifices that had taken Sommervieux's love away from her, she began to understand. A new contrast here. The environment, the milieu of this mansion with its refined luxury is the symbol of complex coquetry. When she is admitted to the boudoir in which, voluptuously recumbent, the idol, "like an antique statue," is receiving the worship rendered to her beauty by an assiduous admirer—in this instance a young cavalry colonel—Augustine grows angry with her own past: "Ah! If I had been brought up like this siren!" Yes, beings are dominated by things. Forgetting her arrogance, abandoning her cruel egotism, moved by her vanity, the duchess gives the weeping little wife the benefit of her own experience by revealing the secrets that protect a wife's superiority over her husband. "Externals, for fools, are half of life, and for that reason many a man of talent is a fool in spite of all his genius." "A science of trifles, but nevertheless important," whose very existence was unknown to the house of a wool merchant. What irony! The duchess is "a strong soul"; the daughter of the merchant, a weak soul. Each is the product of a different background. Augustine was not made for "the powerful embraces of genius." And the final comparison leads back to the principle of habitat: the humble and modest flower that had bloomed in the valley dies when it is transplanted to the high regions where storms are generated and the sun is incandescent.

We could start this demonstration over again, using a score of other novels: *Eugénie Grandet* (1833) or *Le Curé de Village* (1837), where two old houses figure and cause the psychophysiologic complex of two girls born in their shadows, Eugénie Grandet and Véronique Sauviat. Similarly, in *Les Illusions Perdues* (1837), the printing shop of old Séchard, with its dirty, tumbledown appearance and its worm-eaten furniture, assumes the features of an old man who is a miser and hostile to his son. The moral position of Augustine Guillaume facing the Duchess of Carigliano we find identically reproduced in *La Cousine*

Bette: the virtuous Baroness Hulot goes to ask the great opera singer Josépha Mirah to give back her husband, whom she believes is caught in the toils of the famous actress; but another "protector" has already replaced him. Here again is the splendor of the picture frame, splendor spread like a trap. "The power of the seductions of vice" astonishes the dazzled eyes of the baroness by the sheer luxury of furnishings. Although surfeited, *blasée,* like the Duchess of Carigliano, the singer allows her feelings to be stirred by the sublime yet naïve greatness of the weeping wife; once again, the candor of virtue disarms cynicism and the sinning woman becomes the servant of the pure-hearted wife.

The symbolism of material things, their repercussions on the activity of souls, were, in the end, to mark profoundly the novelist's conceptions. Like invisible springs, they actuate the great dramas to such a degree that inanimate things themselves, by their magnetic power, act upon destinies as living beings do. It is possible to sense in advance the system of correspondences that Balzac will eventually push to its extreme limit: the pebble in the fjord has spiritual thought and language.

He was to extend this method to the composition of his portraits. A gesture, a peculiarity of dress, a rent in the coat, an oddness in the costume, a facial feature, the style of hairdressing or head covering, the hair straight, wavy, or curly, and the hair's coloring, the color of the skin: these are the descriptive signs, the documentary signals that give information about the moral makeup of people, about their social status and worldly position, with as much exactness as direct questions and answers. Such details are in themselves the expression of a person's characteristic bent. To them must be added certain words and phrases borrowed from a special vocabulary that intimates the origin of those who use them often. Balzac uses them not only as an instrument of description, but for the portrait, for the dialogue, and even for the equilibrium of the plan. But as his observant gaze grows in acuity and grasps more surely the expressive detail, Balzac also frequently yields to the temptation to overload and extend his descriptions.

One who has lived a great deal in and with *La Comédie Humaine* at length falls under its spell. The choice of a detail immediately brings to mind its moral significance so that, in a manner of speaking, his intelligence inebriated by strange vapors, the reader interprets the behavior of his fellow creatures, not by an original judgment of his own, but by a sort of Balzacian code that has taken the place of the natural exercise of reason and experience. Let us suppose he enters a drawing room or a secondhand dealer's shop (*La Peau de Chagrin*); immediately he evokes what might be called the *loca communia* of Balzacian rhetoric. The same thing is true when he discovers someone whose prototype is a character of a favorite author: a name springs at once to his lips.

The true Balzacian develops for himself the habit of meticulous observation. And this habit has the effect of a shock in reverse; he examines an interior and its furnishings attentively in order to deduce from them the spiritual complex of the man who lives there. In addition, he has recourse to a spontaneous method of operation, a rule of comparison: the collection of prototypes created by his god. This fascinating art may lead those who become subject to it toward a dangerous mirage. Some may answer that it arms them with perspicacity, with experience, with prudence. But the theory of the milieu, the place, the environment, without being a total failure, now has only a relative value. Some novelists continue to make use of it, but there are other psychophysiological explanations, deeper and more scientific, better adapted to the infinite suppleness of human dynamism. Balzac was to invent some even more fantastic.

Part Two · Currents of Ideas

5 · The Philosophical Meaning of the Fantastic Theme

DURING THE course of the years 1830 and 1831, Balzac's production was abundant, even tumultuously so. The mariner's compass may stand as its symbol. His activity shoots off toward the four cardinal points; between times it aims in the intermediate directions. If you mentally picture a shifting of orientation by a few degrees to the right or to the left, these varied genres, because of their composite makeup, might be pushed toward one line or the other, overlapping one or another of the preceding works, to pass, for example, from *Scènes de la Vie Privée* to *Scènes de la Vie Militaire*. Their immediate position depends on the impression uppermost in the mind of the reader.

This image was suggested to me by the expression "literary weathervane," which the novelist uses in an article of May 29, 1830, "De la Mode en Littérature" to announce "the fashion of the coming year." "You may choose between the colorful and the dramatic, between the *fantastic* and the real." He brought out *La Peau de Chagrin* in August, 1831. This novel had a second edition, accompanied by twelve tales, under the general title *Romans et Contes Philosophiques*. In 1832, *Nouveaux Contes Philosophiques* was added to the series.

At first glance the name may seem pretentious, but for the thinking man, there is something *philosophical* in everything, even in extraordinary yarns, even in those of a farcical or macabre nature. *Fantastic* would have been a more fitting word, but Balzac would have none of it. When in February, 1832, the *Contes Bruns* appeared, on which he had collaborated with

59

Philarète Chasles and Rabout, he declared in an article to *La Caricature:*

First of all, let us congratulate the authors of the *Contes Bruns* for not having slipped into some corner of their title the word *fantastic,* the vulgar program of a genre in its first flush of newness, to be sure, but already too much worn by the mere abuse of the word. And yet, if ever the conditions for allowing such a title have been fulfilled anywhere, certainly it is in the volume with which we are presently concerned: eyes without eyelids, body without arms, head without an owner, details of an existence in some other world; here, I believe, there is something of a fantastic nature or I am no judge.

This opinion is perfectly applicable to preceding works: *L'Elixir de Longue Vie, Zéro, La Danse des Pierres, La Comédie du Diable, L'Auberge Rouge, Jésus-Christ en Flandre, La Peau de Chagrin.* The *Fantastic Tales* of Hoffmann, translated by Loëve Viemars (1829), had stimulated the public taste for this style, and Jules Janin followed it up with *L'Ane Mort et la Femme Guillotinée* (1829) and *La Confession* (1830). This vogue reawakened in Balzac a tendency that had manifested itself ten years earlier in his first works: *Falthurne, Sténie, Le Centenaire, La Dernière Fée, Argow-le-Pirate.* Their web is interwoven with a vital magnetic power, able to project its energy a great distance. For the magic spells of Anne Radcliffe or Mautrin, the young romancer little by little substituted agents endowed with a power that he tried to explain scientifically. But in these new works (called *philosophical*), he made use of a piece of shagreen leather, which magic talisman had the virtue of insuring its possessor the satisfaction of all his desires: shrinking a little at each new pleasure, when it was reduced to nothingness, it caused the death of its beneficiary. Or again, there was the elixir that reanimated the dying and kept them alive. There was also the witches' Sabbath in the cathedral where the arches, pillars, and lectern engaged in a dance while the organs played of their own volition. There was also the diabolical pact that would restore youth to the body of Melmoth at the cost of his soul.

It is necessary to make concessions to the tastes of the times. That implacable leather is soon forgotten. That diabolical pact, which was finally quoted on the stock exchange like an ordinary stock, amuses us by its oddity. We take each of the extraordinary events for what it is: a cold allegory. Is it not the mark of a clever artist to substitute natural causes for them? The shagreen is the symbol of the phthisis that devours Raphaël. It is a *deus ex machina,* a magic vehicle that will take us through all the social spheres to see how the *philosophical principles* are applied in them. Philarète Chasles said that *La Peau de Chagrin* and the *Tales* are works "where real observations, full of subtlety, are enclosed within a magic circle." To paint "the fantastic of his epoch" on canvases of authentic veracity—that was the goal of the storyteller. To translate into clearly understandable language the words inscribed on the talisman—that was the goal of the thinker. The colorful evocation of a civilization given over to unlimited enjoyment in the licentiousness of the passions and the profligacy of luxury, shamelessly appearing alongside the wretchedness of human society—that was the incredible but authentic enchantment. The philosophic lesson has to be drawn from it by showing the consequences of its excesses. In Balzac's opinion, these *Tales* are only variations on the theme treated at length in the symphony entitled *La Peau de Chagrin.* In its inner meaning, in its depths, it is a study of mores, satirical in aim, fantastic in form, philosophical in its immediate goal; it consists of searching out the causes of social disintegration.

Let us reconstruct the philosophical system of Balzac. Whence comes the *mal du siècle,* the despair that observers and doctors note especially in the youth of 1830? Never did the frenzy of enjoyment range over so wide a scale of pleasures and sensations, some more subtle, some more violent, where the spirit and the body combined their resources. The more they increased, the greater grows the despair. Every excess demands its payment. Senses become dulled in this terrible game, in the expenditure of nervous strength. The empty place in the soul becomes still more hollow as the appeal to the infinite increases and rises; people become apathetic. The organism can be awakened only by renewed and disordered excitation. Because it requires infernal voluptuousness, the brain conceives and invents artificial pleasures and perfects its instruments of enjoyment. Is not this the goal toward which modern civilization tends? "Debauchery becomes a very great art, like poetry." *Ability* and *volition* united—such is the formula of this egotism. It renews that of Jean Jacques: "The man who thinks is a depraved animal." Balzac repeats it: "Thought must be considered the quickening cause of man's disorganization." As man becomes more civilized, he kills himself, for "life diminishes in direct ratio to the power of its desires." Epicurean wisdom could provide us an efficacious antidote in this other formula: *See* and *know*—discover by means of the intelligence the very substance of the fact, enjoy it intuitively without the contamination that physical possession entails. Once the latter is appeased, it dissolves into abstract ideas. Extract them without fatiguing your organs. These "pleasures and delights will even supply you with themes if you are an artist." A fine code of law that septuagenarian fogies are always unsuccessfully preaching to young people! One of them, after having exposed to Raphaël, the hero of *La Peau de Chagrin*, these theories, gives them a comic twist: "An hour of love" with "a young ghoul" seems more substantial to him than these "phantasmal ideas" and hollow dreams; the thought has killed the thinker. The immobility in life, the moderation and renunciation taught in the past by the elder Balzac are without value for the son. All the characters of the novel—Raphaël, Foedora, the old antiquary, the courtesan Aquilina, who wastes away with disease in the hospital and dies young—prefer to lose none of the beatitude preliminary to the martyrdom of the passions: death is a swap.

We shall examine the scientific value of these philosophical theories, but we shall not discuss the moral import claimed by its inventor but decried by H. de Latouche, Sainte-Beuve, Montalembert. The principal merit of this "poem"—it irritated Balzac to hear it called "a novel"—consists in the portrayal of the extremely unlike environments into which this "oriental enchantment" leads us.

By means of its glow, this "frenzy of invention," this implacable satire, "this colored poetry of the senses," creates the actual sensation of the most dramatic realism, the din of orgies, the soft pleasures of cool idylls. It is a hurly-burly whose movement is speeded with clanking and clicking and the cracking of the whip; the animal tamer torments his beasts, real wild animals roaring with pleasure, never sated, never wearied of their intoxications. Enthusiasm urges the author on and on, pushes him ahead in the dance of colors, rhythms, images, and sounds. His style meanders, his prose undulates, conforming to the changes of scene with unequaled virtuosity. Nevertheless, he remains the veracious "historian" of the nineteenth century slain by a poison: an excess of civilization.

According to their author, the *Philosophical Tales* followed from the axiom that supported *La Peau de Chagrin*. The intensity of an idea or of a sentiment, whether joy or sorrow, disorganizes the vital forces; it strikes down the body as with a bolt of lightning. Here in *Adieu* is proof: in the crossing of the Beresina, the Countess of Vandières is violently separated from her lover. Thereafter, as she sinks into a state of madness, she repeats over and over a single word—"Adieu!" It was the last word that she had uttered to Philippe de Sucy, the officer with whom she was in love. When he finally returns from capitivity, the gentle madwoman does not recognize the man who had never ceased loving her. He attempts a desperate measure to restore her reason. In a setting as faithful as possible to the original he reconstructs the terrible scene of their separation. The mind of the unfortunate woman is shocked into sanity. "Human will comes with its electric torrents" to bring life to this dazed, bewildered body. The woman bursts into tears as she recognizes her loved one; she embraces him. But suddenly "her tears dried, she stiffened into a corpse as though touched by lightning."

In *Le Réquisitionnaire* the same effect is described in the case of a mother killed by sorrow when she finds her lost son. In *Un Drame au Bord de la Mer*, a Breton fisherman kills his son because he fears he will sully the family name; the idea of honor kills paternal love. In *L'Auberge Rouge*, a man kills his friend because the idea of the crime engenders the crime itself: the idea of autosuggestion. In *El Verdugo*, an eldest son is condemned to kill his father and his brothers in order to have his own life spared. He obeys the order of his father, who wishes the name and nobility title of his family to survive: the idea of dynasty wipes out paternal love. In *L'Elixir de Longue Vie*, a son kills his father, the sooner to possess his inheritance: the idea of heredity. *Melmoth Réconcilié* was added to the group in 1835. A man sells his soul to the devil in order to live amid pleasures forever: the idea of longevity. Many deviltries and phantasmagorias run rife in one and another of the tales.

There still remain *Le Chef-d'oeuvre Inconnu* (1831) and *La Recherche de l'Absolu* (1834). The former was a prelude to the tragedy of Louis Lambert. It is the story of a seventeenth-century painter, Frenhofer, whose intense imagination in the quest for the ideal kills his artistic strength. For ten whole years, he works secretly on a woman's portrait, incessantly retouching it in the delirium of his enthusiasm. The balance between his interior life and his common sense has been broken. When at last he shows his canvas to two friends, they see only a chaos of color, a shapeless daub, a mass of confused lines, while he ecstatically contemplates what he thinks is superhuman beauty. The others are unable to bring him to his senses, and during the night he dies.

Balthazar Claës, he who is in quest of the absolute, exhausts himself in a similar drama. This time, the breakdown of nitrogen (a desire which Balzac did not believe was beyond the powers of modern chemistry) is the fixed idea, the mania. Because of the enormous sums required by the experiments, this passion ruins the family of Claës. Claës dies in despair, believing at the last moment that he has discovered the coveted secret.

Much later, *Gambara* (1837) and *Massimilla Doni* (1839), two works concerned with music, were added to the *Etudes Philosophiques*. Music appears under two forms, performance and composition, subjected to the same test as was the central thought in *Louis Lambert*; that is, the composition and its performance are killed by the overabundance of the creative principle. Massimilla, a beautiful and unhappy patrician of Venice, is spurned by her infamous husband, Cataneo, a vicious and debauched old duke. This highly placed maniac sacrifices everything, including his fortune, to search for a musical effect: a perfect chord in the unison of the first string of a musical instrument and the human voice. There lies the point of the novel: thought kills art. Likewise, Prince Emilio Memmi, the lover of Massimilla, exemplifies ideal love annihiliating virile strength.

Balzac set a pace for these adventures that keeps the reader breathless. He is familiar with the art of shortcuts; and at will, he complicates the strangeness of the atmosphere. A kind of poetry made up of blows, surprises, dramatic ferocities, and deviltries breaks loose around figures etched with strokes now delicate, now, and more often, violently energetic—figures colored as if by the light streaming through stained glass. These are some of the narrator's special talents.

Balzac was more poet than thinker. Nevertheless, he took himself very seriously when he set forth his philosophical theories. Poetry was the vehicle of his thought, nourished by a "hidden science" that "carries its synthesis in itself." He expected to publish the physiological formulas, the obliging Félix Davin tells us in confidence; and we have already pointed them out. From the text of these stories, some well-informed reflections and general views emerge. Louis Lambert was to dig them out and put them before us, drafted into formulas suitable for consideration. Séraphîta, having reached the limit of her angelical evolution, lets us profit from her heaven-sent wisdom by offering a structure of pseudo-Swedenborgian philosophy. Her teaching, set forth in the form of broad theses, contains a compact criticism of scientific and psychological methods as they try to prove the existence of God and to define the relationships of the Universe and the Eternal. Later Balzac himself was to compose for our use an "Epitome of Magnetism" in *Ursule Mirouët* (1841) and a "Treatise on the Occult Sciences" in *Le Cousin Pons* (1847) to put within our reach the arguments of his characters and to explain their behavior. Quite often in other novels he suggests a motif of the same order and to the same end, and he was to continue to do so until the very end of his career.

In Balzac we can recognize the physiological system constructed by Cabanis in his *Traité du physique et du moral de l'homme*, perfected by the observations of his disciples Broussais, Bichat, and Dupuytren. Often quoted in *La Comédie Humaine*, these men have as colleagues therein the two cele-

brated doctors Desplein and Bianchon. The documentation
was indeed complete. Balzac declared that he had been able to
"compare, analyze, and sum up the works dealing with the brain
of man that the philosophers and doctors of antiquity, of the
Middle Ages, and of the two preceding centuries had left." It
may be presumed that he nourished his mind with ancient
works—Cardan, Apollonius of Tyana, Paracelsus, Plotinus—
and collected data from them. In this way, he created the
strangest sort of climate, complicated by mysteries, second sight,
and telepathy, and pierced by invisible forces that we divine
only from their consequences. For a moment, all these lend
plausibility to the laws that, unknown either to their authors or
to their recipients, rule the indefinable emanations, explosions,
and projections of thought and, consequently, the reactions of
the actors, their gestures, and their intuitions. "The chain of
causes" continues in the atmosphere of the spiritual world as in
the physical; in both worlds, the ideas that "are real and acting
creations" are operative. In the vocabulary of Balzac, thought
is equal in value to will. Thought designates all the phenomena
of inner life, be they intellective, affective, or volitive. To what
extent does conceptualism differ from voluntarism? Everything
contributes to make us believe that the Balzacian creature cannot conceive of anything at all without immediately, concomi-
tantly, willing it and trying to bring it to reality. Every idea
tends to translate itself into action. It is only a transmutation of
the ethereal substance that nourishes our brains, a sort of flask
from which a magnetic fluid seeps. The moral consequences that
flow from this observation lead to determinism. Balzac insistently reminds his readers that the *principle of causality* is the
firm support of his inductions. It is rather a presumptuous illusion to believe that the chain of causes is so easy to establish
when it is a matter of reconstructing a series of human acts.
His own belief was that it sufficed to "spread over these spontaneous determinations a sort of psychological light . . . by
explaining the mysteriously conceived reasons that have necessitated them." Was he not one of those observers of human nature "capable of measuring the strength of the bonds, the knots,
the fastenings that secretly weld one fact to another in the moral
order?" Let us not forget that he also invokes the authority of

the most celebrated contemporary magnetizers: Dr. Koreff, Dr. Chaplain, Baron Dupotet, Balthazar, and Prince von Hohenlohe. He protects himself with their experiments—and his own. Did he not believe that he personally was endowed with an occult and magnetic power, which enabled him to verify in his own person the veracity of the theories? He believed himself to be clairvoyant.

Finally, let us avoid a misunderstanding of the meaning of the word *philosophy*. In his *Traité des Sciences Occultes*, Balzac tells us that "the different philosophies are all one and the same." The true one, the only one, in his opinion, "professable," is "anthropology." With all possible earnestness, he calls for the creation of an academic chair that would "teach occult philosophy." No doubt it was confused in his mind with Magianism, "the intimate, inner Science of things," "the Science that reveals the march of the forces" diffused throughout all the kingdoms of the universe. Anthropology would be a sort of preparation, a first initiation, which would permit some people to achieve Magianism; it is "the sphere of the causes in which privileged souls dwell," "the gigantic thinkers." He classified himself in that category, just as he believed himself endowed, like Napoleon, with the gift of *spécialité* or second sight—that is, the intuitive knowledge of the fact in its absolute essence.

To be complete in the exposition of these scientific data, we must point out the relationships that Balzac established between them and the observations of the naturalists—Leibnitz, Charles Bonnet, Geoffroy Saint-Hilaire, Cuvier, Lavoisier, and others—by the idea of unity of *composition* in beings. The *homo duplex* of Buffon hung fire in the system. This scientific documentation, displayed somewhat naively, is the short-lived part of his work. The facts with which he proves his physiological laws are connected by the thinnest of threads to the theories he invents, but their supposed relationship authorizes him to throw himself into the analysis of causes and particularly into the description of effects. Science brought Balzac artistic material to be exploited; little more can be said.

We have several times had occasion to allude to the systems of Lavater and Gall, which Balzac made his own, from the very start of his career. The destinies of his characters are prefigured and even necessitated by signs inscribed on their persons and particularly in the lines, the relief, the sculptural form of the face, of which the animal resemblance is appropriate to the character. The physical and social environment, which reacts upon the individual and modifies his physiognomy, creates the specific differences: whence the physiognomic science. Balzac applies with conviction the fundamental principle of Lavater: "Everything we are has an inner cause." He has not made methodical use of all the observations of his master, but he follows him in a general way and then takes it upon himself to establish empirical or fanciful correlations between the propensities and certain facial features, which are often his own.

The same holds true for the phrenology invented by Gall, corresponding to the protuberances of the cranial box. There is little point in citing the title of a novel or the name of a character; one has only to open *La Comédie Humaine* at random to find proof of this demonstration. For example, at the beginning of *La Recherche de l'Absolu*, no less than four pages are necessary to describe in minute details the persons of Balthazar Claës: each of these physical particularities presages the events of his life. "His majestic step is that of a thinker who carries worlds along with him." The protuberances of his forehead, his hair, his eyes, his skin, his complexion, his attitudes, his dress, the equine shape of his head indicate to the observer the feelings, the passions, the manners and morals, the qualities and vices of this human organism. We should also mention the names that Balzac chose with such care, the appellations of his characters: Gobseck, Z. Marcas. Those two syllables bear the "somber significance" of their destiny. "Our globe is full, everything fits in. Perhaps someday we shall return to the Occult Sciences." Here is the conclusion reached by Pierre Abraham in his penetrating study *Balzac et la Figure Humaine:* "It is not with the help of observed facts, but in word images that he is thinking when he conceives and fabricates, unknown to himself, the vast morphology of his *Comédie.* Phrenology, physiognomy —he has used not their debatable results but their fruitful initial idea." That idea has permitted him to establish correspondences of the physical to the moral. They were "associations of ideas set in motion, in the tireless and powerful literary worker, by the words of the French language, by their assonance, by the images which they enclose." He sets down the signs and then interprets them by a code that is personally his own. With symbols, with metaphors, with word images, the artist decrees a destiny.

But where in all this system does moral responsibility lie? There is no protuberance to take care of that. Man is vanquished beforehand in the struggle against the passions. "Poor nervous natures, which the exuberance of your organism delivers without protection into the hands of some nameless genie, where are your peers and your judges?" cries Félix de Vandenesse. By this determinist law, Balzac, great physiologist and great penitentiary, frees his creatures from all sins.

What do all these scientific trappings matter to us? Their artistic triumph consists in the fact that we are not overly aware of the artifice of the psychophysiological law. The scenic play dazzles us. Transported into the illusory and changeable regions of the settings, we lose sight of the framework of the flats on stage. Ensnared by so many beautiful images, struck or charmed by words whose sounds blend into the foreshadowed symbol and strengthen it, we no longer trouble to keep the mind critical or to reflect on the postulates and axioms of the technique, any more than it does itself. Balzac does not bother to be literal and logical. What purpose would the rigor of reasoning serve here, or the inductions that support it? It is by virtue of a transcendent principle that he subjugates us to his apodictical certitude. Why should we exert ourselves in verifying, by our petty, earthly means, a process that has come straight down out of the empyrean? "The power of vision that makes the poet and the power of deduction that makes the savant are based on invisible, intangible, and imponderable affinities that the common people include in the class of moral phenomena, but which are physical effects. The prophet sees and deduces." By virtue of that statement, Balzac placed himself on the level of Balthazar Claës as a genius. His organism picked up fluids in the ether; it drank in ideas there: the fluids and the ideas, brought together in the matrass, the alembic of the brain, recomposed the substance of things in such a way as to evoke reality. Do not speak to him of hallucinations. He has an actual perception of what he recounts about objects and beings and physical circumstances, a perception determined by physiological prefigurations and by presence. There is no longer any past, no longer any future, for an artist of his stamp. For him, everything becomes immediate. He is a wise man, he is a prophet, he sees, he deduces, he states the law of events, the laws of psychism, that which he calls *la mystique*—the science of mystical devotion.

6 · The Occult Meaning of
Balzacian Mysticism

IN THE INTRODUCTION TO *Romans et Contes Philosophiques* (1834), Balzac makes clear the association in his mind of the first part of *L'Enfant Maudit, Les Proscrits, Louis Lambert, Jésus-Christ en Flandre,* and *Séraphîta.* He confessed having had the intention of "running through his work a radiant ray of faith, a melodious Christian metempsychosis, which would begin in earthly sorrows and end in heaven." He already imagined that work as a sort of cathedral, "his cathedral," and he already desired to light it with "divine gleams" so that in it "might shine the pure beauties of the altar." Some of these tales, first published between 1831 to 1835, were already completed; others, especially *Louis Lambert,* were revised. Considerably enlarged, this story was joined by *Les Proscrits* and *Séraphîta,* and the three were republished in 1835 as a single work under the title *Le Livre Mystique.* This joint publication, then, was the fulfillment of Balzac's project: to present them in a way that would allow the general idea and the theories of the Balzacian mysticism to become clear. Previously, all these works had formed part of *Romans et Contes Philosophiques;* henceforward they were to be definitively reunited in *Etudes Philosophiques;* the term *mystique* disappeared, but the content remained. Although these two genres have their roots in the same documentary terrain, the *Oeuvres Mystiques* (Mystical Works) keep their own distinctive character. Not only do they manifest a constructive effort of the spirit, but, still more do they demonstrate a deep-

seated conviction and a proselytizing purpose, both of which are
productive of poetry.

In order to follow their development, their chronology must
be reestablished; it will be necessary to compare data authenti-
cated by extrinsic documents with such events as those presented
to us in the biographical novel *Louis Lambert*. We shall bring
out only the points indispensable for this demonstration. A first
comparison of dates is enlightening: Balzac entered the school
at Vendôme in 1807, when he was eight years old; he left it in
1813 at the age of fourteen, not having completed the fourth
form; he was still a child. Louis Lambert entered the school
in 1811 at the age of fourteen, after having begun his studies
with his uncle, the vicar of Mer; he leaves "in the middle of the
year 1815 at the age of eighteen, having completed his course in
philosophy." He is therefore equipped with enough science and
culture to lend reasonable credibility to "the precocious activity
of his intelligence," to his ability to observe and analyze the
extraordinary phenomena that take place within his person,
and to draw conclusions from them and formulate their laws.
Let us note that most of these experiences happen after 1813.
Let us take at face value the appeal of Balzac to the testimony
of Barchou de Penhoën, his old companion and dormitory
mate: "He was already concerned, as I was also, with questions
of metaphysics; as I did, he often talked nonsense about God,
about ourselves and about nature." Let us remember, as a sign
of religious uncertainty, the objection he made to the chaplain
of the school some months before his first communion: " 'Then
if everything comes from God,' I asked him, 'how can there be
evil in the world?' " And as proofs of mystical exaltation, let
us recall his fervor when partaking of the sacrament for the
first time and the curiosity that led him into clandestine reading
of some works by the fathers of the Church and the acts of the
martyrs. Let us observe that this peculiarity proceeds from imagination and intelligence: the child wanted to renew, in himself,
the steadfastness of the persecuted during their sufferings; he
suspected that this courage is dependent on the personal temperament. He would have liked to discover the means of being
heroic. In dreams, he accomplished so many sublime acts! And
for him, that was both anticipation and realization. He was per-

suaded that he was one of those "Famous Children" (*Enfants Célèbres*)—Pico della Mirandola, Pascal, and the others whose exploits he read with avidity. Only the elements of mysticism seem to us to be clearly demonstrable in the schoolboy.

They may seem insufficient to us, but not to Félix Davin, to whom they "show how precocious, in M. de Balzac, was the germ of the physiological system around which his thought flutters" in his first essays. After leaving the school in 1813, Honoré returned to his family, and then his true acquaintance with the works of Swedenborg and above all Saint-Martin began in earnest. We already know how much this new curiosity owed to his mother's library. We know about his first rough sketches tinged with occultism: *Falthurne* (1816), the "shapeless sketch" of his illuminist dreams; *Jane la Pâle* (1822); the *Traité de la Prière* (1824). The influence of *L'Homme de Désir* is perceptible. This treatise seems to be the first chapter of *Histoire Primitive de l'Eglise* (Primitive History of the Church), which Louis Lambert wanted to write, explaining by physiological causes the steadfastness of the martyrs. The letters that Louis Lambert addresses to his uncle, Abbé Lefebvre, during his advanced studies in Paris, in the three years from 1817 to 1820, exactly express the ideas of Balzac, who at that time was attending courses at the Sorbonne, the Collège de France, the Museum, and the Law School; we have proofs of this in the *Notes Philosophiques* (1818). The *Traité de la Prière* would later reach its objective and its total development in the eighth chapter of *Séraphita*, entitled "Le Chemin pour Aller à Dieu" (The Road that Leads to God), where Balzac again designates it a "Treatise on Prayer."

In *Louis Lambert*, he tells us his inner story, the development of his mystical ideas, not only during his first studies in Vendôme but as late as 1832, when the first edition of *Louis Lambert* appeared. This self-explication continued in 1833, when the greatly enlarged second edition appeared, entitled *Histoire Intellectuelle de Louis Lambert*, again in 1835 when this tale, revised and increased by the *Lettres de Louis Lambert*, was integrated with *Le Livre Mystique*; and finally, in 1846, the date of the definitive edition, following so many others constantly revised. The immense bibliography that the author calls to witness for *Louis Lambert* and *Séraphîta* had grown out of all the information gleaned during his lifetime from the writers on mysticism—a subject very close to his heart.

The problem of human destiny did not cease to occupy his thoughts; rather, it became integral in his activities as a man and as an author. The *Lettre à Charles Nodier sur son article intitulé: De la palingénésie humaine et de la résurrection* (1832) testifies to a "philosophical curiosity" and not at all to religious anguish. His creatures, the accursed child Etienne d'Hérouville, Dante the exile and his companion Godefroid, Louis Lambert and Séraphîta, are pining nostalgically for heaven. They think of it not so much as a place of happiness as the region of definitive clarity. Here on earth all the sanctuaries (i.e., all the religions) are surrounded by *clouds*, by metaphysical obscurities. Each of these characters repeats the words of Dante: "I who am a mystery to myself." They try to pierce the enigma "by interpretation of the divine Word, writ on each thing of this world." They try to see the truth, and their aspiration is so violent that each of them longs for death in order to approach it. Godefroid tries to take his own life to come the sooner into the region of clarity; and for a moment Louis Lambert considers self-mutilation.

Before we attempt an interpretation (perforce always shifting, always disappointing), Balzac's sincerity has to be estimated at its real value. Trying to explain his own fate to himself, he made Louis Lambert his interpreter in order to spread throughout the world beliefs which he thought useful to mankind. We must not forget that he deemed *Louis Lambert* and *Séraphîta* superior to all his other works: "One can write a *Goriot* every day; a *Séraphîta* can be written only once in a lifetime," he confided to Madame Hanska. And again: "Those are books [*Louis Lambert, Séraphîta*] that I create for myself and for a few others." Soon afterward we find more in this vein: "When a book has to be written for everyone, I know very well from what ideas it must derive and what ideas it must express."

"For myself and a few others"—this reticent formula is the language of an initiate. It is said by some that the Martinist initiation had been accorded to Balzac, and a paragraph of the *Traité de la Prière* (1842) gives credibility to this assertion. Van

Rijnberk, in his study on *Martinès de Pasqually*, established the sequence of events, according to recent information, thus: Claude de Saint-Martin had initiated the Abbé de la Noüe, who initiated Antoine-Louis-Marie Hennequin, the famous lawyer, who initiated Hyacinthe de Latouche. The latter initiated his friend Balzac and, about 1825, transmitted to him the doctrine and the occult powers of which the author of *La Comédie Humaine* boasted so freely.

The "theurgic philosophy" on which Balzac relies traces its origins back to primitive, Johannine Christianity and thence back to the most ancient oriental mystagogues. Jesus was one of the great initiates: from the Mosaic traditions, which themselves flowed from the Egyptian, he received the secrets of his thaumaturgic power, which he had transmitted to the apostles and especially to John: "The Apocalypse is a written ecstasy." This doctrine, which comprised "the body of the revelations and the mysteries from the beginning of the world," was publicly taught in the twelfth century at the University of Paris. It was "nebulously" handed down to Madame Guyon and Fénelon and finally reached the Swedish prophet Swedenborg and his perfect disciple Saint-Martin, "the unknown philosopher." It is the "Inner Church," constantly persecuted by the Church of Rome. While the latter endlessly encumbers the Christian religion with external observances, Swedenborg brings it back to its primitive simplicity. He reduces the practices of the cult to a strict minimum and proscribes the intermediary of the priesthood. Balzac, in 1835, did not question but that Swedenborg would be victorious: "Doubt is at the present time tormenting France. After having lost the political government of the world, Catholicism is now losing its hold on moral government. Catholic Rome, nevertheless, will take as long to fall as did pantheistic Rome. What form will religious sentiment assume? What will be its new expression? The answer is a secret of the future" (Preface to *Le Livre Mystique*).

Louis Lambert was a scientific effort to reduce all the forms and all the forces of nature to unity. *Séraphîta* completed this attempt to reintegrate the spirit into this unity by means of an esoteric system. A single principle underlies each of these books:

the full interdependence of the physical and the moral. The observations of the physiologist, more and more precise and numerous, demonstrate it every day; they are preparing sensational discoveries for science. To provide a base for the extraordinary phenomena, for the so-called preternatural gifts of which the illuminists avail themselves—this is Balzac's aim. For occultism he wishes to substitute "scientism" (i.e., total confidence in the infinite theoretical and practical possibilities of science) in order, first, to explain what seems in the eyes of the common people a marvelous power, then to expand its use by people who are sufficiently gifted. The theory is clearly explained in the "Lettre à Charles Nodier." It is an epitome of those mysticoscientific beliefs and tendencies. Man is endowed with "perfectible faculties" and with others besides, which are unknown, nameless, unobserved, or else forgotten, lost, atrophied. They explain the steadfastness of the first Christian martyrs amid frightful tortures: the Primitive Church was the "great era of thought." There the idea *faith* abolished the idea *suffering*. The fundamental argument is the *Homo Duplex* of Buffon: the inner man and the outer man are in perpetual antagonism. The nervous fluid that emanates from the brain and is commonly called the "will" is a force whose mechanism is not yet known, its potential not evaluated, its utilization not realized. Oneiromancy, telepathy, clairvoyance, somnambulism, bilocation, ecstasy, apparitions, diabolical possession, cures—these are phenomena occasioned by a projection of fluid. Thus are explained the miracles achieved by Jesus and his disciples, either by the laying on of hands or from some distance away. By determining the qualitative and quantitative relationships between thought and will, physiologists will arrive at ever more astonishing results. They will find the means of exploring the subtle zone of thought and feeling. Adepts will reach the point of communicating mind to mind, of seeing and reading in the brains of others without having recourse to the carnal senses.

How does this perfection of the organism promote the relations of mankind with the Divinity? This is the target at which Balzac is aiming: "It is a matter of giving wings in order to penetrate to the sanctuary where God hides from our sight"

(*Les Proscrits*). The time has come to "establish religions upon the *inner being* placed within us by the Almighty." It is an instinct comparable to that of animals, but superior by its very object. It designates that beginning of intuition which simplifies knowledge of the Word; and it places the individual essence in contact with its echos—the Word being the thought or consciousness that God has of himself. "The Word moves worlds." "To believe is to feel God; God must be felt." This experimental, immanent certitude prevails over all the other proofs presented by the philosophers. It is the theosophical faith, by which each one of the creatures, the whole of creation, communicates directly with the higher spheres. "Everything speaks and everything listens here below"; in all the kingdoms, in all the spheres, everything participates in the elementary correspondence with the Divine. The pebble, the toad, the flower, thought, which is a spiritual flower, the clouds, all communicate by means of the Word, all are in communion in a sort of fraternity. Unceasingly they evolve through divers "states of existence" toward the superterrestrial Unity. Humanity, personified in the androgynous Séraphîtus-Séraphîta, has reached the stage of angelization, according to the doctrine of Swedenborg. By a process of progressive dematerialization, it is accomplishing its last spiritual metempsychoses, which prepare it to be reintegrated into the Universal Principle. In proportion as it advances toward this triumph, in the midst of earthly ordeals and indifference, its nature becomes lighter, so to speak; it becomes capable of performing all the preternatural acts we have enumerated. This ascension is achieved by virtue of an energy natural to everyone. Thought mounts from sphere to intelligential sphere and finally reaches the goal of its destiny. There, the prime idea from which all the others flow will be known in its infinite essence. Jacob's ladder, his struggle with the angel, are symbols of voluntary efforts. The Balzacian supernaturalism is summed up in one of the axioms uttered by Louis Lambert: "*By uniting his body to elementary action, man can attain to light by his* INTERIOR." The young illuminee is already satisfied with a negative criticism of Christian truths; in abundant tautologies, he expresses hypotheses on the materiality of thought and its magnetic energy.

Séraphîta advances further into the domain of knowledge. In the chapter headed "Clouds of the Sanctuary" she admits to the skeptical pastor, Becker, the impotence of reason to pierce the enigma of the world, to solve the problem of destiny. She examines the existence of a God that the idea of infinity by which man is assailed and pursued seems to postulate. With an almost furious energy, she accumulates the objections and contradictions raised by traditional theses, maintained *pro* and *contra* by materialists and spiritualists. Thinking that she has destroyed their claims, she argues from the standpoint of her experimental certitude of the Divine: I believe in God because I have felt God. Ah! What mockery! Has not every science, whatever its object, begun with an act of faith in a principle? Physics, for example, recognizes a force distinct from the bodies to which it imparts movement. But physics knows nothing, absolutely nothing, of the nature of that movement; it judges only the effects. How, by these methods, could our intelligence find an instrument of knowledge when it is a question of God's existence and essence? An adequate reason for the belief is entirely subjective; as for its object, it is not demonstrable. It increases in amplitude and in depth proportional to the fervor of each believer.

The sixth chapter of *Séraphîta*, entitled "The Road that Leads to God," points out to us the only means we have of achieving this angelization: Prayer. Balzac expounds for us, at length, the plenitude and magnificence of the revelations that he thought he had received in recompense for his theosophical faith. "Who will make you believe," he cries, "the grandeur, the majesties, the force of Prayer?" This term denotes the transcendent state of an enraptured soul in contemplation: it tastes with "ringing certitudes" the most exquisite enjoyments, "the most suave . . . delights of a divine intoxication." We know, of course, that the author is expressing these flaming desires, these aspirations, this vision of God, with words and phrases borrowed textually from *L'Homme de Désir* of his beloved Saint-Martin. For that reason, we doubt that his ecstatic transports have attained the *extra*literary zone. All the same, thanks to him, certain spirits in their search for God succeeded in finding Him. One such was the Dutch painter Verkade, a member of the "Nabis" group: the reading of *Séraphîta* transported him into a supernatural world and set him on the path of piety, which led him to the monastery of Beuron, where he became a monk. All religions are "poetical" and lead to the same end. In the very words of Saint-Martin, the high speculations of Illuminism "poured the light of heavenly love and the oil of inner joy" into the soul. And Balzac defined the effects of this religion thus:

This doctrine gives the key to the divine worlds, explains existence by transformations in which man travels toward sublime destinies, frees duty from its legalistic downgrading, applies to the sorrows of life the unchangeable gentleness of the Quaker, and prescribes scorn of suffering by inspiring an indefinite maternal "something" for the angel which we are bearing to heaven. It is stoicism with a future. Active prayer and pure love are the elements of that faith which comes out of the Catholicism of the Roman Church in order to return to the Christianism of the Primitive Church (*Le Lys dans la Vallée*).

There is nothing, however, that forbids one to remain within Catholicism and practice its rites, as Henriette de Mortsauf does. We shall see the importance of this latitude.

It is necessary to know the origin and the nature of the ideas that Balzac expounds in *Louis Lambert* if we wish to comprehend their poetic role and the philosophical bearing of the novel. These theories are founded upon the materiality of thought and will and upon their identity. The ideas are emanations, "marvelous modifications of the human substance," of the "electric and entirely physical substance" of which the actional being, our "inner being," is composed. This being, "by a completely contractile movement," collects this substance, then, "by another movement," projects it outward, or even delivers it "to material objects." These abundant tautologies leave the idea "in the unknown limbos of the organs where it is born." This deluge of images does not give us the slightest indication of the nature of the "king of the fluids." "To what," asks Balzac, "unless to it, may we attribute the magic by which the Will enthrones itself so majestically in the look, in the glance, in order to strike all obstacles with lightning, at the com-

mand of the genie?" The novelist portrays himself as besieged
by ideas. When he closed his eyes, ideas came in droves about
him; mysterious or brightly clear, they fluttered and swarmed
around him in the air. "The infinitely tiny detail" verified the
exactness of the idea by the immediate interpretation that he
found for it. This experience was repeated over and over at a
dizzying rhythm. We know that he pushed observation and, with
it, description, to the fleetest nuance, to the minutest grain, to
the least perceptible mite. He pursued the idea and forced it
to yield its slightest meaning. Everything became an idea, because to understand was to see in advance, by "a glimpse of the
causes"; to think is to paint. The idea animates the material object, and the object arouses the idea; it is like vibration in space.
These ideas have a life of their own, by themselves and by their
effects, realized in the inner vision. They are a complete system
within us, similar to one of the kingdoms of nature, a sort of
flowering. "They are like myriads of stars. They also live outside. They assail us; we are obsessed by them, as they act, now
one by one, now in groups." *Les Aventures administratives
d'une idée heureuse* (1834) is a historical demonstration of this
psychophysiological doctrine, conducted with wild and comic
energy. It is conveyed by the spectacle of an idea that comes
into being, grows, chews up and devours men and children and
hopes and fortunes, assumes the shape now of a man, now a
woman, and traverses the centuries.

For the poet, a visionary by profession, ideas are perfumes,
colors, sounds, forms. He is an artist. When he thinks, his
imagination unleashes impetuous genii to assault the idea. They
take possession of it, carve it like a block of crystal, like a precious stone of which each facet, by its different angle, reveals
a more brilliant reflection, a more secret shade of color, a deeper
luster. Here the romantic resumes full sway. If the sentiments
that are unveiled to us in one of the characters are not unexpected, the symbolic idea that expresses them is quite unforeseen. Let us take the example of Abbé Birotteau: "His shifting
lusts" put him in the position of being looked on as a juvenile
lead contemplating with admiration the woman he is to love,
as a lover bidding a most tender farewell to his first mistress, as
an old man saying good-bye to the last trees he has planted.

When Mademoiselle Gamard passed from undercover revenge to open hostilities against Birotteau, he "could no longer doubt that he lived under the sway of a hatred that kept an always open eye upon him." The reader at once thinks of a fowl fascinated by a beast of prey. Already the Gamard woman has assumed the profile of one in the eyes of her victim, who is "aware every moment of the hooked, tapered fingers of the lady ready to plunge into his heart." The shape spreads its wings wide, its outline becomes sharper, it spins about in the field of vision, which it fills with threatening orbs: the metamorphosis is completed. "Happy to live by a sentiment so productive of emotions as vengeance, the old maid enjoyed soaring and hovering oppressively over the vicar, as a bird of prey soars and hovers oppressively over a field mouse before devouring it." Not a phase of the chase is forgotten: "She had conceived long since a plan that the bewildered priest could not fathom and that she was not long in putting into action." Who, having once observed them, does not see the maneuvers of the sparrow hawk tightening the circles of its flight before swooping down upon a bird frozen by terror to the ground? If anyone should follow up almost all the important characters of *La Comédie Humaine*, he could multiply these examples of grandiose projection, increasing the statures and the gestures to the stars, or plunging them into the depths of the abyss.

There is the terrifying performance that takes place under the roof of old Grandet, "a bourgeois tragedy without poisons or poignard, nor spilled blood, but, relative to the actors, more cruel than all the dramas accomplished in the illustrious family of the Atrides." There is Mademoiselle d'Escrignon, who "survives her brother, her religions, her destroyed beliefs." Understand her disappointment at seeing her nephew Victurnien—a marquis—marry beneath him by choosing a bourgeois heiress. In her sorrow, she appears "greater than ever," comparable to "Marius in the ruins of Carthage." There is the wretched Pierrette Lorrain: to give her story "immense proportions it suffices to recall that, shifting the scene to the Rome of the Middle Ages, upon this vast stage a sublime young woman, Beatrice Cenci, was brought to the scaffold" by the same persecutions, factions, and infamous passions, that led Pierrette to the tomb.

There is Pons, "le chineur," the mocking banterer, who, to satisfy his passion for ancient masterpieces cheaply, cleverly utilizes a course of action like that "so painfully sought after by ambassadors to effect the rupture of alliances." There is Camusot, the examining magistrate, who, to satisfy his passion for truth, yields "to a thousand suppositions" like a jealous wife and "rummages through them with the dagger of suspicion as the sacrificer would rip open the belly of his victims."

Constantly the idea calls up the image that disguises the actor of the drama being played: the idea puts a new mask on him, raises the height of his buskins, and, varying thus the phases of the part he plays, makes apparent to the eyes the shades of thought and feeling. From these poetic metamorphoses comes forth a character more imposing, or more delicate, or greater, one whose visage becomes more expressive and takes on a colorful relief. Balzac thus reveals his intellectual passion. He tries unsuccessfully to exhaust his perceptual materials, but the substance constantly renews itself—even more abundantly from his imagination. *To ideate* (a neologism he might have borrowed from Bonald), *to poeticize an idea, to gild ideas with poetry, to broaden ideas:* by these expressions the writer clearly designates the two faculties that, like two magnetic poles, attract the elements on which his inventive genius was sustained.

We cannot here undertake a philosophical appraisal of the Illuminist system or of the psychophysiological problem, but let us look briefly at some of the judgments formulated by Balzac himself. In *Louis Lambert* and again in the Foreword of 1842, he affirmed that his hypotheses on "this new moral world" cannot "*disturb* the certain and necessary relations between the worlds and God," nor "*shake* the Catholic dogmas." This claim is contradicted by the role of simple messenger that he attributes to Jesus Christ, by the exclusively magnetic explanation that he gives of the miracles of Jesus. Christ is thus stripped of his divinity and his omnipotence by the proscription of the elevating and sanctifying grace; that grace would have no usefulness in this rationalistic supernaturalism.

Between these contradictory opinions the fundamental idea

of *Jésus-Christ en Flandre* preserved a means of conciliation. In its first part, this tale was fantastic; in its second, mystical. Each preserved its own significance, the first philosophic, the second occultist. The first part had appeared in two fragments, *Zéro* and *La Danse des Pierres.* These titles are verbal symbols. The Church of France in 1830 = o. It is an old woman fallen into the gutter: *jam foetet.* A passerby says of her: "That thing's round like a priest's skullcap. . . . It's black and empty. Was it really a living woman or an entelechy?" The church, a divine institution, which by means of its Founder's word hurls a permanent challenge at the pernicious powers of the centuries, seems to have collapsed. It has turned back into an idea, as it had been before its transformation by mores and monuments. It is an "entelechy," that is, an active force, a dynamic power, but neutralized for the time being, as the idea of incredulity is now subjugating the idea of faith.

La Danse des Pierres takes up the theme in a more gripping way. After the fall of Charles X, Balzac is in a church, witnessing a witches' Sabbath. All the stone blocks of the edifice become dislocated, and they begin to dance to the music of the organs, which are playing all by themselves. This dream "is a gripping vision of religious ideas devouring themselves and crashing down one on top of another, ruined by incredulity, which is also an idea." We can no longer be astonished that ideas, "those living forces," rise up against each other and fight. Some of them "wither away from lack of strength or nourishment." They rarely die. The third part of *Jésus-Christ en Flandre* shows how long-lived they are. The spirits that are directed to the progress of enlightenment and perfectibility have deserted Catholicism. But the humble people, "the pariahs of society, those banished from its universities and its schools, remain faithful to their beliefs, and with their moral purity they preserve the force of that faith which saves them, whereas the upper classes, proud of their great capacity, see their ills increase together with their pride, and their sorrows together with their enlightenment" (Introduction to *Etudes Philosophiques*).

The idea of faith has in reserve marvels of civilization yet to be realized. Instead of stopping short at a pessimistic conclusion, the storyteller adopts the attitude of the initiates. While trying to spread the doctrine of Illuminism, which for him represents truth, he likewise encourages the crowd to practice Catholicism. But only Martinist and Swedenborgian esotericism nourishes and keeps alive his own inner being.

As for the Romantic material with which he overloads his canvases—empyrean settings, archangelical processions, angelical ascensions, concerts of astral music, golden sistra, harps, hymns, celestial conflagrations, and so forth—he personally confessed to Nodier that they are "illusions" *with which he loves to nourish himself,* and which he inserts as additions to his psychophysiological theories. They are poetical visions on which he confers an ecstatic meaning. As a result, in *Séraphîta* he has introduced on the same plane religious meditation, artistic vision, and the reveries of sleep; although different in modes, they lead to the same transcendental objective, to that personal revelation of the higher abysses where the spirit meets the Absolute.

One may wonder: did Balzac believe in a personal God? At the moment when the androgynous Séraphîta, removing his earthly envelope, reached the shore of Heaven in the form of a seraph transfigured in "a point of flame," he calls loudly: "Eternal! Eternal! Eternal!" He "then takes possession of the infinite." Does this outcry designate merely the single substance to which every living being returns, be it material or spiritual, to reintegrate itself in its primitive state with the universal soul from which it emanates? At various times, however, Balzac denied that he professed pantheism. His thinking was quite confused on this point, as was that of his contemporaries Lamartine, George Sand, and Musset. In agreement with Jean Soulairol, the following posthumous passage by Victor Hugo may perhaps be considered as the argument of *Séraphîta;* following the Chant of *Les Voix* in the great edition of *Dieu,* it runs:

Swedenborg prit un jour la coupe de Platon,
Et, pensif, s'en alla boire à l'azur terrible . . .
Il revint éperdu, chancelant, effaré,
Ployant sous la lueur farouche des étoiles,
Voyant l'homme à travers des épaisseurs de voiles
Et de tremblants rideaux de lumière où sans fin
Multipliés, flottaient l'ange et le séraphin.

[Swedenborg one day took the cup of Plato
And, thoughtful, went out to drink beneath the fearful azure . . .
He came back bewildered, staggering, affrighted,
Bowed beneath the fierce glow of the stars,
Seeing Man through folds of veils
And shimmering curtains of light where, endlessly
Multiplied, floated the angel and the seraph.]

To the Romantic generation, by melancholy made a prey to the chimeras, ever disillusioned in its quest for the sole happiness, Séraphîta, to convert it to enthusiam, opened a way leading upward toward divine hope. This theodicy, like that of *Louis Lambert,* is based on Neoplatonism, and its creator Plotinus figures among the authors cited by Louis Lambert. Whether it be a question of God, of the Word (Logos), of the emanation of individual souls and their return into the universal soul, or notions of virtue and prayer, the resemblance, or rather the identity, is perfect. Despite certain appearances, "fundamental differences separate this philosophy from the Christian doctrine and not only in the theology of the Trinity but in the mystic and moral doctrine that leads to union with God. . . . This union is the fruit of intellectual *abstraction* and not of *grace*, which has no part in it," any more than the effort of will has, because virtue is but "a simple removal by the soul of a foreign element, matter, which is accomplished almost automatically." [1]

At the end of *Physiologie du Mariage,* an old exile boasts of having brought back from Germany the doctrine of a poetic and transcendantal Christian. Let us understand that Balzac's thought had been steeped in this same theosophical current. He had studied, more or less intensively, some works of Jacob Boehme; he had borrowed from the *Abrégé des Oeuvres de Swedenborg,* with an introduction by Daillant de la Touche, and two works of Saint-Martin, *L'Homme de Désir* and *Ministère de l'Homme-Esprit.* He had read *La Nuée sur le Sanctuaire, ou, Quelque chose dont la Philosophie orgueilleuse de notre temps ne se doute pas* by Eckartshausen. He came under other contemporary influences connected with the philosophy

---

[1] Cf. Father Cayré, *Patrologie et Histoire de la Théologie,* Vol. I. This refutation of Plotinism is valid for the mystic system set forth in *Séraphîta.*

imported from Germany: Madame de Staël, Pastor Ancillon, Baader, not to speak of the naturalists and the savants. Did Balzac do more than vulgarize the system of the Illuminists? However infatuated he may have been with his predecessors, he tried to temper their enthuiasm "by the Cartesian genius," to clarify their nebulous theories, "to bring that flood of furious phrases into line with logic." Just as he reconciled theosophy and Catholicism, so he joined Illuminism to scientific rationalism. Here is their point of junction: It has often been remarked how opposed are the occultist mysticism and the materialism of the philosophers and Encyclopedists. The latter forbid any introduction of mysticism into the system of nature, whereas Martinism is saturated with it. The correspondences, the language that binds together all beings, and all kingdoms, from the grain of sand to the plant, will presently take on a kind of consistency. Balzac admits a physical continuity throughout all the spheres. We have already mentioned this chain of causes: it is the *ladder idol*, instituted by Bacon and mocked by Joseph de Maistre. It penetrates even into the metaphysical world and advances continually, thanks to the improvements expected of our faculties.

What Balzac called mysticism influenced his life and his work profoundly.[2] Strongly attracted by temperament toward solid, concrete, sensual enjoyments, he was no less overjoyed to fly off toward more ethereal regions. Despite these "sublime impulses," he was always opposed to engaging personally in the minute practices of devotion.

In addition to the novels already mentioned, there are others in which the characters are guided by Illuminist beliefs. Would Balzac persevere in them to the end?

On June 21, 1840, he declared categorically to Madame Hanska that *it was his religion*; on July 12, 1842, that *it was the bottom of his heart*.

You know what my religious beliefs are; I am not orthodox and do not believe in the Roman Church. I think that if there is any plan

---

2 Cf. in Henri Bergson, *Les Deux Sources de la Morale et de la Religion,* pp. 323 ff., the essential differences that exist between ancient mysticism (from which Swedenborg, Saint-Martin, and Balzac received inspiration) and Christian mysticism.

worthy of the name, it is the human transformations that send the being marching toward unknown zones. That is the law of the creations inferior to ours; it must be the law of the superior creations. Swedenborgianism, which is nothing but a repetition, in the Christian sense, of ancient ideas, is my religion, with the addition that I make to it of the incomprehensibility of God (June 21, 1840).

He was looking for something else, and he found nothing safer to shelter his hope than to return to the old Church to which he had so often before directed his admiration, as a bird wearied with too daring flights settles, wings folded, upon the golden cross atop the familiar spire.

On March 13, 1850, in Poland, at the very ceremony of his marriage to Madame Hanska, Balzac received communion after going to confession. After his return to Paris, his health did not improve; and at his request, the priest of his parish came several times to converse with him. In that mouth, said Dr. Nacquard, "religion was no longer anything but the highest expression of the Universe." From his hands on Sunday morning August 18, the dying man received extreme unction, making a sign to show he understood. At half past eleven that evening, Balzac was dead.

Balzac saw no contradiction in this alliance of occult mysticism and Catholicism. Rather, for him these two religious forms completed each other, usefully if not necessarily; mysticism took the place of the dogmas, substituted for them a sort of collection of scientific notions on magnetism, psychophysiology, and evolution. This esoteric doctrine in no wise rejected participation in the exoteric law of Catholic morality or its practices: the Swedenborgian declarations that we have just quoted date from the same epoch as the writing of *Ursule Mirouët*, published in August and September, 1842. This novel translates that state of the soul and makes use of its data. Once more the novelist breathes into characters of fiction his own convictions, which thus pass from his life into his work. Mysticism becomes the material of art. It often becomes confused with the fantastic. While it may aim at producing the same effects, it distinguishes itself from the other, however, by its ob-

ject, which restricts itself to the relationships of the soul with
the divinity or with the region of the absolute, in virtuous acts.
When Balzac thus introduces preternatural events into the romantic web, in his eyes they assume a probative value; in ours,
they gain in gravity, which gives a more profound nature to the
story. Our severity, our stiffness, revolts at accepting these
facts as probable when used as dramatic means to give more
body to a plot, to prepare its progression. We know nevertheless
that Balzac believed them to be possible, that he said he had
observed such things in reality; therefore, we adopt his candor
and invest ourselves with it to enter into the behavior of his
personages.

Let us recall that in his letter to Nodier (1832) he had insisted on the psychological facts of oneironancy, on "the somnambulism of the inner being," on "the phenomena, so notably
excentric, of sleep," in which space and time are annihilated.
Nine years later, *Ursule Mirouët* was the Romantic utilization
of all those theories. Minoret-Levrault had stolen and burned
the will of his uncle, Dr. Minoret, who had bequeathed his
wealth to his ward and goddaughter Ursule. The deceased appears to the girl several times in her dreams; he reveals to her
the criminal actions of Minoret-Levrault, which have defrauded
her; he points out how she can have justice done. Ursule wins
that justice with the help of her parish priest, Chaperon.
Ursule is piety personified. The priest hears her confidences
with complete approval; he does not for a moment doubt the
authenticity of the apparition or the orders that the deceased
has specified from the beyond. He even makes use of them as
arguments to bring the guilty Minoret-Levrault to repentance
and to reparation. All through the novel, occult mysticism plays
a considerable role. And it was to be used again in *Le Cousin
Pons* (1847). Balzac sets before us his ideas on divination, visions, and phenomena "proved, authentic, born of the occult
sciences," in a whole chapter: "Treatise on Occult Sciences."
Nodier in *Smarra*, George Sand in *Lélia* had allotted a place to
the strange and fantastic. We are aware that it was a genre very
much favored by the Romantics.

The remarkable feature of *Ursule Mirouët* is the intimate
union of the two elements, the preternatural and pure Cathol-

icism. The explanation of the phenomena tends to explain what the Catholic Church calls miracles in terms of the play of natural forces as yet not clearly understood: our will, and the presumption of survival of posthumous faculties. Chaperon, the parish priest, a type of sacerdotal perfection and total faith, joins science and broadmindedness to those eminent gifts. He has no repugnance about ratifying with his religious authority the authenticity of those extraordinary phenomena. He explains them to Ursule by means of Balzac's theory of ideas: living creations of man, subsisting by themselves with their own life in the spiritual world, "having forms imperceptible to our external senses, but visible to our inner senses under certain conditions." Ursule has been "enveloped" during her slumber by the ideas of the Doctor and by those of the guilty party, Minoret-Levrault. She has seen the acts of which these ideas were the essence, as time and space are nonexistent during sleep. After having brought on upheavals, occasioned sensational turns of events, and prepared the definitive crisis, these same events provide the final solution of the drama.

Occult mysticism is one of the most powerful motive forces of *La Comédie Humaine*, very frequently employed in the building of plots and characters. How many of them, like Henriette de Mortsauf, Ursule Mirouët, and La Fosseuse, are endowed with occult faculties or, like old Mrs. Cibot, are subject to their influence!

7 · The Aesthetic and Romantic Utilization of Catholicism

IN SEPTEMBER, 1831, *L'Eglise* [1] was published in the *Romans et Contes Philosophiques*. During the preceding days of carnival, February 14 and 15, 1831, Balzac had seen with his own eyes a delirious crowd sack the church of Saint-Germain-l'Auxerrois and pillage and burn the archiepiscopal palace. How many masterpieces of ancient art profaned, stupidly annihilated! How many pieces of beautiful furniture, incunabula, and rare editions thrown into the Seine! These scenes of savagery on Monday and Shrove Tuesday, Mardi Gras, "that new Festival of the Fools," had aroused his indignation. He had described them in his "Lettre sur Paris" of February 18, published in *Le Voleur*: "Such was the Catholicism of 1831. . . ." If that horrible sight was not the determining cause of Balzac's rapprochement with the Church, it is certain that it strengthened its conclusion. Was not this conclusion firmly indicated a few months after-

1 Published on this date, original edition, in the second edition of the *Romans et Contes philosophiques* by the publisher Ch. Gosselin. This tale was republished by the same firm, first in June, 1832, in the *Contes philosophiques*, then in March, 1833, in the third edition of *Romans et Contes philosophiques*. A fourth edition was published by Werdet in September, 1836, in the *Etudes philosophiques*. A fifth edition appeared in 1846 under the title of *Jésus-Christ en Flandre*, with which *L'Eglise* was incorporated, in the *Etudes philosophiques* of *La Comédie Humaine* published by Furne et Cie. The reader desirous of going into all the details of the religious evolution of Balzac may consult with benefit the recent critical edition of *L'Eglise* (Paris: Librairie Droz, 1947), by Jean Pommier, Professor at the Collège de France, to whom I am indebted for an important rectification; the interesting variants of the preceding editions are brought out and commented on.

ward, in September, 1831, in this sentence from *L'Eglise:* "Such was the situation in which I saw the most beautiful, the vastest, the truest, the most fecund of all human ideas." And in the mind of the thinker, it was an idea that had reached maturity. Let us recall the Balzacian theory: "Sometimes the idea . . . wearies us by a long confinement, then develops, becomes fruitful, and openly grows big in the gracefulness of youth, adorned with all the attributes of a long life; it endures the most curious glances, it draws them to itself and never wearies them; the inspection that it provokes commands the admiration that long-elaborated works always call forth." The word *église* had been opened before the eyes of the child like a colored album whose every page multiplied the marvels. "By their mere physiognomy, words put new life into the creatures of our brain, which they clothe as with vestments." Let us watch these creatures rise up one by one and people the notion of Catholicism with images. Taken by his mother to the ceremonies, to the Te Deum of Imperial victories celebrated in the cathedral of Tours, Honoré was greatly impressed by the sacred hymns, the presence of the pontiff, the glitter of the priestly ornaments; he preserved a vision of it that later revived all its nuances in numberless descriptions. This adolescent, aged fourteen, returned to meditate alone in the shadow of the great stone nave, to wander about in its dim light seeking sacred thrills in "the majestic horror"—or the "unbelievable sublimities"—of the silence and also "the religious picturesqueness," "the affecting sounds of the religious harmonies set in motion by the cathedral bells." At the age of fourteen, he read the *Lettres édifiantes,* and his young imagination took delight in following the good missionary fathers of Paraguay who went plunging "into the primeval forests" to convert the savages. He heard his father, in spite of being an atheist and a good Voltairian, state solemnly that the Catholic Church, "looking at it only from a political viewpoint, is unparalleled for the good that it has generally done in advancing civilization by its mildness and general unity by an equality of justice owed to all men." The lesson would bear fruit. In one of his first works, *Histoire Impartiale des Jésuites* (1824), the young author praised the successes of the fathers, founders of model villages, "apostles and legislators." "Has there ever appeared in the universe a more beautiful proof that, faithfully observed, the Christian religion leads a state to happiness?" That is the cornerstone upon which the thinker was to build his politicosocial system.

Here is the first foundation laid in 1829, in *La Peau de Chagrin:* "We owe to the *Pater noster* our arts, our monuments, perhaps our sciences, and, a still greater benefit, our modern governments. . . ." This phrase might serve as an epigraph to the fantastic tale *L'Eglise,* in which are enumerated all the works that the monkish orders are accumulating in the sciences, the arts, literature, and charity for the good of humanity.

In January, 1832, Balzac took a decisive step: he joined the neolegitimist party. In a collection of literary pieces, *L'Emeraude,* he published "Le Départ," a sentimental article on the departure into exile of Charles X. "On that vessel, the arts in mourning accompany him." "The meaning of the word Catholicism, so often hurled like a reproach at the head of the old man we are deporting," here takes on its full breadth and wears all its adornments: "luxury, the arts, thought," all "those beautiful things that make a fatherland great and strong." Ostentatious tastes are essentially aristocratic and royal. What can be expected of a middle-class government, of a rule by selfish mediocrities? The legitimate king "is carrying France away," that is to say, the privilege of the immense power that appropriates the money "necessary for experiments that take a long time to show results, for the slow conquests of thought and the subtle enlightenments of genius." All these caresses of hope hovered over the already well-known author. Quite as much as royalty, the Church had shown itself as inspirer and protector of the arts, fosterer of artists.

The word "Church" represents now "a swarm" of ideas that assail him joyously. One of them—let us keep following his theory—projects its fluid; Balzac wants to try for a deputy's seat. He prepares his candidacy and publishes in the *Rénovateur* (May 26 and June 2), the neolegitimist organ, a sort of electoral program, his "Essai sur la Situation du Parti Royaliste." Let us mark this essential passage in his statement:

The best society must be that which, while giving bread to the proletarians and offering them the means necessary to learn and to possess, nevertheless restrains the probable excesses of the suffering part of the nation face to face with the part that is well-off or rich. . . .

Of all the means of government, is not religion the most powerful to persuade the people to accept its sufferings and the constant labor of its life? Finally, is it possible to have a religion without symbols, without action, a purely intellectual religion?

All the royalist doctrines are implicit in these two thoughts, which are summed up by the Catholic religion and the legitimate monarchy.

Legitimacy, a system invented more for the welfare of the peoples than for that of the kings, derives from the impossibility of governing the people when the state recognizes equal rights for the man who possesses nothing and the man who possesses much, for the man lacking in ideas as much as for him who has attained to intellectual power.

Catholicism has the authority of deeds on its side: the finest philosophical thoughts are powerless to prevent robbery, and discussions about free will perhaps even counsel it, whereas the sight of a cross, whereas Jesus Christ and the Virgin, sublime images of the devotion necessary to the existence of societies, hold whole populations in the path of wretchedness and make them accept indigence. . . .

Thus, the royalist party is philosophically rational in its two fundamental dogmas: God and the King. Those two principles are the only ones that can keep the ignorant part of the nation inside the boundaries of its patient and resigned life.

By its harshness, this concept of Christianity singularly diminished the place of the charity and the brotherly love that the Master had joined in a single precept with the love of God. The dialectician went on to demonstrate that these theories of political absolutism, derived from Bonald and Joseph de Maistre, result in the well-being of the laboring classes and the increase, vitality, and prosperity of the family, that preeminent social cell. One would hunt in vain in all this writing for any of the marrow of evangelical tenderness.

Le Médecin de Campagne (1833) is an imaginary essay on the practical applications of these politicosocial theories in the field of the government and administration of a canton, completely restored by them, passing from death to life, economically and morally. The results are admirable, naturally, and all opposing obstacles are swept away in their advance. Here, clearly stated, is the religious position of Bénassis, the country doctor, Balzac's mouthpiece and the instigator of these transformations:

Formerly, I considered the Catholic religion a heap of prejudices and cleverly exploited superstitions which an intelligent civilization would make short work of. Here, I have recognized its power by the very value of the word that expresses it: Religion means *bond*. And certainly the cult—in other words, manifested religion —constitutes the only force that can bind together the social species and give them durable form. Here, finally, I have breathed the balm with which religion soothes the wounds of life; without discussing it, I have felt that it fits admirably into the impassioned mores of the nations of the South.

What good would it do to comment on that last phrase, especially? Observation of the facts, historical results, sentiment, these are enough to decide in favor of adherence to moral Catholicism. What is the use of *discussing?* What purpose would be served by plunging into metaphysics? The bias with which our apologist—for he claims this role—approaches the notion of the Church in *Le Curé de Village* (1836) is always the most striking, the most positive, the most glaring: earthly interests, material prosperity, the social order. All that is what Abbé Bonnet envisages when he is dreaming, in the Seminary of Saint-Sulpice, of his future apostolate. To chose a neglected corner of the earth, there "to prove by his example . . . that the Catholic religion, considered in its human works, is the only true, the only good and fine, civilizing power." [2] This "corner" turns out to be an out-of-the-way town in Upper Limousin, Montégnac, whose inhabitants are real savages. By his mediation and his zeal, he, the very humble country vicar, would miraculously improve the physical and moral state of the uncultivated land and backward population. The experience at Montégnac, like that at Voreppe, proves that the Catholic religion is the supreme social ferment, as well as the only brake on the passions. Constantly Balzac refers to this definition,

2 This is the same argument used by Father Chaperon on Dr. Minoret, whose materialism is tottering, to get him to decide to become a convert to Catholicism: "My dear doctor," said the good priest, "you will soon have understood the grandeurs of religion and the necessity of its practices: you will find its philosophy, in its human aspects, much loftier than that of the most daring minds" (*Ursule Mirouët*).

which he enounces for the first time in *Le Médecin de Campagne*: "Catholicism is a complete system of repression of the depraved tendencies of man." It is above all because of this faculty that it becomes "an instrument fit for governing," "a political necessity," "the only power that can sanction the civil and political powers" and subject the masses to legal obedience.

The reflection of the vicar of Montégnac, speaking of the Church—"considered in its human works"—and that phrase of Bénassis—"without discussing it"—do they indicate a mental reservation on Balzac's part? Is he giving us to understand that the dogmatic verities have no importance in his eyes? Quite so. And we know it already. These texts have no need of any commentary. They reflect the idea of Catholicism envisaged as a "code of social morality." Its dogmas are admirably fruitful myths, for example, that of the Eucharistic communion, which is the bond of universal brotherhood and sociability.

The complete exposition of the Balzacian Catholic system would involve many nuances. It would be erroneous to accuse the novelist of religious ignorance on the basis of a few errors of detail in casuistry and in liturgy. In fact, he seriously meditated on the essential dogmatic data of Catholicism: numerous remarks prove it. Let us chose this one from *Le Catéchisme Social*: "Catholicism is the most perfect of religions insofar as it condemns the examination of things already judged and allows the entrance, if made through the Church, of the secular complements of religion, which thus tends to come nearer to God. The fate that the heresies have prepared for Europe proves in favor of Catholicism. In the Church, revelation is continuous; it is limited among the heretics." It was not carelessly, but knowingly, that for himself he rejected the authority of the teachers of the Church. He lost no opportunity to stress all the greatness that he perceived in it.

Very soon, besides, the stiffness of his conservatism became attenuated and softened by a feeling of pity for the working class, which Saint-Simon and Lamennais inspired in his heart. Like their models, Saint Paul and Fénelon, Balzac's parish priests are endowed with the sympathetic faculty, which is the authentic mark of the Saint-Simonian apostle, the artist-priest.

They adhere to the doctrines of the Future. Such priests as Janvier, Bonnet, Chaperon, and Brossette closely associate their pastoral ministry with the popular interests; their hearts burn with tenderness for the humble and the dispossessed, the pariahs of society. Balzac thinks of himself, in *Le Livre Mystique*, while writing in *La Duchesse de Langeais* (1835): "While Lamartine, Lamennais, Montalembert, and several other writers of talent were gilding with poetry, renewing and broadening religious ideas, all those who were bungling the government made the bitterness of religion felt." He even went so far as to regret, in an article in the *Revue Parisienne*, September 25, 1840, that the Roman Curia had refused to take "the strengthening potion, the elixir" of "Catholic democracy," which Lamennais had proposed. By fitting "this reform" to the circumstances, he thought, "by letting it come from the bosom of the Church," the Pope "would have made it salutary," and by it "he would have saved the thrones." At about the same time, in his *Catéchisme Social*, he entitled a chapter "De l'Esclavage" (On Slavery). "Before our eyes there exist nameless slaves, more unfortunate than the named slaves of the Turks, than the slaves of the ancient world, than the negro. They are the factory workers who are almost allowed to die of hunger and exhaustion by their masters." Their miserable condition had in 1838 provoked Lamennais to a violent pamphlet, *De l'Esclavage Moderne*. Before that, Benoiston de Chateauneuf and Villermé, members of the Academy of Moral and Political Sciences, mandated by that society, in 1832 had undertaken investigations into the condition of the workers in the factories. At almost the same time, the Viscount of Villeneuve-Bargement, their colleague, was starting the Catholic social movement, and Balzac followed them. He mentions the statistics of Benoiston on the number of foundling children; he admires this savant (*Physiologie du Mariage*, 1829).

In 1842, he began publication of the first part of *L'Envers de l'Histoire Contemporaine*. In it, he shows pious laymen joined together in a charitable association under the name of "Frères de la Consolation." They dress the social wounds of greater Paris by their works, which are helpful to people of all classes, the shamed poor as well as the workers. In order to

study the needs of the latter and to improve their material and
moral condition, one of the Brothers of Consolation, Monsieur
Alain, becomes "foreman in a big factory in which all the workers are infected with communist doctrine and are meditating
social destruction, the throat-slitting of the bosses. Thus he will
gain entry into a hundred or more households of poor people
led astray, no doubt, by their misery even before they were by
evil books." This "budding institution" was to have real and
numerous replicas in the Church of France, during the second
part of the nineteenth century; its conditions, its imaginary
beginnings in the prose of its founder, the charitable exploits of
its members profited greatly from the models that were supplied
by the Société des Conférences de Saint Vincent de Paul,
founded by Frédéric Ozanam, and the Société d'Economie
Charitable, directed notably by the Viscount Armand de
Melun. Their initiative and their pious industry are all to be
found in the Société des Frères de la Consolation. Balzac and
Melun were acquainted, having met quite often about 1835,
says the latter in his memoirs, at the literary soirées of Prince
Metchersky, prince and poet, which were attended by numerous
men of letters.

   L'Envers de l'Histoire Contemporaine (1842–48) is therefore
both a poem of Christian charity and a chapter in the history
of the Church in France. The basic meaning of this novel lies
in the advice that Madame de la Chanterie, mother superior of
this institution of men, and later on Monseur Alain, dean of the
Brothers, give to Godefroid, the initiate or new postulant: to
believe strongly, abandon oneself totally into the hands of God,
"be a docile instrument under the fingers of Providence, an-
nihilate all self-esteem, eradicate all vanity and self-compla-
cency," practice material poverty to the point of "sordid"
avarice for one's self, in order to expend all one's possessions
in alms. Among these injunctions, the most urgent, without
forgetting prayer, concerns humility, i.e., self-effacement. While
they are dispensing their good deeds, the Brothers represent
themselves as the agents of some pious person. Their good
works are directed only toward loving Jesus Christ in the form
of his suffering brothers. This active charity is the visible translation of the inner and divine love. "Thus, for us, misfortune,

misery, suffering, grief, evil, from whatever cause, in whatever
class of society, have equal rights in our eyes. Above all, whatever may be his belief or his opinions, a wretched man is a
wretched man, and we must not try to turn his face toward
our mother, the Church, until we have saved him from hunger
or despair. And, moreover, we must convert him more by our
example and our mildness than otherwise, for we believe that
God helps us in this. All coercion therefore is bad." Madame
de la Chanterie has risen to the summit of perfection not only
by resignation and patience in "frightful" misfortunes, but also
by the sublimity of the pardons that she accords to her tor-
turers. "She is a living image of Charity."

It is the custom of the Brethren of the Consolation to read
and meditate on a chapter of the *Imitation* every day so as to
acquire a taste of the afflictions and crosses of existence, for the
love of Jesus Christ. The *Epistles* of Saint Paul are their social
manual. It is necessary for them to have "absorbed into their
hearts and intelligences the divine meaning of the epistle . . .
on charity" before they aspire to the exercise of their apostolate.
Here we are plunged into the heart of the purest Christian
supernatural. Balzac touches on the idea that leads to total
understanding of Catholic meaning: brotherhood in Christ. It
is the Pauline formula: *In Christo Jesu*, the mystical identifica-
tion of all Christians with the Christ through grace. Balzac
makes a clear distinction between the two concepts united by
Jesus in the word *Love* and by the apostle Paul in the word
Charity. From charity or love of God toward us, which permits
our union with Him through grace and confers on our acts a
meritorious worth, flows the active, effective love of one's neigh-
bor or charity toward him, which is exercised through works of
spiritual or temporal mercy. By divine grace such works have
eternal scope and effect, and there results, among people thus
united by Catholic charity, "an immense infinite feeling,"
which has its "delights." It is "a sublime friendship" free of
any pettiness and disappointment. It is the bond of the tiny
community presided over by Madame de la Chanterie: the five
gentlemen feel for this woman "a soul-to-soul love," which
"religion permits." Such certainties are exalting. Godefroid experiences a fullness of life from them, and his strength is in-

creased tenfold. "To live for others, to act in concert as one man, and to act by oneself like the whole group together! To have Charity for a leader, the most beautiful, the most animated of the ideal figures that we have made of the Catholic virtues, that is to live!" It was by trying to "annul himself" that he discovered this immense power: thus he is recompensed for his "abnegation." Unfortunately, since the Revolution, individualism has killed "association," "one of the greatest social forces"; it has substituted philanthropy for charity. Every time the occasion presents itself, Balzac condemns the former, because vanity is its sole motive. He adds: "Only the Catholic religion can produce discipline," without which no association, charitable or other, can subsist. "So any association can live only by means of the religious sentiment, the only one that masters the rebellions of the spirit, the self-seeking of ambition, and the appetites of all kinds."

The conception of Catholicism as it is presented in *L'Envers de l'Histoire Contemporaine* expresses admirably the all-conquering virtue of pure charity, that which makes one see in any man a brother to cherish and to succor. How that conception had deepened since 1831! Balzac was then writing the ending of *Le Curé de Tours*. He expressed himself as being very skeptical about a doctrine that the true Church demands: the universality of faith and precepts. "This moral cosmopolitism, the hope of Christian Rome, might it not be a sublime error? It is so natural to believe in the realization of so noble a chimera, in the brotherhood of men. But alas! The human machine does not have such divine proportions. The souls sufficiently vast to espouse a sentiment reserved for great men will never be the souls of ordinary citizens or heads of families." No theologian accepts individual universality in an absolute sense. It seems that Balzac, at that moment, did not believe such a thing possible, even if it was limited to a few men in the different countries of the world. He does not believe that unity of faith creates a universal brotherhood among all men who profess the same belief. After having shown the evolution of the altruistic sentiment on the natural plane—family, tribe, clan, city, caste, religion—he sees its definitive boundary in the fatherland. Humanitarianism or internationalism are ideas that only "the leaders

of the age or of the nation," such as Peter the Great or Innocent III, can conceive.

From then on, his thought had never ceased to scan the
riches that Catholicism represented to him. From 1831 until
the end, *La Comédie Humaine* is bathed in Christian atmosphere. Even when the influence of the Church is attacked by
one character, it is so that another may defend it and evaluate,
justify, and praise the blessings of which it is the author.

Is it mistaken to consider Balzac an apologist for Catholicism? In what measure may we concede this title to him? To
dodge the answer would be to hold cheap a responsibility that
he voluntarily assumed and often proclaimed, in *La Vieille
Fille*, for example. Once and for all, let us disregard the seeming conflict between his inner thought, his Martinist beliefs,
and his Catholic-inspired teachings. Like many theosophists,
he was convinced that this dualism in no wise sullied his conscience or in any way weakened the strength of his position or
the value of his defense, this, from his point of view, being all
the more disinterested. It is permissible, if you like, to regret
this state of mind, but it is a fact that must be reckoned with.
On the purely literary plane, it throws light on the composition
of several novels. On the moral and religious plane, Balzac's
Illuminism is *res judicata*. I shall not be the least embarrassed
when, shortly, I shall meet it intruding into the soul of the
Catholic and mystical Henriette de Mortsauf, as it mingled also
with professions of Catholic faith in the soul of the novelist. Criticism is still far from having determined all the points of diversity by which a genius, who cannot be gauged by ordinary
measure, erects proof of his greatness in giant dimensions. It
may be represented as a relief map on which the peaks of a
mountain range stand out. We will not level them off. They
must be approached one by one. There is not one religion in
Balzac—there are several. For the present, his Catholicism is
under consideration. Neither the *Scènes de la Vie privée*, nor
Le Médecin de Campagne, nor *L'Interdiction*, nor *Béatrix*, nor
La Duchesse de Langeais, nor *Le Cabinet des Antiques*, nor
César Birotteau, nor *La Vieille Fille*, nor *Le Curé de Village*,
nor *Les Employées*, nor *L'Envers de l'Histoire Contemporaine*

(except for a single remark),[3] nor *Les Paysans,* nor still other novels, has anything to do with Illuminism. They portray the mores, manners, and morals of the aristocracy and the middle classes under the Restoration and under the reign of Louis Philippe. These works of the imagination, slices of real life, called forth judgments from the novelist. He opines, he approves, he also condemns. Virtues, vices, faults, fashions take on living faces from contemporary models. The Duchess of Langeais incarnates the hypocrisy of the conventions and the good manners of upper Parisian society. The formula "Would you forbid the holy table to a lady of the Court, *when it is the accepted custom* to approach it at Easter?" is as applicable to religious practices as to the other article of the worldly code: a conformity useful to the political party that wishes to get from religion a base for staying in power. To describe this Pharisaical abuse is not the same as to approve it, and Balzac denounces it often, especially when depicting the Faubourg Saint-Germain *(Duchesse de Langeais).* He mocks the great ladies: they rarely go to church, but their apologetic flow of words pours out "in stereotyped phrases," in "neo-Christian speech sprinkled with politics." That is what their pious effort is reduced to *(Autre Etude de Femme).*

Two conditions are imposed on anyone who wishes to appraise sanely the Balzacian concept of Catholicism: this concept must be set back into its own time, it must not be considered with the mental habits of a present-day Christian, and lastly it must be seen in its chronological entirety, with due heed to its evolution.

When Balzac undertook to defend Catholicism, Chateaubriand, Joseph de Maistre, Bonald, Lamennais, Frayssinous, and Ballanche had cleared the way for him. Having studied those authors in the preceding decade, he adopted their vindicatory methods. When the vicar Janvier wishes to convert Commandant Genestas, he first shows him that the Catholic religion pro-

---

3 " 'Does God reserve these last, these cruel tribulations for those of his creatures who are to sit in his presence the day after their death?' said Alain, unaware that he was artlessly expressing the whole doctrine of Swedenborg on the Angels." This remark of Balzac's does not keep him from admiring the spiritual vitality of the Catholic dogmas.

tects the "interests that touch him most closely" (*Le Médecin de Campagne*). He becomes the echo of Monseigneur de Frayssinous. The latter, to his own regret—"the spirit of the times forces me thus to abase my ministry"—envisages religion only "in its relationships with human interests"; religion looks after the preservation of property, wards off anarchy, and nurtures resignation in the poor. As for the argument drawn from the *fecundity* of the Church in all fields—art, literature, holy aesthetics—it was equally in style at that time. Chateaubriand, Ballanche, Lecordaire had exploited it because it accorded with Romantic sensibility. Let no one slander it. There will always be men who will let themselves be won over to the faith by impressions of the beautiful: between 1830 and 1840, they were legion. It would be unjustified to reproach Balzac alone for his "Catholic façade."

In addition, the constant evolution of his religious thought toward an ever more substantial and purified Christianity must not be overlooked. It is impossible to forget the eulogy of religious practices (*Le Lys dans la Vallée, La Muse du Département*): the scrupulous probity and the supernatural resignation of César Birotteau, the tormented contrition, the overcruel expiations, the popular charities of Véronique Graslin, the numerous conversions, amongst them those of the two doctors, Bénassis and Minoret, the merciful and unflagging pardons of the pious Baroness Hulot with regard to her infamous husband. Above all, there is the admirable flowering of heroism in the Brethren of Consolation. Their mystic garden is perfumed with all the odors of sanctity, moistened by the flowing waters of the theological virtues: faith, hope, and charity. It is heartwarming, even today, to retire into this spot. What a road has been traveled since 1830! *L'Envers de l'Histoire Contemporaine* is the final outcome of the story *L'Eglise*. In the latter, only two little words are reserved for charity, for the monks "serving the poor"; all other thought is absorbed by solicitude for showing the magnificent influence of the Church in the aesthetic productions of the centuries. In the other, nothing, nothing at all for the externals, for sacred luxury, for the garish wealth of a doctrine inspiring artistic geniuses; nothing for political conservatism. All the effort of the believer concentrates on and hides in inner secrecy in order to perfect the mysterious beauties of the soul reserved for the sight of God alone. *Omnis gloria ab intus,* while the *service of the poor,* the suffering members of the mystic body of the Church, fills this darkness with fraternal devotion, all the more efficacious for being detached from show. Oversimple faith, the instinctive belief of simple creatures, formerly so much preached, Balzac let triumph belief, rationalized in humility, forged in trials: it was the fruit of prayer and meditation. To pluck it, it was necessary to make onself worthy by perfection and to set foot on "the royal road of the Holy Cross."

For many people, the declaration of 1842 announced in the "Avant-Propos"—"I am writing in the light of two eternal verities, Religion and Monarchy"—covers the narrow concept of Catholicism restricted to the defense of property and worldly interests; it could not be otherwise, it is said, because *L'Envers de l'Histoire Contemporaine* did not appear until 1848, six years after the foreword. This reasoning is false. On October 11, 1846, Balzac confessed to Hippolyte Castille: "I have recoiled for six years before the immense literary difficulties to be conquered" in order to succeed with this novel. In 1848, when *L'Initié* (the second part of *L'Envers*) appeared, a final note by the author confirmed that this "work was begun in 1840," that is, two years before the foreword to it was written. It is necessary to return to the myths of *Zéro, La Danse des Pierres,* and *L'Eglise,* the three stories that, joined together, became *Jésus-Christ en Flandre.* The "religion" of 1842 was no longer "a little night lamp" whose flickering light barely allowed a broken little old woman, the Church of 1830, to recite her prayers in a dismal retreat. It had become a hot burning flame, haloing in a luminous sheet of fire a girl of archangelical beauty. This girl was waving toward the future a long fiery sword to set the world afire with her charity. Such was the myth that fitted the Church of 1842, personified in the Brethren of the Consolation.

The Catholicism whose Balzacian evolution we have just set forth represents the essential part of a doctrine that came closer and closer to the conformity necessary to the validity of his vindication. The errors—and there are some—in no wise change the interpretation of the system. The novelist made use of it

not only for the defense of society, but for artistic purposes—
to give a character of realism to his creation.

Catholicism . . . consecrates in all its institutions the great struggle
of life, the combat between the flesh and the spirit, matter opposed
to divinity. Everything in our religion tends to overcome this
enemy of our future. It is the characteristic by which the Catholic
Church differs from all ancient religions. Our religion, as I have
said in *Le Médecin de Campagne* [and Balzac repeated it in *Béatrix*,
La Muse du Département, "L'Avant-Propos," *Le Catéchisme Social*,
and many novels] is "a complete system of repression of the depraved tendencies of man." . . . Madame Mortsauf is an expression of this constant struggle. Unless the flesh uttered its last cry
I would not have created a figure both true and typical in orthodoxy.

One would expect that this definition would become the soul
of the characters torn between faith, "the great anticipation of
eternity," and the violences of the passions, especially of love.
We are wrong. Where in *La Comédie Humaine* is that young
man, full of sap in his youthful vigor, as he was depicted by
Bossuet in *Le Panégyrique de Saint Bernard*, impetuous in his
desires, but controlling his ardors at the touch of the divine
grace that inflames him with superhuman strength to scorn the
blandishments of sensual pleasures? Where is that believer
described for us by Paul Bourget in *Le Démon du Midi*, that
Christian chaste and pious, struggling a great while against his
faith before succumbing to the temptations of a guilty love
that sinks not only his own self but also his dignity as a Catholic
leader? Balzacian Catholicism is the religion of disappointed
men, deceived in their hopes, beaten by life—tired old men.
Those who are converted bring to God the remnants of a storm-
tossed life, worn out and withered. Stronger than any supernatural motive, their own experience brings them to this
change, when in loathing they see themselves on the decline
of life and their strength diminishing. They no longer have any
choice: the world no longer concerns them. An end has to be
reached, and "the Catholic religion ends human anxieties better
than any other." Thus speaks Father Janvier to Commandant
Genestas, showing him, in the manner of Pascal, that it is necessary to make a decision and to wager:

"But even if it were not so, I ask you what you would risk by believing in these verities?"

"Not a great deal," said Genestas.

"Well, then! what do you not risk by *not* believing?"

Balzac takes particular pleasure in describing "the application of Catholic repentance to civilization." This is his second principle of literary creation. Bénassis and Véronique Graslin thus escape the inner torment that ravages their beings after the sin. How pathetic it would have been to see unroll before our eyes the struggle of the flesh against the spirit if the novelist had kept to his program! He eludes the difficulty by a conjuring trick. In Bénassis, in the course of his disorders, an absolute indifference with regard to Christian principles occasions no struggle: his disappointments alone bring him back to God. In Véronique Graslin (a woman of the upper-middle class who pretends to be very pious), hypocrisy, hidden by superior technique, masks the crime: "I have hidden my passion in the shadow of the altars." Thus she avoids entangling herself in the horrible scandal of which she is the prime cause. She had taken Tascheron as her lover. He is a young workman, much younger than she is. He murders an old man while trying to steal his treasure, which would have provided him with the means of fleeing to America with his mistress. In this case, it does not seem that faith presents any obstacle to the desires of the flesh. Repentance comes to the woman only on her deathbed ten years later. In spite of appalling penance, Véronique is never able to erase the memory of her guilty pleasures. The regret for having caused the death of her lover takes precedence in her heart over that of having given offense to God. To repeat, *La Comédie Humaine* "consecrates" the victories of the flesh over the ever-defeated faith, but it takes its revenge by offering the edifying spectacle of repentance for the good of civilization.

In Balzac's view, the case of Madame de Mortsauf is different. She embodies that "constant struggle," she is "a figure both true and typical" of the Christian woman, tempted by infidelity to a husband who is a brute. The repressive virtue of Catholicism here takes on its full meaning, because this creature is the

Lily of the Valley, who the Demon of the South has not wilted with his drying breath, who will be cut down by Death still spotless in her splendor.

Balzac had often undertaken the painting of the nuances in the soul of an unhappy woman in his psychological novels: *La Femme de Trente Ans, La Femme abandonné, Le Message, La Grenadière, Madame Firmiani.* Except for the first one, their adventures do not unfold in extraordinary circumstances. The tenuous, delicate analysis of the sentiments that people the barren wastes of a deserted mistress, a misunderstood wife, supplies all the charm of these recitals, veiled in a gentle melancholy, shadowed by memories whose bitterness and despair are occasionally broken into by a persistent bittersweetness. Religion played no part in the dramas in which the essentially human happiness of Madame de Beauséant, of Madame d'Aiglement, or Lady Brandon occupied the stage. It was as though religion had not actually occurred to those souls, yesterday given over to the enjoyments of love; it was there, not decried, not disparaged, but rather ignored by a sort of facile forgetfulness, driven, in these sorts of intrigues, by mundane usages. Religion played no consoling, sustaining role in the hearts of these lovers, now defeated and aching with loss and abandonment. *Le Lys dans la Vallée* completed this series of portraits with the portrayal of the pious and deceived woman. Balzac intended to rewrite Sainte-Beuve's *Volupté* (1834) to avenge himself for a malicious article by Sainte-Beuve. The two heroes, Amaury and Félix de Vandenesse, show that it is impossible for man to overcome the senses by a platonic love affair unless they are subjugated by religious vows or by a deep and living faith. Of the two heroines, the one in *Volupté*, Madame de Couaën, surrounds herself in such reserve and modesty by her chaste silence that we would not dare to imagine any reflection on her lofty honor. The heroine of the *Lys*, Madame de Mortsauf, undergoes the assaults of temptation "under the open sky," we might say. We know every detail of her struggle; all phases of it, with their slightest details, are exposed before us. She is an unhappy woman of refined, aesthetic emotions, whose heart is trampled by a husband cranky and hypochondriacal. Suffering from the coarseness and violence of his boorishness, her feelings little by little are invaded, then submerged, by her love for a young man who admires her and who consoles her with a full measure of devotion. Only one thing prevents her from giving herself to him: her Christian faith. All the art of the novelist lies in the tenuous analysis of the sentiment and its nuances, in the intuition of the secret fervors, the alternations between spontaneous tenderness, then contrition, then withdrawal, which supply the key to the inner torments. The external incidents are of slight importance: imagination supplies poetic material at small cost. Everyone knows that the love of two lovers turns a desert into a universe populated with sensations.

Here Catholicism passes from social morality to individual morality, from the doctrinal plane to that of casuistry. "Petty things become great." For a pious conscience like that of Henriette de Mortsauf, a word, a murmur, a silence, a gesture, a handclasp, a smile, a sigh, a permitted thought, a regret, although not accused of ill-considered levity by the worldly code, can sometimes become grave faults in the judgment of a confessor if these acts have been inspired by an express intention, by an unrepressed guilty desire. All those things may offer to the partner, the lover, testimony of a triumph over the constraints of faith. No kind of attack made by the seducer can surprise us, because in order to work out this strategy, Balzac used his psychophysiological theories and the resources acquired by experience. Among them, romantic religiosity was a good tactic with a pious woman. In accordance with the taste of the times, the lover borrows from the Catholic liturgy some expressions of adoration; from the sacred ritual, some formulas, some groveling attitudes, some litanies, some invocations that, by a poetic profanation, have been turned from their mystical meaning in order to do service in the cult of a carnal idol. In this way, his oaths take on the grave, touching character that a supposed eternal sanction bestows upon them: *et nunc et semper*. They are wrapped in a cloud of incense stolen from the immortal Divinity, and these perfumes weaken the will of the woman whom they intoxicate. Faust has recourse to all the evil spells in order to fascinate his prey.

The crisis experienced by Henriette de Mortsauf, the struggle that she wages, is the preeminently dramatic material supplied

by Catholicism to the novelist. The resources that Corneille
derived from it in the alternations of sentiments which Pauline
manifests toward Poleucte are well known. By transfering this
situation to contemporary society, Balzac's sharp sense of observation enabled him to make heartrending the phases of
passionate intoxication, of perturbation, of inner combat. But
since he wanted grace to triumph over the flesh, he should have
made the contacts, the uplifting and sustaining powers of Divinity more clearly felt through the temptations. This he was
unable to do: he lacked the spirit of the supernatural. He
did not possess the idea of sin, the sentiment of guilt, the horror
of carnal instincts, the feeling of defilement. He did not comprehend the strength and energy bestowed by grace that has
been obtained as a reward of struggle. He had discovered in the
history of mores a rather trivial theory. Catholicism has en-
nobled and refined love, has made it great, and has adorned it
with exquisite delights. Catholicism has made it "an ideal kingdom, full of noble sentiments, of great trifles, of poetry, of
spiritual sensations, of devotion, of flowers of morality, of enchanting harmonies, situated well above vulgar coarseness but
where two creatures are joined together in one angelic spirit
and lifted up by the wings of pleasure." These sentiments are
taken from *Béatrix*, and echos of them are perceptible in *Physiologie du Mariage, La Fausse Maîtresse, La Rabouilleuse*, and
in certain articles. They repeat the idea that gallantry has made
use of Christian modesty to vary, embellish, multiply, and
dramatize the enjoyments of love. What resources in those
words for a Romantic novelist! What a useful means for
spicing an intrigue—the haunting memory of sin and forbidden
fruit! This Romantic conception rests on a false principle: when
religious sentiment refines the scrupulousness of a woman's
heart, it makes the pleasure of her fall all the more ardent by the
contrast of emotions; all her fears, all her hesitations are ship-
wrecked in the storm of happiness. "The hope of pardon makes
it sublime." Balzac goes so far as to consider Protestantism as
"the death of art and of love" because it exempts the woman
in love from moral scruple. These are pagan ideas that might
sometimes be justified by the weakness inherent in lukewarm
souls practicing a conformist and superficial Christianity, for

example, the Duchess of Langeais. But, having chosen as the protagonist of his story of conjugal felicity a Countess de Mortsauf, having depicted her as very pious, very fervent, going often to communion, he ought to have known that sin, even in thought, cannot dwell in the heart together with the love of God. Temptation in a condition of such acute crisis as he describes cannot endure for many years: this would be to live in a permanent emergency and very close to mortal sin. Whatever he may say, no confessor could tolerate it, much less authorize it. Imagine the problem he would have to solve: all its circumstances are set forth in the posthumous letter from Henriette to Félix. Reread it. Henriette is twenty-eight years old, Félix twenty-two. She is completely disgusted with her husband; Félix is characterized by a very ardent and sensual temperament that brooks no moral restraint. For eight years, from 1815 to 1823, until the death of Henriette, they see each other almost constantly. They live under the same roof and share the intimacies of the same home for months and months at a time. How can this woman call herself honest and believe herself to be honest in the Christian meaning of the word, when by confessing to her friend the tumult of her senses, she ceaselessly fans his desire in private conversations held in the moonlight or in the shade of accomodating bowers? Their talks have one single subject: the splendors of true love, the laudability of renunciation and sacrifice. He interrupts with declarations ever-increasing in warmth; she answers with half-avowals, palliated yieldings, poetic sighs, tears of regret, jealous angers. She, the fair preacher, is a pedant convinced of the opposite of what she preaches to her fervent admirer about Holy Love, to her "too-much-beloved one." There is in this situation an intemperance of imagination and an unbridled lack of verisimilitude. Balzac, who (in *L'Auberge Rouge*) boasted of consulting the *Dictionnaire des Cas de Conscience* in use among the older ecclesiastics of his time, has missed a chance to avoid a serious error in psychology and in physiology. Thus it is that by making use of an inner drama created by religious beliefs, he has left the path of literary aesthetics to stray in the serialized novel, the *roman-feuilleton*.

Henriette de Mortsauf regularly exposes her soul's states to

her confessor, old Father de la Berge. Although "austere" and
quite "severe," he gives proof of an excessive indulgence: "certain" that separation from her beloved would cause her death
(how strong their passion must have been!) he allows her to
keep him close at hand, provided that she love him as one
loves a son and plans to have him marry her daughter. This
subterfuge proves the sublety of an overly crafty casuist.

Balzac has cast himself more than once in the role of father
confessor, with touching good will but too manifest maladroitness. Confessors and directors of conscience crop up often in
La Comédie Humaine. They too easily fill the office of *deus ex
machina,* as does Father Loraux between Count Octave and
his wife Honorine (*Honorine*). It is within the bounds of
imagination that he had known some black-robed ecclesiastic
capable of schemes as shady as those woven for self-profit by
Father Fontanon (*Une Double Famille*), Father Troubert
(*Le Curé de Tours*), Father Cruchot (*Eugénie Grandet*), and
the vicar Havert (*Pierrette*). But we are astonished that after
the death of the wise and understanding Father de la Berge,
a woman as intelligent as Madame de Mortsauf would confide
the guidance of her soul and the solution to very difficult cases
to such a nullity as Abbé Birotteau, whose entire acumen consists of "being moved to pity instead of reprimanding." His conduct at the bedside of his dying penitent is lacking in all
critical sense. When she has reached the edge of the eternal
abyss, she lets herself, a "new Chloe" be carried away by a
sensual delirium. Clutching her lover close to her, she shrieks
into his ear these words like a little girl asking for a doll: "How
can I die before I have even lived . . . I want to live. I want
to ride horseback, too! I want to taste everything, Paris, the
celebrations, the pleasures. . . . I want to be loved, I'll commit
follies, like Lady Dudley" (her rival). Hearing that, the poor
bewildered confessor falls on his knees; and with hands clasped,
raising his eyes to Heaven, he mingles the Kyrie Eleison of his
litanies with the ramblings of the woman.

This death scene as it was depicted by Balzac was very di-
versely appraised. It is known that Madame de Berny—a
woman of taste and experience, level-headed and sure in her
judgments—condemned it. Among the critics, there were those

who considered it sublime, who admired it as one of the most beautiful and moving passages in the book, as a powerful and true symbol of the two rival natures in which the wife and the lover are face to face. Does not art live by contrasts? The sensitive souls are agonized, in their turn, by the despair of this woman. She has struggled all her life to keep her wifely virtue and honest dignity. And now, all of a sudden, at the moment when she is about to appear before her Sovereign Judge, she denies in an outburst those Christian principles that have sustained her for eight years and proclaims that she was grossly mistaken. Care is taken to warn the reader twice that these are "impulses of madness," alternations between heavenly resignation and earthly despair, that the perfume of the flowers "acts too strongly on the dying woman's nerves." "Thus the flowers had caused her delirium; she was not a party to it. Earthly loves, the festivals of fertility, the caresses of the plants had inebriated her with their perfumes and doubtless had reawakened the thoughts of love that were dormant in her since early youth." Those are bad reasons, childish reasons. It is necessary for us to believe that the novelist realized this. To make us accept the cogency of this mental condition, he calls on the eloquence of two priests, "men divine," he imposes the sentence of a doctor on us, and his own commentary we are very familiar with. All that does not convince us at all. Henriette de Mortsauf, confessing to her husband, and in a ridiculous posture, her platonic love for Félix—or Véronique Graslin confessing publicly to an archbishop her guilty love affairs with Tascheron, during a mass celebrated after an extravagant ritual —shock both verisimilitude and the conventions. In other places, *La Comédie Humaine* gives examples of this incomprehension with regard to spiritual realities.

The most typical, the most amazing example of this is offered by Esther Gobseck, nicknamed The Torpedo (*Splendeurs et Misères des Courtisanes*). This "prostitute of the basest species," of the Jewish race, is placed by a pseudo-priest, Carlos Herrera (in reality a convict who has broken his parole), in a Parisian convent where daughters of the highest Parisian aristocracy are brought up. There she prepares herself, for several months, for baptism and her first communion at the same time that she picks up the manners of a high-born lady, in order to return thus transformed to her former status as the secret mistress of Lucien de Rubempré and carry him to the peak of worldly honors and success, reigning like a Ninon, a Marion Delorme, a Du Barry. Balzac is competing with Eugène Sue, Pigault-Lebrun. The young readers of the fair sex would weep. They would think that this is what the Catholic religion is, that the thoughts of carnal and pagan love, the vanities and the coquetries harmonize with the introversion of the heart when a young person partaking of the sacrament for the first time, proud of her attire and her appearance, approaches the altar, advances toward her heavenly betrothed, amid all the acclamations (even though silent) with which she feels herself surrounded beneath her lily-white veil. Voltairian irony, the skepticism of the boulevards did not inspire this tableau; it would be better if they had. We do not criticize it from worry over the "uplifting" genre, but because of the challenge that it brings to the sane, authentic, penetrating, realistic interpretation of an almost trivial fact: the simplicity of the faith in the heart of a girl. The faith of intuition, of feeling, the attribute of rough, unpolished natures refused any alliance with reason. In Balzac's eyes, it was the only faith, the only profound and powerful faith; it was *la foi du charbonnier*, "the faith of the charcoal-burner," in other words, simple faith. He thought he was presenting it as a reality in this prostitute, Esther Gobseck, an unselfish nature if ever there was one. Her conversion is an insult to good sense, it defies all physical and moral impossibilities. It would be easy but unpleasant to prove it.

Finally, let us notice that the Catholic data of *Le Lys dans la Vallée* are contaminated by the Martinism of which Henriette de Mortsauf is a very fervent adept. A very searching study should be made of this religious dualism, which is rightfully attended by an absolute incompatibility. This woman has visions and premonitions. She has that "surprising faculty" of seeing the fate of those she loves as it unfolds far away; she "hears a gentle voice, which wordlessly explains to her, by mental communication," the counsels that she must give them. Thus the mystical state in which prayer plunges the illuminati manifests itself. Twice in her life she arrives at the entrance to the heavenly sanctuary. The castle of her inner life is carpeted with poetic images. While she believes with certainty in her gift of clairvoyance, she allows her confessor to attribute these marvelous deeds to divine intervention. She is reticent with her two directors of conscience and hides from them her Martinist convictions, which authorize these sentimental extravagances.

This situation corresponds exactly to Balzac's. It does not allow us to consider the case of the heroine as the case of a completely Christian woman. A question arises: To what degree does this situation make possible the sanctifying influence of the sacraments in that soul? *Le Lys dans la Vallée* is a finished specimen of the religious system that its author professes: a formalistic and traditional Catholicism, completing and purifying itself in Martinist Illuminism, which infuses into the spirit solicitude for social and altruistic activity. It is what he calls, after the Unknown Philosopher, "active prayer." This novel is a perfect working out of his doctrine. But Henriette is a failure as a representation of the struggle of the spirit against the flesh.

If one wishes to estimate fairly the artistic value that a novelist imparts to Christian sentiment, it is almost indispensable to compare *Le Lys* and *Volupté*. They differ in their alloy and their fashioning. Sainte-Beuve had a profound acquaintance with Christian dogma. With spirit of curiosity he had explored the sacred literature, plundered the mystical essences of certain Fathers of the Church. His unfettered intelligence laid a wager to steal furtively the secrets of consciences. He had just been involved in a religious crisis. Did not all that prepare him to describe the inner tortures that tormented a Christian, tempted by the appeasement of the senses, convulsed in the lascivious traps of carnal beauty, when, angry under the yoke imposed on him by platonic slavery to a woman, he hardened in licentiousness a heart revolting against the divine law?

Unlike Sainte-Beuve, Balzac had not been subjected to the storms of faith, nor had he yet extracted from an assiduous study of the sacred authors and the Fathers of the Church the marrow of saintliness or the ascetic capacity that it inspires even in an admiration lacking the efficacity of grace. The egoism of his sensual nature had dimmed the idea of stigma (if indeed he had ever had it) with each new amorous entanglement. There no scruple kept his desire in suspense. Let us recall how, at the start of *Le Lys dans la Vallée*, Félix lets himself be carried away by the frenzy of temperament that suddenly overcomes him and pays to the beauty of Madame de Mortsauf a hommage of which the least that can be said is that it proves a tumescent animality. The grave, prolonged restraint of Amaury, followed by his inward tumult, is far more pathetic. What circumspection in Sainte-Beuve in that slow rise of feeling in which a hungry desire starves itself! Art makes the temptations more insidious. In Balzac, what sometimes vulgar emphases there are! The drama takes place, if we dare express it so, only skin deep, producing its effects with little effort. On the other hand, with what insinuative gaze the subtle psychologist follows the meanders, the eddies, the deviations of temptation that succeed the evasive impulses. Not a single one is left out. He notes the cruel wounds that the sharp goads inflict on this weakened soul, impoverishing its noble substance at the whims of proud, bold impulses, some even prodigally overgenerous. He neglects none of the obsessions, haunting memories, ready weaknesses, falls into the mire followed by bitterness and disgust, shot through with false resolves and stray impulses. He proceeds without haste, but with a firm step; an observer as patient as a clinician, he halts his advance at the slightest new sign.

Of the two heroines, the true lily [4] is Madame de Couaën; no slightest trace of blemish appears to sully her spotless halo. An unshakable belief has forever lifted her soul to the heights of the misty whiteness grazed by the wing of the archangel. Her

4 I do not know if it has already been noticed that among the many borrowings of Balzac from *Volupté* could be numbered the very title of his *Lys dans la Vallée*. "I had perceived down there," I answered, "a slender white form in the shadow, and I thought it was you; but it was only a lily—a big lily—which from here—see there? with its tall and slim figure, and its whiteness in the shade of the foliage, might be taken for a girl's dress." Amaury to Mme. R.): "Aha! you are trying to reconcile that with your lily . . ." (*Volupté*, II, p. 59, original edition; Renduel, 1834). It is also claimed that Countess Guidoboni-Visconti suggested to Balzac this title, translated from that of an English story, "The Lily in the Valley," published in London in 1820, which she had made known to her friend.

anguished human love never extends beyond the maternal zone; it is completely unselfish [5] and undespairing: does not all its value lie in its sincerity? Her ingenuousness cannot suspect the fault or the imprudence that she commits by captivating the heart of a young man. Madame de Mortsauf pants ceaselessly for the relaxation of furtive caresses; ceaselessly she sighs for that solace. The writer creates his character according to his own pleasure. That does not prevent his method of action, *operatio sequitur esse*, from betraying its own essence. He draws from his inner depth characters who share in his own nature, even should he, as he does here, shape their souls from a material that he borrows from divine inspiration. Balzac and Sainte-Beuve have treated their subjects in accordance with the leanings and penchants of their respective temperaments; one more than the other had received his intelligence from secret sources. He might be called an old man expert in the directing (regimen) of souls: in Amaury's he ascertains its mysterious touches of grace, then its march forward and the eddies that it causes. He marks the progressive equilibrium of the will strengthened by force from on high and regaining little by little the vital rhythm of the higher instincts. It has often been said that Racine was his god.

What the author of *Volupté* makes very appealing in the character of Amaury, the author of *Le Lys* has awkwardly and vainly attempted in Madame de Mortsauf. She remains a prey to her fever without its ever being tempered by the cooling, refreshing calm that proceeds from grace. Divine help is thus reduced to nothingness (divine succor plays no part in the drama), as we have shown in the psychological study of this woman. There is one very striking similarity: the two writers mingle in the souls of their respective personages the influences of Martinism and of pure Christianity. Henriette de Mortsauf and Amaury each proclaim that they are each one respectively enlightened by the pleasant teaching of *L'Homme du Désir*.

---

5 "She granted me the favor," acknowledged Amaury, "of loving me in the same way she loved her eldest son." Madame de Mortsauf spoke in like manner to Félix, but lying mentally to herself, hesitating between hope and subterfuge. Instead Madame de Couaën was completely sincere. See *Le Lys* (Conard edition), xxvi, 143, 253, 312.

But while in him there results a fervor subservient to the Church, in her it engenders an independence of spirit favorable to the passion that torments her. Finally, Sainte-Beuve is silent concerning the way Madame de Couaën practices her religion. Is this due to a sense of decency? Or to fear of profaning the sacred ministry? Might it not, rather, be due to a skill that art bestows? Not once does he let her director of conscience, her confessor, intervene in the conduct of this amorous friendship. Is that adjective suitable to the affection that Madame de Couaën has for Amaury or is it not? Right up to the last moment we do not know. Or if we decide to suit ourselves, then let it be our responsibility. Balzac, on the contrary, makes each of the two successive confessors of Madame de Mortsauf bear the responsibility for the perplexing and risky situation in which her divided heart is struggling; a more perspicacious decision, which their calling should have dictated, would have settled the matter quickly.

Sainte-Beuve's versatility led him to reject as too clumsy so rudimentary a tool, which was used to excess by George Sand, Eugène Sue, and the writers of serials. He preferred to leave in the secrecy of the sanctuary the opinions and the counsels that a skilled pastor dispenses, under the gaze of the angels, to lost sheep. One page of *Volupté* proves it to us: no one has made a more respectful judgment on the merciful and reassuring role assumed by the directors of conscience. The death of Madame de Couaën, a scene of sublime grandeur, moves one profoundly, the scene is clothed in the eloquence of the symbols expressed in the ritual movements. It shows the tranquil steadfastness of the dying woman, confident of the impending certainties of her liberation. Chateaubriand never achieved this pathos, and Balzac rigged it out in theatrical fancy dress. The consummate art of Sainte-Beuve and his sense of modesty allow us "faintly to discern a shadow" which the sorrowful soul of his heroine had carefully veiled. He employs retractile movements in order to dispense emotion in proper amounts, to instill unexpected and rapid effects into the drama. In this supreme ceremony, where the tragedy of the flesh is played out, the writer handles awesome objects with respect and surrounds the sacerdotal character with majestic veneration. Jocelyn acts and speaks like an actor, Birot-

teau like a ninny, but Amaury like a real priest, submissive to the
thrice-holy God whose will provides consolation for the humiliated, contrite sinner. The disturbing memories are effaced, the
poisonous acquiescences set aside. The power of the spiritual
realities manifests its august origin and girds with a supernatural
energy the loins of the sacred minister. His faith transfigures
him in the presence of this dying woman formerly so coveted,
so lusted after with impure desires, now forever extinguished
and repented. The sacred formulas that Amaury pronounces
as he runs his consecrated fingers over the organs of the sinful
senses and anoints them with atoning oil [6] spur us to understand their significance. Sainte-Beuve interprets their translation and adapts it to let us divine the tumult of the subcon-
scious. He makes full use of the aesthetics of the sacrament.
His intent becomes our perspicacity. Suddenly the "curtain"
which that intangible Christian had held closed over her heart,
even in the presence of her friend, is drawn aside. Suddenly
we are aware of the groundwaves that spread over the bottom
without ever ruffling the glassy surface of the lake of Ireland,
the image which for Amaury symbolized the lily-white majesty
of Madame de Couaën, daughter of green Erin.

Before this picture so marked by serenity, the inflated style
and the noisy glitter with which Balzac overloaded his descriptions of the deaths of Madame de Mortsauf and Madame Véronique Graslin testify to incompetence and maladroitness: his
daring could not compensate for them. It was difficult for him
to conceive that invisible beauty which is not at the mercy of
sensations. An evil genius cut him off from the light that filters
down to this our world from the home of eternal love. He would
not discover a ray of it until *L'Envers de l'Histoire Contemporaine*, the last of his novels. By what dispensation was Sainte-
Beuve able to make the opposite quality his own? In any case,
in *Volupté* his talent purged his work of the Romantic altera-
tions and the irrelevances that tarnish the Christian intent of
Le Lys dans la Vallée.

If in these two novels we consider Catholic life itself, in terms

6 In the sacrament of extreme unction, in the Roman Catholic Church,
the anointing with oil of the body—on the eyes, ears, nostrils, mouth,
hands, and feet—usually is administered just before death. [Trans.]

of its exigencies and its profundities, it is Sainte-Beuve who implies it as the focal point, the center of the action. He is the true realist whose art consists of unspoken secrets, of halftones, but who nevertheless solemnizes the dogmas. Is it necessary to say that Balzac always runs to anticipated, conventional forms? He sees everything on the outside in order to illustrate a theme of his own composing.

At all events, Balzac put realism at the service of the Catholic idea. He had grasped its poetical beauties. First he competed with Chateaubriand and Lamartine in depicting external settings. Keep in mind, for example, the painting of the evening prayer at Clochegourde. But he was above all the initiator of the novel of ideas, which some call the apologetic novel. This genre was lying in limbo, stifled under the dust of gloomy, tiresome authors. Their mediocrity spread a lackluster greyness over the splendors of their faith: they gave their readers a distaste for it. *Le Médecin de Campagne, Le Curé de Village, L'Envers de l'Histoire Contemporaine* were so many daring flights into a deserted sky. By these endeavors, the Romantic spirit, always in quest of the marvels of Christianity, got rid of the worn-out mawkishness of former times. It found its artistic material in the shapes and the settings of everyday life, in contemporary mores, even in the lower strata of society. In these it had discovered problems awaiting literary solution, more vital, more thrilling than the languors of *René* and *Atala*. It engaged Catholicism on the terrain of social reforms and charity. Before Bourget, Barrès, Bazin, Baumann, Péguy, before Bordeaux, Mauriac, Bernanos, and many others, there was Balzac.

Not everything is decayed in his apologetic work. In the eyes of the faithful, this earns him a glory that they will not allow to be proscribed. For it continues to effect what he was aiming at: an influence on minds, an influence favorable to the well-being of the masses and to their moral progress. He defined the great laws that dominate human life. He showed factually that individuals, like society, expose themselves to the worst ordeals and afflictions whenever they stray from the Decalogue; he shows that in it resides the secret of heroism. We see it translated into virtues in Bénassis, Véronique Graslin,

Madame de la Chanterie and her disciples, César Birotteau, Judge Popinot, the Marquis of Espard, Bourgeat the water carrier, Chesnel the notary, Dr. Mirouët, Pierrette Lorrain, Ursule Mirouët, Madame Hochon, Marguerite Claës, Eugénie Grandet and her mother, the old peasant "mother of the foundlings" (*Le Médecin de Campagne*), and so on. Their biographies offer us a kind of *Christian Elevations on the Mysteries of Sorrow*, which might have a cover, like that of *Le Médecin de Campagne*, illustrated with a vignette representing Jesus bearing his cross. All these Christians stand firm on an earth of tangible wretchedness to be consoled, tribulations to be born with utter resignation. They do not get lost among the phantasmagoria; their Calvary and their Ascension are realities. Each of us feels the better for associating with such people, living symbols of the eternal truth, toward which, said Balzac, "every writer with common sense must try to bring our country back." For Catholicism, at least, he was not mistaken; events proved that his experimental apologetics was right, and it was taken up by numerous imitators.

8 · Political Ideas

BALZAC, in the "Avant-Propos" says that he places "Catholicism and Royalty, two twin principles," on the same plane of historical evolution. He favored legitimacy, that is, absolutism, and not a constitutional monarchy. His career as a man and as a writer—1830 to 1850—was passed under the reign of Louis Philippe, and he never ceased scorning the July Monarchy: "If I cannot live under an absolute monarchy, I prefer the Republic to those ignoble bastard governments, without foundations, without action, without principles, which unfetter all the passions without deriving any benefit from any of them and, for lack of power, keep the nation stationary." In the king, he saw the permanence of a strong and energetic power, a motive force for progress, an arbiter of the classes in their own interests, divergent or contrary, and alone capable of curbing exactions and shocks—the defender of justice. "He who says power says force." Therefore, he condemned universal suffrage: "He who votes, debates. Debated powers are nonexistent." The masses are not converted by individual discussion. "The proletarians seem to me the minors of a nation and should always remain in tutelage. . . . This is a just and necessary thing." There is an opposition of nature between the masses and the law that often runs contrary to the interests of the individual. An assembly will flatter the individual at the expense of the law, and the public weal will suffer thereby. Power, being repressive by nature, has need of a great concentration in order to oppose a resistance equal to the popular movement. Balzac considered parliamentary government an evil; he made a pithy criticism of it: an assembly debates when it should act. "The power and the law, then, should be the work of a single person." The effective irresponsibility of ministers arouses the ambitions of mediocrities.

Equality is a chimera with no basis in the nature of things. The order of social superiorities proves quite the contrary: "superiority of thought, political superiority, superiority of wealth": "art, power, money, or otherwise: the principle, the means, the result." However, it is necessary for the people to have agents or representatives for granting or refusing imposts. It is necessary that the best intellects, endowed with a strong will, be able to rise above the crowd and be provided with means to receive a superior education and to reach the higher echelons of society and power. A distinction must be drawn between "liberty" and "defined and characterized liberties"; the former is a noxious utopia, the latter are beneficent realities. Religion alone can establish the balance between the supreme power and the suffering, laborious mass, by holding the former within the bounds of justice, by commanding the latter to utter resignation, and the rich to charity. For the individualism that resulted from the Revolution, there must be substituted the cult of the family, the real social cell. Balzac is intolerant of liberty of the press, regrets the peerage, the right of primogeniture, and the equal division of property between offspring; he vituperates the Civil Code.

Such, in brief, are the political ideas of Balzac. These ideas flowed from the education he had drawn from the works of Joseph de Maistre and Bonald, "those two eagles of thought" whom he had adopted as masters "very early" and by very deliberate choice. "I have meditated long and deeply on the building of societies," he wrote to his friend Madame Zulma Carraud at the end of June, 1830. "My thinking on the theories of Hobbes, Montesquieu, Mirabeau, Napoleon, J. -J. Rousseau, Locke, and Richelieu did not start today." He said that "if the well-being of the masses must be the particular thought of politics, then absolutism or the greatest possible concentration of power, by whatever name it is called, is the best means of reaching this great goal of social stability" (*Le Départ*, 1832).

These political conceptions are not completely identical with the traditional theory of the French monarchy: there was some Caesarism in the portrait of the chief of state as he drew it. These opinions are to be found clearly set forth in *Le Médecin de Campagne* by Dr. Bénassis, in *Le Curé de Village* and *L'Envers de l'Histoire contemporaine*. Other novels and some articles and letters strengthen these convictions and cast light on them.

At many points, Balzac's political predictions have been realized: the fall of the July Monarchy, the accession of democracy, socialism, and communism. He explained them by the selfish inaction of the bourgeoisie, its passion for acquiring wealth at the expense of social justice, and the blindness of the government in regard to the seething of the proletariat. He stigmatized "the frightful wretchedness upon which Parisian civilization rests." *La Comédie Humaine* abounds in portraits of unworthy nobles and intriguing, legacy-hunting priests; but this gallery should not be held against the political sincerity of its creator.

The judgment of Taine (see the end of his study on Balzac), in his *Nouveaux Essais de Critique et d'Histoire*, has often been repeated: "C'est Saint-Simon peuple" (i.e., "He is a plebeian Saint-Simon"). In the *Etude littéraire et philosophique sur la Comédie Humaine*, by Marcel Barrière, one may read a parallel between the memorialist of the seventeenth century (J. L. Guez de Balzac, 1597–1654) and the novelist of the nineteenth, painter of mores: "In France, they have both been as pitiless as Dante and at the same time as comic as Molière about vices and excesses of power. They have filled the same judicial office. . . . The powerful railleries of Balzac and of Saint-Simon on the absurdities and the abuses of their epoch have produced the same result" as the verdicts of Tacitus on the men in power in ancient Rome. These verdicts "weigh heavily on their fame."

Does this mean that we should subscribe to the words of Victor Hugo in his speech at the tomb of Balzac and include the latter "in the strong race of the revolutionary writers?" The idea has had strong support. "A great social accusation rings through *La Comédie Humaine*." Its author shows the undersides, the wheels and gears, the subterranean forces, the wings of the theater, the interests of his time: "the ascension to power of the middle class with its powerful industrial and commercial development, the movement of the aristocracy in the direction of the triumphant bourgeoisie, the penetration and the transformation of one social stratum by another, brought about by other conditions of existence, the setting up of a new class, toppling the old ways of life, bringing its own into all domains." These are the words of Marie Bor, in *Balzac contre Balzac (Les Cahiers de l'Eglantine)*. In *Père Goriot*, we hear the violent indictment of social ethics by the convict Vautrin. He teaches young Eugène de Rastignac "the revolt against human conventions." To succeed, it is necessary to place oneself above laws, of which "not one article does not reach the absurd"; it is necessary to despise all men, to use them as a means to success. It is necessary "to see the meshes by which one may pass through the nets of the Code." Blondet says likewise: "The laws are spiderwebs through which the big flies pass and in which the small ones stay caught" (*La Maison Nucingen*). This concerns businessmen like Du Tillet and Finot, bankers like Nucingen, usurers like Gobseck. All the conventions, all the rules were annihilated when Rastignac had understood the lesson of Vautrin: "He saw the world as it is, the laws and morality powerless against the rich, and he saw in wealth the *ultima ratio mundi*." He would convert love into an instrument for winning wealth. His scruples of honor and honesty would not stand against the glitter of gold and the luxury it brings. Yes, "gold at any price!" cries Lucien de Rubempré, brought up by Carlos Herrera, the emulator of Vautrin (*Jacques Colin*). The first pricks of conscience, like those of Rastignac, vanish quickly before the Golden Calf, the idol of temptation, which all the ambitious ones, all the pleasure-seekers, madly adore (*Les Illusions Perdues*). They are legion in *La Comédie Humaine*. Money extends its scepter over a crowd of human beings who exhaust themselves in the race for wealth. What family dramas, resulting from inheritances won insidiously, heiresses coveted, rivalries over pecuniary interests, corruptions, shocks! There is not one novel that does not reflect—and in any social environment whatsoever—the venal passion, the rage to possess in contempt of right and virtue, in order to enjoy and to enjoy again:

"Money gives you everything, even daughters!" cries old Goriot in his death agony. He discovers that the love of his two daughters has never had any motivation but the desire to win for themselves their father's millions; they have minted their affections; money sets Delphine against Anastasie like two hyenas. The omnipotence of money rules the passions; it perverts the traditions of honor; it takes the place of reason in society: "Intelligence is the lever with which you move the world. But the fulcrum of the intelligence is money."

If we wish to be informed concerning the role of the banks and usurers under the Restoration and the reign of Louis Philippe, *Eugénie Grandet, La Maison Nucingen,* and *César Birotteau* show us the collusions of the Nucingens, the Kellers, and the Du Tillets in politics. Gobseck and old Grandet represent the passion for gold: it clouds the moral sense; it extinguishes the more important feelings. Balzac devoted a comedy to it, *Mercadet.* That is the name of the protagonist, a cutpurse, around whom revolve a whole band of rogues, swindlers, discount brokers, gamblers, usurers, wreckers of society—the dregs of finance.

From the fact that he charted the seamy side of civilization and politics—the excesses engaged in by powerful bankers to the ruin of honest citizens, bankers who were men of importance but pirates often favored by legal protection—is it to be assumed that Balzac is a demolisher of order and society? As a painter of the mores, a historian of his generation, he describes all forms of abuse. As a lover of justice he denounces them and condemns them. As a social clinician, he confronts them with remedies. Whatever was, whatever is the regime in question, the lynxes of society, the profiteers, have teeth too long to be unable to coerce their prey. It is not wrong of the novelist to describe their methods of stripping their victims. He is accomplishing a work of political and social purification. Who would not be willing to be a revolutionary in Balzac's fashion? To unveil abuses, in whatever domain, is the first condition of their reform. The plutocracy had a conspicuous representative in the person of the adventurer Du Tillet. Balzac laid upon his wife, Eugénie de Granville, the work of characterizing the deeds and actions of her husband. "Murders on the highway seem to me acts of charity in comparison with certain financial schemes" (*Une Fille d'Eve*). Her husband was convinced that an absolute monarch alone was capable of protecting the people, considered an easy prey, an abundant pasture, by the profiteers of public and private funds.

Such is the conclusion of *La Maison Nucingen*. Two fraudulent bankruptcies allow the banker Nucingen to amass an immense fortune. He ruins a host of people who have accumulated savings by hard work. He obtains capital by means of dishonest speculation, but finds the means to get around the law. So Blondet says that it is necessary to come "to absolute power, the only place where the enterprises of the Mind against the Law can be checked. Yes, despotism saves nations by coming to the aid of justice, for the right of grace has no reverse side. The constitutional king who can pardon the fraudulent bankrupt returns nothing to the plucked victim. Legalism is killing modern society." And André Bellessort here pleads the dénouement of *Tartuffe*. Legalism would evict Orgon from his property. But the absolute monarch, "with sovereign power," breaks the contract that stripped the victim of all his possessions in favor of the impostor, hands Orgon's fortune back to him, and puts the traitor in prison.

Did Balzac persevere in his monarchist opinions to the very end? Alexandre Weill, in his *Souvenirs*, relates a conversation that took place at his table, between Balzac, Eugène Sue, and Heinrich Heine in the summer of 1847. "The discussion was very animated." In very energetic terms, Balzac expounded his antirepublican, antisocialist, anticommunist principles to his table companions. Yet on April 20, 1848, he wrote to *Les Débats* a letter that would be considered a profession of political faith. It was an answer to the clubs that had called on him to explain his ideas. "From 1789 until 1848, France, or Paris if you prefer, has changed the constitution of its government every fifteen years; is it not time, for the honor of our country, to try to found a lasting form, a durable empire, a permanent domination, so that our property, our commerce, the credit, the glory, in short all the riches of France, shall not periodically be called in question? . . . so that the new Republic shall be powerful and wise, for we need a government that signs a lease for longer than fifteen to eighteen years, at the exclusive pleasure of the lessor! That is my desire, and it is the equivalent of all the professions of faith." [1]

The elections for the Constituent Assembly took place on April 29; Balzac received only a score of votes. "My opinions on power, *which I want strong to the point of absolutism* [italics mine], put me quite out of the running for the Assembly," he wrote to Madame Hanska on April 30, "and my letter was likely to bring me few votes from the current incompetent bourgeoisie. So I knew I would not form part of the Assembly where they have put a song-writer, Béranger, and five workmen! Just the same, it is enough to make you weep." In short, Balzac did not change in his political opinions. His rallying to the Republic was merely provisional; he would have joined the opposition while waiting for better days. According to the sally of Heine which ended the conversation at Alexandre Weill's, Balzac saw the solution of the problem in a republic governed by monarchists. A comparison of texts proves its exactness, and it is sharp. The terms in which Balzac deplored the departure of Charles X into exile (*Le Départ*, 1832) and the end of the legitimate monarchy are identically those with which he would rally to the Republic, if that institution would protect and favor "everything that makes a nation great and prosperous": the arts and the artists, commerce, which depends on everybody, their glory, property, and acquired wealth.

1 M. H. J. Hunt, *Le Socialisme et le Romanticisme en France, Etude de la Presse Socialiste de 1830 à 1848* (Oxford: Clarendon Press, 1935), p. 215, contradicts the conclusions of Norah Atkinson, who, in *Eugène Suë and the Serial Novel*, 1929, stated that the ideas of Balzac were "definitely socialistic."

Part Three · Technique

9 · Character Structure

IN 1842 Balzac brought out the first part of his complete works under the title of *La Comédie Humaine*, published by Furne. It would be pleasant to believe that the title had been suggested to him at the beginning of 1835 by a young English friend, Henry Reeve, to whom he had revealed the plan of his future work. "If Balzac has need of a title for this great labor, which, we read in his *Memoirs and Correspondence*, is to fill forty large volumes in octavo, I shall take the liberty of suggesting the imitation of the *Divina Commedia* of Dante, for this modern 'commedia' is *tutta diabolica*—the Diabolic Comedy of Mr. de Balzac." According to Ferdinand de Gramont, a friend of Balzac, it was Auguste de Belloy, another friend and an unpaid secretary of the great writer, who, on his return from Italy in 1841, imbued with a vast admiration for the *Divine Comedy*, proposed the overall title of *Human Comedy*, as a contrast to the trilogy of Dante.

According to the "Avant-Propos," "the original idea" of something that would make his work into an organic whole had haunted Balzac's brain for a long time, "like a dream, like one of those impossible projects that one caresses and allows to fly away: a smiling chimera that shows its woman's face and immediately spreads its wings as it flies off into a fantastic sky." The idea arose from a parallel between *humanity* and *animality* based on *a unity of composition*. This, raised to a principle, had attracted the thought of savants and theosophists. Fancying himself to be both, Balzac became interested in the question; he followed the arguments in which Cuvier and Geoffrey Saint-Hilaire crossed verbal swords; he studied Swedenborg on this subject, as well as Saint-Martin and Baader. Whatever its actual worth, this principle, added to the systems of Gall and Lavater, gave the novelist immense resources for the development of his characters according to the law of species in harmony with the environment in which they evolve. It increases the dimensions of his inventive genius. In addition, it permitted the observer to order under one great conceptual arrangement the overwhelming riches that were constantly amassed by his insatiable curiosity about life and knowledge. In this sense, it may be said that *there* is the generating and unifying formula of *La Comédie Humaine*. It translated the fundamental disposition of a temperament that was innately systematic and could not be satisfied by analysis, no matter how detailed: "It is not enough to be a man, it is necessary to be a system."

The revelation took place when, according to the happy expression of Félix Davin, Balzac's spokesman, in his Introduction to *Etudes Philosophiques* (1835) the author had *isolated* "from his numerous insights into humanity" the inner meaning of the general formula that guided him in "this progressive elaboration of an idea originally indefinite in appearance." That is, to use the novel as "the history of mores, manners, and morals," the "great history of man and of society," a design that this same Davin stated in 1834 and Balzac was to express in this formula of the "Foreword" of 1842: "French society was to be the historian, I was to be only its secretary." The function he alloted to himself was to express in words each of the faces of the social world in tableaux which, taken together as a whole, would offer, in a vast diorama, the gigantic perspective of human society.

Because he was heard to repeat it frequently, we know how much his art owes to that of Walter Scott. It is well established that the Scottish novelist was his model from his earliest essays: his youthful works, *L'Heritière de Birague, Clotilde de Lusignan,* and later *Le Dernier Chouan* retain more than one imprint in which the hand of the instructor is recognizable. As his experience developed and grew richer, he penetrated deeper into the poetic and technical secrets of Scott, a painter as well as

creator of *dramatis personae*. Representing the social types of a
historical period, Scott animates them as much by the dress
and attitudes of the supernumeraries and their ancient setting
as by their sentiments and the stage dialogues. Balzac comments
thus in the "Avant-Propos": the pictures of Walter Scott relate
to different epochs; nothing relates them to one another or
ties them together. Their author was lacking in the coordinative
power that would set a goal for his artistic effort. Balzac did
not want any such lacuna in his own work; instead of choosing
his subjects from history he would take them from the present;
he would observe what he saw happening in all walks of life.
He would be the nomenclator, the classifier, and the annalist
of his own times. Like a good archeologist, he would describe
all the pieces of the "social furniture." He would describe all
types of the drama. He would keenly examine all the plays of
facial expression so as to penetrate to the very core of the being,
to seize all its secret and passionate driving powers. Thus it is
the whole of society, an abridgement, a microcosm, that is put
before the eyes of his readers, who are offered samples from
everywhere, reproduced in all their particularities; and while
the readers are contemplating the effects, the causes will be
shown to them. Balzac goes further still, and higher: as a moral-
ist, he would judge the individuals and the social groups while
showing the real dangers that threaten them when they stray
from the eternal principles that govern mores.

As a parallel to the historical vein of which Walter Scott had,
in his view, been the discoverer, the young beginner exploited
another vein that had been revealed to him by his flair, as if by
a natural gift—imitation does not enter into it. He was already
digging into what would become the inexhaustible mine and
the wealth of his work—the observation of *contemporary* mores.
One day he was to claim this as the principal source of his inspiration. Observation is the Muse; he, the humble amanuensis.
We have already pointed out the signs in connection with the
Romans de Jeunesse and the *Code des Gens honnêtes*: flashes
of customs, portraits, characters, settings, actual experiences.
In everything is to be found the authentic background of Honoré in his youth. Thus becomes manifest his growing taste for
the document written from life, for the external details which

characterize an epoch and its ways and by that very fact preserve its time. Let it suffice to point out, in *Argow-le-Pirate*, the picture of the Gérard family, and in *Wann-Chlore*, the portrait of Madame d'Arneuse: it is easy to recognize in them models borrowed from the Balzac-Sallambier family. The beginner is groping in search of a process whose usefulness he vaguely comprehends. He is rather like a painter doing one sketch after another, chalking in postures and faces for the final, big production. One who has followed these unconscious preparations is not astonished when he sees them lead to *Les Scènes de la Vie privée* (1830)—a comprehensive tableau. Little by little, the artist has been reassured about the good results of his technique, he has invented his genre, he has found his formulas. One of them will embrace the others: highlighting the representative personages of his epoch and "strongly embodying" the social categories that he observes. A dealer in cloth, Monsieur Guillaume; an artist, Théodore de Sommervieux; a great lord, Count Fontaine; a magistrate, Count Granville; a great lady of the Faubourg Saint-Germain (in several models); and so on—individualized types, sketched in his own way with their gestures, their attire, their tics, their surroundings. Thus the engravers of the time illustrated the editions of *La Mode*; Balzac made himself the historian of things and men after having studied them with critical curiosity: his eyes carefully captured what escaped other less ferreting, or less furtive, glances. "Those women," young Louise de Chaulieu was to say about her aunt, Princess de Vaurémont, "carry off with them certain secrets that paint their epoch." In this instance it concerned "the inimitable movement that she imparted to her skirts when she threw herself into her easy chair. She also had certain motions of the head, a way of uttering words, of darting glances. . . ."

One fine morning in 1833, an idea suddenly emerged from its larval state and burst forth shining. Balzac saw it so beautiful, so rich with promise for the fabulous development of his future work, even for the perfecting of his already accomplished work, that he was impatient to have someone share his emotion and his joy. He rushed to his sister Laure Surville, ever his confidante, and forced her to listen to him then and there: "I shall become a man of genius," he cried. His gropings had found an opening. He had just discovered at last the mechanism that would insure the universal and vital movement of the whole *Comédie Humaine:* this was the systematic return of the same characters through all the novels. Although it is possible to detect earlier a few rare and timid moves in this direction, it is in *Le Père Goriot* that the technique was definitely applied for the first time, in September, 1834. Here was a find without parallel. For once lacking in judgment and perspicacity, Sainte-Beuve ridiculed it in *La Revue des Deux Mondes*, November 1, 1838, calling it a "false idea contrary to the mystery always attached to the novel."

What effects Balzac's fertile inventiveness was to draw from that admirable mechanism! When an already known character enters another novel, he brings a whole past with him: he complicates the action with all the resources and all the powers of which his personality has given proof elsewhere. Under penalty of lacking logic, under penalty of lessening reality, the novelist must keep track of those previous happenings in order to hold the hero in line with his temperament and his behavior. The first requirement is that the author must have them already assembled in his memory and present in his mind. What an impressive faculty that presupposes when you think of that crowd —more than two thousand characters! Balzac developed a pride in this fecundity, a necessary monstrosity that he dared compare with divine power. "To create, always to create! God created for only six days!" he confided to Madame Hanska. His overflowing imagination was, of necessity, to be restrained by this process. It no longer would need to multiply the adventures, to set forth the antecedents, to prepare the incidents, to motivate the blows of fate: mere appearance on the scene would suffice. Each character, on entering, presents himself before us as an old acquaintance, we make bold to say, whose destiny we can forecast. Marsay, Trailles, Tillet, Vautrin, Rastignac, Nucingen, and all the others! Any one of them has but to take a part in the novel's action, and we await the new daring of which he is capable. We are moved when Madame de Beauséant shows herself, or Countess d'Aiglement; their misfortunes have already touched our feelings. One or another of the Balzacian characters has but to appear, to utter a word, make a gesture, and our memories are awakened. We are alert now. The interest of the plot is doubled by our participation, which carries us back to underlying schemes glimpsed elsewhere. What resources this dramatic permanence was to put at the disposal of literary talent!

We owe to the pages of very penetrating analysis that Maurice Bardèche has devoted to this artistic enrichment in *Balzac Romancier* our better understanding of both its depth and its extent. "Balzac creates out of whole cloth a sort of Romantic perspective by means which are peculiar to him, giving a future or a continuous present to stories which he relates and making his imaginary characters, characters which belong to us as well as to him and whose witnesses we become." And again: "He has given a positive importance to the periods during which some character does not appear. Deliberate omissions, periods of obscurity or absence are used by him later to gain more contrast when setting opposite each other two profiles chosen at different moments." The image of these personages becomes sharper, stands out progressively more fully as each one's destiny carves, full face or in silhouette, with strokes of wretchedness, of greatness, of virtues, of crimes, or of mere middle-class foolishness, the stigma of vulgarity or the features of nobility. Thus this juxtaposition of several portraits of the same person, "taken at different epochs," forms a "virtual image" that does not exist in any of the individual portraits and is the true image of the personage." This new technique, Maurice Bardèche continues, "permitted Balzac to give each character, no longer a single and fleeting image, but an image real and living throughout his whole work. He had just invented what has since been found again only by Marcel Proust, the 'third dimension' of imaginary characters."

The various *Dictionnaires biographiques*—or *Index—des personnages fictifs, anonymes, des personnes réelles, des allusions littéraires de La Comédie Humaine,* by F. Lotte, constitute a perfect instrument for research. Each of these two thousand persons is alloted a biobibliographical entry, thus giving the *curriculum vitae* an appearance that wipes out the idea of fiction by its documentary proof and leaves instead a historical record. Going through these documents, we remember the career of the character in whom we are interested, we pass through the social groups in which he moved. We also note the general characteristics of universal man, which persist in and show through all accidental appearances, however diversified by the environments.

But a Balzacian becomes more attached to what, for him, remains the only humanity. From the day when the proportions of his work, the anticipation of his future efforts, created before Balzac the immense tableau of French civilization in the nineteenth century, he was no longer concerned with composing one novel and then another novel, but with launching into space a new planet, another world of which he would be the father, endowed by him with a dilating force. He would be inspired, true enough, by the mores and the customs in vogue on earth. Not only did he dream of "competing with civil status" but of competing with the whole planetary system, with the result that we can formulate the principal, even the organic, laws that govern the progress of the Balzacian universe and rule its different kingdoms. Such a thought—the substance of the entire work—cannot be limited or circumscribed; it grows as the work grows, following the principle of Spinoza, since the life course of each being transmutes the acting force of the mother substance. We are no longer astonished that Romantic reality places a screen before authentic reality and absorbs all the vitality of its creator. Balzac is absent from everything that is contingent to his work, from everything that is for others most necessary and most solid. He deems its presence importunate, for it upsets the plan of his creation. He repulses it. Remember that sudden interruption of Sandeau, when the latter was returning from a visit to his seriously ill father: "That's all very fine! But let's get back to reality. Who is going to marry Eugénie Grandet?" Other remarks testify to this absolute. Is not the most significant and the most telling thing the final appeal that the dying Balzac, in his crucial illusion, made to Bianchon, the famous doctor whom he had called as a last hope to the bedside of so many desperately ill people?

As soon as he had discovered his technique, the novelist set to work to exploit it to the full. In the republication of several novels, and particularly in the reissuance of *La Comédie Humaine*, he did not hesitate to change the names of numerous characters from works earlier than *Père Goriot*—for example, *Les Chouans, Eugénie Grandet, Madame Firmiani*. Because he was constantly preoccupied with strengthening the original nature of this world of his own making, he multiplied the return of his characters. "It is a useful reservoir of walk-ons," is the happy formula of Maurice Bardèche. How very useful to have them within reach, always available, always ready to act, all of them capable of thowing themselves into the plot to make it reach a conclusion or to start off anew! Just by seeing them, by hearing them, we are obsessed by their presence; their names take on a definitive meaning, equivalent to the allegory of vice, of passion, of virtue, whether presented in halftones or in washed out or deepened colors. The avarice of Master Cornélius or of Gobseck is not the same as that of old Grandet or of Hochon; the ingenuous love of Ursule Mirouët is not that of Pierrette Lorrain, any more than the lewd debauchery of Philippe Bridau resembles the senile deliquescence of Baron Hulot. Let us say, in passing, that the psychological description in Balzac does not lead to excessive schematization or diagraming; on the contrary, it leaves a very personal stamp, made up of infinite nuances; it is this which gives so much life to similar types. Like the real world, his work contains the most diverse samples within a given category.

In order to verify the preceding assertions, let us choose one of the simplest characters, one whose conscience is all of a piece and without depth: Abbé Birotteau, the protagonist of *Le Curé de Tours* (1832). This priest is the *individualized type* of selfishness, as it is shaped by the psychophysiological restrictions of ecclesiastical celibacy, ending in deviations of temperament: meticulous and refined searching for material well-being, ridiculous pettiness, puerile ambitions. He carries out the duties of his ministry with the punctuality of a civil servant. He is the regular confessor of the boarding schools, a class of customers that does not entail involved or complicated cases for him. He is devoured by a desire for the canonry that eventually brings about his ruin, even his death, after submerging him in misfortunes to his person and his possessions. The crisis lasts only a few months. The deep reasons for it must be sought in the lengthy psychophysiological explanation alone; the antecedents of the man play no part in the matter and are merely pointed out in a brief allusion to his peasant origins and his poverty. Three years later, Balzac again pushed the vicar onto the stage, this time in *Le Lys dans la Vallée* (1835), to entrust him with the soul of Madame de Mortsauf. The choice of the lady of the manor was premeditated. She thought her former confessor "virtuous" but "uncouth, austere, severe." She knew on good authority that Father Birotteau was totally incapable and utterly lacking in perspicacity. Did she not hear her friends, Madame des Listomère and Monsieur de Bourbonne (a former musketeer, an old rake of a bachelor) mock often, but not maliciously, the vacuous remarks of "our dear Birotteau"? With "that gentle angel who becomes moved to tears instead of reprimanding," as the penitent said, she was sure of not being forced into categoric decisions. It was she who would rule that impulsive and erratic but meek and compliant old man and bring him to follow her own desires. How could he lay down a line of conduct for others, he who for his own salvation, even in earthly matters, stopped in bewilderment at the slightest difficulty? What veiled irony lay under the unctuous eulogies with which Balzac bedizens Father Birotteau, "one of those men whom God has marked for his own, investing them with mildness and with simplicity, granting them patience and mercy!" By virtue of the degree to which they are pushed, these qualities border on stupidity. It is not surprising that the *philothée* would judge such a man inaccessible to the sublime beliefs of Martinism; she hid her own beliefs from him, and this dissimulation opens a perspective on the slender authority that she grants to her confessor. She would not be constrained by him from the sentimental extravagances authorized by her Illuminist cult.

By bringing Father Birotteau into the plot of *Le Lys dans la Vallée*, Balzac had recourse to *dramatic utility*. A situation that we have already judged paradoxical from the Christian point of view could not arise except through the ineptness of this priest.

Let us reconstruct the genesis of a character from the data available on his psychology. First of all, an idea enters the consciousness of the novelist. As in the present case, the idea attaches itself to a theory: here it is celibacy considered as the physiological cause of imbecility. Synthesizing a psychological case, the novelist formulates the idea in two or three lines (as he does in *Pensées, Sujets, Fragments* or in the *Correspondance*). As this idea is personalized, a phantom takes on consistency: features, physiognomy, gestures, environment, setting, scenes are combined around the primitive concept. The type is formed, the idea individualized. It would also be appropriate to show, by means of examples, the force of attraction on and cumulation with other characters; such examples are indispensable in bringing out certain aspects of the protagonist. Thus, the role of Monsieur de Bourbonne in *Le Curé de Tours* leads Balzac to endow him with the character of Monsieur de Rousellay de Valesnes, who figured in *Madame Firmiani*, until finally he exchanges the first name for the second: the interaction of the accessory characters guides the novelist.

In *Le Curé de Tours*, Balzac has pictured the Abbé Birotteau in the last year of his life. Two years later, to strengthen the climax of *Le Lys dans la Vallée*, he found it necessary to use the vicar, whose weak personality is admirably adapted to the particular situation and who, as a result, forms part of the little circle of inhabitants of Tours brought to the stage. This carries us back a few years in time. It should not be said, as it has been, that the priest was resuscitated. The events of *Le Lys* take place four years before his death; the incidents that bring him to the fore stretch forward by a rectilinear movement, toward new circumstances; the personage stands out in sharper relief without any other causes than those already known coming into play. That is the way the world goes; very often, after someone's death, we hear of things in which he was involved prior to his death. Why should Balzac be criticized for this piece of realism? One remark is essential: between the salient facts of the novel and the sometimes fleeting or futile observations of and allusions to public doings, the synchronism is perfectly established in *Le Curé de Tours, Le Lys dans la Vallée*, and *L'Histoire de la Grandeur et de la Décadence de César Birot-*

teau, where, for the third time the vicar makes his entrance on stage. This exactness defies the most minute verification of the calendar and of historic trivia. It is not impossible to catch the novelist at fault on this point, occasionally.

Sometime in 1831 or 1832 (conjointly, that is, with *Le Curé de Tours*), Balzac, if we may believe what he wrote to Madame Hanska, was already thinking about *L'Histoire de la Grandeur et de la Décadence de César Birotteau*. On October 11, 1846, he wrote to Hippolyte Castille: "I have held *César Birotteau* for six years in sketch form, dubious of ever being able to interest anyone in the figure of a shopkeeper, rather stupid, quite mediocre, whose misfortunes are plebeian, symbolizing what we make so much fun of, *petty Parisian trade*. . . . One fine day, I said to myself: 'He must be transfigured, by making him the very image of honesty . . . and this seemed to me a possibility.' " He had already called him that "stupid Socrates, drinking his hemlock in the shade drop by drop." Three ideas dominate the conception of this character: first, stupidity; then, unappreciated honesty; finally, scorn, which is the result of moral impotence. These three features had already marked the physiognomy of Abbé François Birotteau in the preceding novel. Although this resemblance is not always the inevitable consequence of one and the same atavism, common observation attributes it to that cause. By virtue of that principle, Balzac, fully convinced of the chain of cause and effect, immediately thought of giving the perfumer to the vicar as a brother. At the mere name of Birotteau, the imagination of the readers of *Le Curé de Tours* would start to work; they would feel at home in an atmosphere that both naturally and socially would envelop them once more. By this device, Balzac quite logically was led to pick up again, in the dimly lighted mine, an as yet unexploited vein: the peasant origin of the two brothers, their upbringing as orphans and as protégés of a duchess who would interest her friends, the great ladies, in the future of the two children.

The novelist understood, later, that the apotheosis of stupidity that he confers on the vicar was not justified by the stagnation of celibacy. Such a mystery amounted to a congenital defect: that psychophysiological complex must take on its resemblance

in the economy of nature. The daring and somewhat pretentious theories piled up in *Le Curé de Tours* contradicted those
which had been expressed in the *Physiologie du Mariage* and
were to be restated in *La Cousine Bette,* following a Jansenist
text. The propensity of the vicar toward physical comfort became in *César Birotteau* simply a matter of plasticity of temperament and upbringing. Balzac was not ruffled by the overturn
of his previous theories. He no longer needed them when he recounted the origin of the two brothers: François and César,
as they should, resemble each other like two brothers of a
good blood line. Their psychology had developed in a straight
line, logically and expectedly, because their creator had from the
beginning laid down the principles from which the behavior
of his characters must necessarily flow: "The man is given,
with his character fixed, and his acts follow from his character."
That remark of Albert Thibaudet concerns not only Goriot, but
Birotteau, Cousin Bette, and most of the Balzacian people. The
absence of psychological Romanticism and the immutability
of the characters permit the reader to foresee in what direction
their destiny will take these creatures: they carry out the actions
expected of them; they experience the sentiments required by the
situation, because everything is commanded by conditions already established once and for all. The nature of these profound
causes cannot be changed along the way. These types and these
portraits stem from the classical tradition and particularly from
the French moralists who, by their analyses of fixed characters,
project into the abstract, outside the real, the very images of
life. But, by his descriptive strength, this great visionary creates
in these abstracts a center of irradiations; his art is prevented
from becoming monotonous in spite of the fixity of the supposed scientific laws that govern these series of effects and tie
them together. Balzacian characters are rarely seen cracking the
molds in which they have been conceived and belying the prepared fate that their creator has established and the reader too
easily deduces.

The stronger the personality, the more rigorous the enchain-
ment: I am thinking of Rastignac, of Philippe Bridau, of the
Gobsecks, of Marsay, of Tillet, of Finot, and all their like, and
many others besides, the whole collection of beasts of prey; they

all obey the skillful method of their trainer. Even Vautrin, as he accomplishes his horrible exploits, conforms to the law of his physicomoral organism and his environment.

It sometimes happens that the automatism and stiffness of the characters crushes the life story as their creator had imagined it for them. When César Birotteau, reduced to the last extremity, backed to the wall by the threat of failure, begins to hold his own against the mob of creditors, he calls his brother to the rescue. In a three-line note, whose laconicism speaks volumes about his terrible embarrassment and his business crisis, he entreats the vicar to send him "all the money he can lay hands on, even if he has to borrow some." The reader tells himself that the perfumer is totally lacking in perspiciacity. When the priest's answer arrives, it is just what we expected: an overflow of fraternal affection that expresses itself in distressingly stereotyped commonplaces. Its style is comic, in view of the anguished situation it is intended to alleviate. The abbé is full of touching sentiment; he is prodigal of his heart. But intelligence, comprehension of the perils that threaten his brother? Absolutely no! He sends all he possesses, six hundred francs, together with four hundred that his benefactress, Baroness de Listomère, has consented to lend him—one thousand francs, when it would require a hundred times more, as César had given his daughter Césarine reason to hope. The priest is totally lacking in practical sense. Even if we limit ourselves to a risky estimate, as is usual in the course of conversations between incompetent people, he is incapable of estimating the important sum that a commercial establishment like *La Reine des Roses* represents. He could have found out two years previously, during his stay at his brother's house. The missive is a shining example of the ability of its real writer: it becomes a document of his—Balzac's—state of mind, his irony. Held together by uplifting words and supernatural encouragement, the consoling phrases submerge themselves in an apparent confidence in Providence. But what hackneyed metaphors to translate that resignation! "When you have overcome this passing squall in your navigation. . . . Remember that I am a poor priest, who goes trusting in God like the larks in the fields, traveling my little

path, without noise. . . . whose hands will always be lifted up
to heaven to pray God to send down his blessing. . . ." And
"the storms of the world" and "the perilous sea of human interests" in which poor César is struggling! Balzac enjoys to the
full underlining the bleating simplicity of the vicar, the insipidity
of his counsels at such a moment. A verse of the fable, "The
Coach and the Fly," sums up the appositeness of his advice:

> A monk was reading his breviary
> He was taking plenty of time.

The perfumer's wife sharpens his ineptitude by prompting her
husband, as he reads the letter aloud: "Just skip all that and
see if he is sending us something. . . ."

All these shafts evidence an intentional persiflage; as in Bayle,
Diderot, and Voltaire, a liking for quips is alive in Balzac. But,
it will be said, the vicar asks for them by his stupid conduct.
In this case, careful examination proves that Balzac sacrificed
the reality he had decreed to the rectilinear, mechanical development of his characters, for which he had previously laid down
the conditions. It sometimes (as here) happens that subse-
quent events do not tally with the directing idea. In this very
novel, at the moment when the author informs us about the
antecedents of the Birotteau brothers, we learn that the vicar,
during the Revolution, "led the wandering life of the nonjuring
priests, tracked like wild beasts and guillotined, at the very
least." These words are very clear: they mean the vocation to
martyrdom, freely accepted by Father Birotteau. The refusal
to take the revolutionary oath supposes his absolute scorn of
suffering and comforts, and there is a flat contradiction of the
tamely bourgeois ideal to which we saw him vulgarly succumb
in Le Curé de Tours.

A man of that stamp, all the more so if he is a priest, does
not become false to himself, even when he grows old. There
is piquancy in finding the proof of it in the Relation des peines
et des dangers encourus par les prêtres du diocès de Tours, con-
damnés à la déportation en 1793, par un déporté.[1] The teller is a
confrère of Abbé Birotteau and not at all fictitious. The charac-

---

1 See Léon Aubineau, Les Serviteur de Dieu, Journal d'un Confessor
de la Foi (Paris: Vaton, 1852, in–12).

ter of the latter was falsified by Balzac somewhat frivolously, without due consideration for verisimilitude and documentary truth, in order to justify the principle of its development and the two inexorable laws of its structure; the consequences of celibacy, for which those of atavism are substituted. How can it be admitted that an intelligence endowed with sufficient acumen to have weighed the motives forbidding him, at peril of his life, to join the schism of the priests who accepting the revolutionary oath would have been capable of committing such errors of judgment as those quoted in the letter under consideration? Balzac plays his game: he has to win it even at the expense of logic and contrary to fact, but the Birotteau brothers have to lose it *because it was written.* Let us not claim to see in this any unexpected psychological Romanticism; no event whatsoever had come about that could cause the sudden change in the vicar's mentality.

Since we are reproaching Balzac for the automatism of his characters, we should rejoice that the mechanism broke down here. This behavior is closer to moral nature. Unfortunately this gap cannot be explained.

Nevertheless, the principles on which Balzac bases his judgments, or according to which he manages his players, do not have all the scientific value he attributes to them. The importance that he gives them and the repercussions of their discussions that we hear throughout his work have as their object, not knowledge, but the triggering off of artistic impressions. They provide the author with means of development, with springs that drive his exploration through all the strata of humanity; they are molds for the casting of thought. His deductions and his conclusions are then added to the theories, the intuitions, the primary systems with which he supported his creation. This creation, by these means, finds an inexhaustible source of nourishment, capable of providing for the countless struggling masses that have originated in an inspired imagination. It succeeds in coordinating its movements by means of a mechanism whose wheels and gears are quite easily disassembled.

We have observed how the character of Abbé Birotteau was unburdened of its antecedents in *Le Curé de Tours.* They are made known to us in the very last phase of existence. By a flashback, the novelist had to explain to us the "profound causes" of Father Birotteau's misfortunes in some way other than celibacy. The foolishness with which the intelligence of the two brothers is afflicted manifests itself as the sign of a mysterious fatality inherent in their blood. It made "their minds unfitted to follow back the chain of inductions by which a superior man gets back to the causes." This congenital impotence blinds their understanding, which is unable to foil an ambush; they are bewildered by the slightest intrigue. How could this simpleton of a vicar free himself from the toils in which he is held by the crafty tricks of two monsters of astuteness, the Gamard woman and Troubert? The fate of François and César will be the same as that of their brother Jean, slain in the battle of the Trébia: "The destiny of the Birotteau willed no doubt that they should be oppressed by men or by events wherever they might make their stand." The intervention of the ancient *fatum* greatly simplified the origin of the storms in which the fortunes of the three brothers were wrecked after a favorable beginning. Their unlimited ambitions had fired the wrath of divinity. Why did not the modest vicar remain satisfied with the fine setup that Canon Chapeloud had bequeathed him? Twenty years of covetousness had ended in the dreamed-of success and blessedness. Why then did he aspire to the canonry? The excessiveness of this pretension was to ruin the happiness already acquired. It was the sign of an unconscious pride. A man doesn't get mixed up in schemes unless he is "great of soul or a rascal" and not "a mere clumsy egoist," "an overgrown baby" sixty years old. He does not depend on others for the success of plans that are dear to his heart and keep him awake nights. Why did César the perfumer let himself be intoxicated by the ambition of wealth?

This recourse to fate introduces into the ordering of the intrigue and the structure of the character a *deus ex machina* whose ephemeral existence has exactly the duration of a metaphor. Worn as it is, it suffices as an admissible motif for such lamentable misfortunes; it manages to coat an adventure of the sacristy with epic glaze: that is clearly what the uninformed reader thinks. In reality, this mythological concept forms part of the Balzacian metaphysic. When tribulations transform a

Sabine de Grandlieu or a Henriette de Mortsauf into victims of conjugal love, Balzac attributes it to the evil spell of the "fatal genius." "Here the genius of evil is too visibly the master, and I dare not accuse God." Whatever may be "the poetic configuration" under which he pictures this "entelechy" to himself, be it angel or demon, he considers it a force contrary to good; these two opposite principles have created the world half and half. This opinion, tinged with Manichaeanism, interests us here only from the literary point of view. It concentrates on a typical personage a preternatural magnetism that forces him to act in the way expected of him. His disaster merges into the decree of a higher power. We become convinced that the distress of a Birotteau awoke in the mind of Balzac all the philosophical echos of his meditations on the essence of evil and the eternity of matter. Any Birotteau, be he François or César or Jean, once more loses his human appearance to return to his initial disincarnated state: an idea.

The characters of *La Comédie Humaine,* like the novels themselves, are the habiliments of a general idea. Each one is summed up by a maxim, a myth, an aphorism, or perhaps by the evocation of a historical personage or legendary hero with whom the fictitious personage is identified. This rational support might give a mechanical aspect to the characters if passion did not come to excite them with intense ardor under the flood of images. The images carry away the mind of the reader; they toss it about on the crest of the foaming waves. It is understandable why Balzac claimed the title of poet even more than that of novelist. We have stressed this imaginative force in relation to the role which he attributes to ideas. It is regrettable that the key to these symbols is supplied as the metamorphoses pass before the eyes of the reader. He must undergo "these downpours of metaphysics" against which Taine so carefully opened his umbrella. Balzac's art would gain in mysterious undulations if he had left it to us to discover the meaning of the images. Too often the author asks permission "to leave the drama he is relating to assume for a moment the role of critic" *(Le Curé de Tours).* His explanations tend to knot more tightly the threads that attach the behavior of the characters to the psychological laws governing passion. Passion remains "the element," primordial, fundamental, by which his poetics fashions the social mobility of his novels. "Passion is all humanity" ("Avant-Propos"). "By drawing up the inventory of vices and virtues, by bringing together the principal actions of the passions, by depicting the characters," Balzac wants not only to write "the history of mores" but also to isolate and define natural principles. In that way his philosophic system possesses a value subject to the critical examination of specialists.[2]

No observation, however small, seemed negligible to him. What importance has the façade of the house where he is conducting an investigation for the psychologist? Whether palace or hovel, the spot hides realities that set in motion rivalries that are the same, stemming from passions which are identical; the same "social teredos" or borers carry out their secret ravages therein. The tragedies of the sordid Vauquer boarding-house have as much importance as those of the mansion of Count Serizy. For an artist, the interest engendered by an intrigue does not lie in the social importance of the persons involved but in the intensity of their passions—as Balzac often said. Le Curé de Tours is "a tempest in a teapot, but that tempest nevertheless developed as many passions in the souls as would have sufficed to carry out the greatest interests of society." According to our theorist, passions are almost always generated by an antisocial reaction, that is, when the individual sets up his particular interests against the order demanded by the common good. This idea had come to him very early, as is indicated by the fact that the sermon of Abbé de Montivers in Argow-le-Pirate (1824) exposes several situations that arise from just this conflict. In Père Goriot, Vautrin's indictment of legal injustices and the hypocrisy of men attains epic eloquence and corrosive violence. This pirate is the typical outlaw, the personification of antisocial passion. Young Rastignac, in whom the bandit instills his own passion, was to have as peers and companions all the "corsairs in kid gloves" of the Scènes de la Vie Parisienne, all the sharks of the financial world. Such exploits

---

2 See Paul Césari, Etude critique des passions dans l'oeuvre de Balzac; Gaston Rabeau, "Balzac et le Christianisme," in "Chronique philosophique," in Enseignement Chrétien (October, 1944).

occur in hovels just as they do in mansions. Colleagues—and very fundamentally so—are the sly, criminal rustics of *The Peasants* and the petty, jealous, vain, middle-class citizens of *Ursule Mirouët*.

Balzac considered *Ursule Mirouët* his "masterpiece of the painting of mores" (letter to Madame Hanska, May 1, 1842). He was discovering nauseating greed in the souls of heirs and heiresses, and, as a result, drew repulsive pictures of the social jungle: "wild beasts," "reptiles," "scorpions," "sow-bugs" covet their prey and lie ceaselessly in wait to surprise it. They are envious creatures. The study of each individual character, however, shows the keen intelligence of the psychologist, who has varied all the colors of moral ugliness. All the aspects, all the forms that greedy inheritance can take, whatever the age, sex, temperament, upbringing, or social position—he has conjured them up. Fleeting suggestions, unforeseen changes, need but a few colorful words to transfix them. Cynicism is added to the contagion of moral beauty, which continues to function in the blemished heart, the heart poisoned by the enjoyment of evil. The dialogue, even more than the portrait and the narration, allows Balzac, like a painter, to bring out in the temper of the personality those colors that come from the farthest depths of the soul. When Portenduère, Ursule's chivalrous fiancé, finds himself face to face with the hideous Goupil, then goes to challenge Minoret-Levrault in the presence of his wife Zélie, his frightful accomplice, there are nuances such as only a great genius can devise. Humanity, panting, drags itself out before the man who can transfix it with unerring perception. Such artistic power gives to each creature its characteristic personality, and to each character his singular appearance, both of which veil the mechanism of the automaton.

The inconsistency allowed by Balzac in the structure of Abbé Birotteau's character is, I concede, exceptional. It is, moreover, instructive. A Father Birotteau who makes a god of his belly is inappropriate when a beloved brother is struggling in the abyss and calls for help. Then the favorite passion of the ecclesiastic can no longer guide the inspiration of the author as he seeks the reason for the unhappy destiny of the three Birotteau brothers. He thinks he has found it; he sets it forth in grave terms as a general idea; the idea fits all the particular cases to the same pattern, even if it means forcing or squeezing one or another of them. In actuality, of course, passion insures the person dominated a continuity of gait, gestures, and words by which the vice is translated and betrayed. There is logic in the passion of Grandet, Vautrin, Gobseck, Hochon, Nucingen, the Rougets, father and son, Philippe Bridau, Hulot, and Cousin Bette. They are so monstrous that we hesitate to admit them among the authentic representatives of human weakness. Flattering portraits, but flattery favoring the ignoble and the ugly. They are the "exceptions."—No, Balzac answers (to Hippolyte Castille in 1846), for I have met the originals of Vautrin and Desplein. Then he states the two principles of his literary creation: "What is life? A heap of petty circumstances, and the greatest passions are its most humble subjects"—"I have undertaken the history of the whole of society. I have often explained my plan in this single phrase: 'A generation is a drama with four or five thousand remarkable characters.' This drama is my book. If, in order to achieve such a great result, I should sometimes make an exception, where would be the harm? Do you believe that Lovelace exists? There are five hundred dandies in a generation, and between them, they constitute this modern Satan" (see *Clarissa Harlow*, by Samuel Richardson). The argument is unanswerable with regard to the truth of the portrait. The painting is done from life, from an infinity of real details. These powerful personalities make use of the same objects as do the humblest mortals! But they have their own particular manner, as each one of us has his or hers. Hence the diversity of types to incarnate the same passion or the same vice—avarice, for example, which plays such a big part in *La Comédie Humaine!*

What variety in the same species! In *Les Paysans*, Balzac himself yields to the pleasure of enumerating them:

Do you remember, possibly, certain masters of avarice already pictured in preceding *Scènes?* First the provincial miser, old Grandet of Saumur, as avaricious as the tiger is cruel; Gobseck the discounter, the Jesuit of gold, enjoying only its power and tasting the tears of the wretched until he was able to tell their vintage; then Baron Nucingen, raising financial frauds to the heights of politics. Finally, you doubtless recall that portrait of domestic parisimony, Old Hochon of Issoudun, and that other of one who was a miser by virtue of his spirit of family solidarity, young La Baudraye of Sancerre! Well, now! Human sentiments, and avarice more than most, have such different gradations in the different layers of our society that there was one miser left on the stage of the amphitheater of the Studies of Mores: Rigou was left! The selfish miser, the one full of fondness for his own enjoyments, that is, cold and brusque toward his fellows, in short the ecclesiastical miser, the monk who remained a monk [Rigou is a former Benedictine who broke his vows in favor of the Revolution] in order to squeeze out the juice called "good living" and who became a secular in order to snap up the public moneys.

Two others should be added to the list: Master Cornelius and Eli Magus. It would be interesting to justify the judgments leveled by their creator, at these miserable types by analyzing each one, showing in their development and their reappearances in the total work the struggles, intrigues, and maneuvers that these misers go through in order to satisfy their vice. This would not exclude but rather favor other violent passions in some of these people. Their primary tendency accelerates its movement toward a more ample object, just as it exerts itself in the direction necessitated by its beginning; avidly it seizes the slightest advantage to increase the thirst for more extensive possessions. At the same time, their characterization becomes an extraordinary alto-relievo as the details pile up in unbroken continuity; they take on body and richness. Thus passion maintains their vitality in their own element: in spite of intensity and dimensions, the characterization no longer seems strange to us, but natural. And this is the point that must be emphasized.

To demonstrate this point, let us take the character of Henri de Marsay. His numerous "reappearances" [3] endow him with a

---

3 [The text gives the word "reparutions"—*Trans.*] This neologism, created by Ethel Preston, expresses better than "réapparition" (reappearance) the notion of the method specially studied by this critic, in her *Researches on Balzac's Technique: The Systematic Return of the Characters of the Human Comedy* (Presses Françaises, 1927). Each of the people who reappears is the object of a personal inquiry, reporting his deeds and movements in each novel, with his psychological analysis and his dramatic role. This information would be complemented by consulting A. G. Canfield, "The Reappearing Characters in the Human Comedy," *Revue*

particular importance: he figures in twenty-six novels. He is one
of *The Thirteen,* a secret organization of companions who put
themselves above the laws, both human and divine, for mutual
help in satisfying their immense ambitions in all fields, but he
is the principal actor in only one novel, *La Fille aux Yeux d'Or.*
There we learn about his origin and his upbringing; together
the two give us the key to his whole destiny. Natural son of a
lord and a marquise, he is taken in charge by his aunt, an old
maid. She puts him in the hands of a preceptor, Abbé de
Maronis, a corrupt priest who depraves his pupil. Henri is gifted
with everything anyone could desire: intelligence, good looks,
wealth, high connections, elegance, and distinction. "He has
the courage of a lion and the cleverness of a monkey"; "his
gaze is steady, calm and intense as that of a tiger." He is irresistible; his conquests are past counting, but among the most
notorious, let us name Delphine de Nucingen, Lady Dudley,
and the Duchess of Maufrigneuse. He is the king of the dandies
and the mold of fashion, the oracle of all the drawing rooms.
There is not a great lady who is not anxious to count him
among the habitués at her receptions. And yet what cynicism!
What scorn in his remarks! "There is always a precious monkey
in the most angelic of women" (*Autre Etude de Femme*). "And
what is woman? A petty thing, a collection of imbecilities"
(*La Fille aux Yeux d'Or*). All his morality is summed up in the
result of his preceptor's teachings: "He did not believe in men
nor in women, neither in God nor the devil." That statement
makes intelligible the whole development of his personality. A
skeptic, a pessimist, an individualist, he is constantly in revolt
against the principles of social morality: "It is powerless against
a dozen vices that are destroying society and that nothing can
punish. . . . Man is a buffoon dancing on the edge of a prec-
ipice. . . ." "Marriage is the silliest of social institutions. . . ."
There is nothing ideal about love: "It is consciousness of pleasure given and received. . . ." The statesman must "always be
able to keep control of himself . . . in short, have within his

d'Histoire littéraire, 1934, Nos. 1 & 2. *The Genesis and the Plan of the
Characters in Balzac's Work,* by Helen Altzyler (Alcan, 1928), offers an
essay on the creative and spontaneous work of Balzac in the structure of
numerous Balzacian types, in its relation to the lives of the originals.

inner self a cold and disinterested being who takes a spectator's role in all the movements of our life, our passions, and our feelings and who whispers to us, with regard to everything, the decree of a sort of moral computor. . . ." Having only contempt for the masses, he has no pity for their sufferings. Nevertheless, Marsay becomes prime minister after the Revolution of 1830, "leaving an immense reputation as a statesman, the extent of which was incomprehensible. . . ."

Machiavellianism, political cleverness, sarcastic, insolent irony—these were the weapons that made him formidable to men and women alike throughout his career, from 1815 to 1834. The magnetism of "the illustrious de Marsay" creates in the whole *Comédie Humaine* an ambiance—an atmosphere—indispensable to the evolution of many intrigues and numerous characters; its permanence holds a portion of wordly society fixed firmly in immortality—and condemns it. Quite late, Balzac reveals the secret of this life and unknots the enigma of such universal skepticism (*Autre Etude de Femme*); Marsay's life becomes a commonplace fact and, for that reason, appears very normal to us. The novelist's technique is an example of consummate skill. The first love of de Marsay had been sincere, even wild with generosity. He had suffered such cruel disappointment that, heart and soul, he had been thrown into hatred: he took his revenge in perverting others. His pessimism is explained; all his anarchistic behavior becomes natural. First of all his origins, then his upbringing, and then his own experiences made an elegant pirate out of him. He came to enjoy, without bitterness, all the evil that he observed and caused.

If we check on the majority of Balzac's personages in this way, we will be inclined to conclude, with Ethel Preston, that Balzac knew how to tie together, from one novel to another, the accidental elements of his plots in pefect conformity with the character of his personages. He knew how to handle with the greatest of ease this whole immense configuration, and he did so "with a sense of sequence that, while not absolute, is none the less remarkable."

Of all the passions, love is the most pervasive; all the gradations of this sentiment bring forth an infinity of extremely diverse touches and types. There is not a single novel in *La*

Comédie Humaine that does not include several studies of woman loving or beloved. Balzac's artistic sensitivity—his curiosity about psychology—his tendency toward moralizing—his claims to being a social historian—his temperament as a sensual man, quick in his susceptibilities, prompt to conceive a passion for the delights of the heart or the flesh or both—all impelled Balzac to determine the character of a new heroine, just as his observation or his imagination might show her to him. His dreams of the perfect woman, of the most harmonious figure, corresponded to his desires, his obsessions, his illusions, his intoxications of the moment; these dreams peopled his work with creatures and with phantoms. It is possible to plot the curve of his own impression, to recognize the chimeras of his own incantations. Each of his youthful works (1820–24) has as its central heroine a girl who is a prey to her first sentimental emotions. Marie de Verneuil (*Les Chouans*)—we have previously commented on this—offers us a synthesis of all the preceding sketches: the young author was here translating all the aspirations and torments of his sensibility. This freshness, this bloom, was to leave its stamp forever on his personality and his talent. All the girls and young women of the *Scènes de la Vie Privée* are poetical creations, virgins with a halo of purity, lily-white fiancées who hide beneath their chaste veils their sorrows and disillusionments. It would be necessary to name them all, but we shall find them again in *La Comédie Humaine*, angels of modesty, overflowing with devotion, always ready to sacrifice themselves for the happiness of the chosen one. Eugénie Grandet, Henriette de Mortsauf, Pierrette Lorrain, and Ursule Mirouët compete with the Sisters of Charity. In their love, there is a hint of the maternal. Would it be rash to attribute it to Balzac's natural disposition?

Partly from egoism, his idea of the role of woman, "her religion," was "to present heaven and earth" to her lover, to seize in the exaltation of love (even heroic love) the end and object of the sovereign instinct that makes her find in another being, one whom she admires, the blooming of her total self— her ego.

The duel of marriage and love often inspired the novelist's inventiveness. As in the *Scènes de la Vie Privée, Une Double*

Famille, La Fausse Maîtresse, and *Une Muse du Département,* he often concluded in favor of society. Most of his novels end on a note of melancholy and disenchantment, as do *Honorine* and *La Femme Abandonnée.* Reasons of "high social importance" may force the wife "to undergo debasing sharing," "which a mistress must regard with hatred, because in the purity of her love lies all its justification." Romantic doctrine colors this subterfuge with a moral beauty that lures and deludes so many women in *La Comédie Humaine.* On the whole, and in spite of so much comic satire on marriage, there is no doubt that the writer sided with the political religious institutions that subject the individual to the law, that safeguard of the family and society. Here we only wish to point out the base on which rests the fresco of love with all its retinue of figurants and figurantes, symbols of all the passions engendered by the wily and cunning god with his inexhaustible quiver. *Les Mémoires de deux Jeunes Mariées* is love-passion deified, passion that burns and devours with a malignant fever the women whose prideful egoism idolizes itself. These women kill those whom they wish to enslave in the belief that they love them; and love destroys itself. Therefore, it is much better to be satisfied with wise moderation: the family also provides worthwhile joys. There is the marriage made for money, plotted by a Machiavellian mother who wishes to enrich herself by using her daughter at the expense of her son-in-law: *Le Contrat de Mariage.* There is the novel of cruel and worldly coquetry: *Béatrix, La Duchesse de Langeais, Le Cabinet des Antiques,* and *Les Secrets de la Princesse de Cadignan.* They paint love as it was lived "in the parish of St. Thomas Aquinas" under the Restoration and with all that comes a Diane de Maufrigneuse: the vanity of her scepter as it subjects a crowd of great lords or little coxcombs who pompously ruin themselves. There is provincial love in *La Vieille Fille,* love that throws all the social world of Alençon into turmoil when Mademoiselle Rose Marie Victoire Cormon, a well-ripened heiress, becomes the pawn of two political clans, the liberals and the legitimists.

Balzac has made a place for the courtesans, candid Aquilina, poor Coralie, unhappy Esther, Mirah the singer, and how many others whose natural goodness, total and sincere devotion, ig-

norance, and moral unconsciousness partly explain and attenu-
ate the horror of their disordered lives and their downfall; he
puts something like a pale reflection of human dignity upon
their foreheads. It is necessary to move still further downward,
toward that ignoble stable where the senile lechery, incurable
and cynical, of the libidinous old men grunts with a dull, hollow sound, puffs and blows in dazed stupidity; there we find
Baron Nucingen, Baron Hulot, Crevel, old Dr. Rouget and his
son. We could not possibly be led through the damned souls
of lewdness "to his prey attached" in a more atrocious way.
Balzac does not, however, waste any time on suggestive scenes.
Inexorable painter that he is, he shows the debasements and
the aberrations into which demoniac sensuality plunges its
possessed victims. The veracity of his realism keeps his witnesses
(who must feel humiliated for the human species) in such
horror as Dante might have created—and in terror. When we
have passed through this gallery of the passions of love, we
come out hallucinated. Is it possible that before our very eyes
so many diversities have expressed a single sentiment? Poetic
tenderness, fervent in its generous promise—platonic and divine
ardors—ethereal unions "of soul to soul," fleeing forever from
false, mendacious contacts—sensual furies—peaceful and profound happiness on the family hearth—prideful and despotic
domination—noble self-sacrifice and devotion to duty: who
has better set forth the contrasts, the magical effects, the sometimes astonishing and subterranean connections that allow genius to expand its conceptions in an attempt to equal the broad
bosom of Nature? [4]

Two novels, perhaps the greatest and certainly the most somber of *La Comédie Humaine—La Rabouilleuse* and *La Cousine
Bette*—show in horrible confusion the passions, lowliest as well
as loftiest, coming to grips with natural, social, and divine laws.
Instincts are unleashed with explosive force; their paroxysms
reach superhuman height. Here no longer is a personage, a character: here is abstract passion endowed with destructive dynamism, the possession of the individual by a sort of demon oper-

4 After Léon Emery, *Balzac: Les grands thèmes de la Comédie Humaine* (which has three chapters devoted to the forms of the passions of
love), pp. 93–153.

ating in a visionary jungle. Balzac goes so far as to say that "noble sentiments pushed to the absolute produce results similar to vices." Saintly Baroness Hulot supplies proof of this. Driven by a spirit of self-sacrifice as baffling as it is extraordinary (worthy of Mary the Egyptian), she was about to sink—"with the majesty of her virtue"—into dishonor. She was about to yield to the infamous solicitations of Crevel so that he would grant the loan that would save the family honor; her faith saves her. An anarchical pessimism emanates from these scenes; they maintain the stamp of the old novels of terror, the fantastic genre. By virtue of realism, they destroy reality. So many dissolute, lewd horrors could not be conceived by savages, for their moral stagnation would prevent it. We become skeptical. Can we admit that civilization can engender such abominable monsters? In the presence of these repulsive creatures, exhaling the putrefaction of morals, before this foul physical and moral decrepitude, might our disgust with humanity turn to despair? Shall we wonder whether, in order to give full artistic effect to his visions, the painter has not hurled a challenge at Satan? Whether the author, as a man pursued by thoughts of this battle, has not taken bitter pleasure in pillaging the city whose laws he had sworn to defend? While on the immense fresco that we might call *The Black Mass of the Passions* the monsters stand out in horrific splendor, do not the gnomes, guardians of morality, responsible for the punishment of criminals, made fearful by so much perversity, disappear into the innermost dark recesses?

Well, no! We reject this conclusion, urged upon us by some critics. The honest man, upright and healthy-minded, reacts spontaneously in another direction—the one toward which Balzac has tried to provoke him. He is captured by an immense pity for those depraved beings. Deeply moved, he admires the lofty virtues, the unsullied probity, of the ideal creatures who rise up eager to defend the rights of human dignity in these novels. As a citizen, he comes to a better understanding of the necessity for those higher principles that keep society from corruption. It is those principles that keep the honest man from sliding into such a deep abyss. Let us say it directly and immediately: the art of Balzac is bracing and tonic.

10 · The Structure of the Novels

SAINTE-BEUVE, in his article on Balzac's death said: "There are three things to consider in a novel: the characters, the action, the style." In this table of basic values, he does not use the word "composition," but three pages later he writes that "Sue is perhaps the equal of Monsieur de Balzac in inventiveness, fecundity, and composition." *Composition* is thus included among three rather inferior qualities in which a Eugène Sue can be rated ahead of a Balzac.[1] To appraise the originality, the talent, and the merits of the latter, let us continue to examine the techniques he adopts. We have already touched on several: description, observation, documentation, a system of philosophy, ideas, and passions. For Balzac these last two are not abstractions but vital forces, incentives that rush, so to speak, into the human organism and into Nature; their confluence is such as to be virtually invisible. His fecundity displays itself in the tremendous range of nomenclature in the titles that make up *La Comédie Humaine.* We have studied his technique of the characters. Before passing on to that of the style, we must stop to consider his technique of *action.* We must examine what it owes to *exposition,* to *plot,* and to *dialogue,* in order to form a judgment on the *composition* of the Balzacian novel. Finally, there is a much-debated question that cannot be avoided: Does not the Romantic art of *La Comédie Humaine,* up to a certain point, make use of the resources of dramatic art?

1 See Albert Thibaudet, *Réflections sur le Roman,* p. 186.

The action lies in the various movements, whether spiritual or physical, brought about by causes directly observable or vaguely foreshadowed, which make a situation evolve from one crisis to another and carry it on to a climax. This is like action in the theater, but with many differences. First, on the stage time plays only a minor role, its duration rarely exceeding twenty-four hours. Second, the dramatic author must rigorously limit himself to the most significant episodes or those judged indispensable to the progress of events or to knowledge of the characters. The novelist, on the other hand, may make other uses of the duration of time: he prolongs at will the development of a situation; he accumulates and joins together, in his development, many minor episodes, even if they may appear to be almost insignificant, as they are created by his fancy or by the requirements of his characters, who, once they have been conceived, develop their activities under the eye of their creator and outside of his volition.

The plot is the combination of the circumstances, incidents, and characters that form the nucleus of a crisis and awaken interest or curiosity in the reader: it generally revolves around an amorous rivalry. The romantic action, then, receives its impetus and its impact from all the other elements of the composition. Here we can only mention them and point out briefly some examples of the groupings and the results that they bring about. We should like in this way to point up and make tangible all that the evolution of the novel owes to the genius of Balzac. These simplified remarks will be in the nature of surveyor's stakes set out for future and deeper exploration.

Let us cast a retrospective glance over the body of novels published after 1830. *Les Chouans, Physiologie du Mariage*, and *La Peau de Chagrin* we shall consider only as the final experiments and the last preparations, in spite of their success. These works are of a value different from that of everything preceding them. They are the consummation of the previous attempts, but they are still sketches, rough drafts, essays in construction, however rich in meaning. At the same time, they mark the forward movement of a talent that now possesses the definitive molds into which it will pour the precious metal whose alloy will finally determine the true consistency of the work of art.

In 1830, the superb flowering of *Les Contes Philosophiques* and *Les Scènes de la Vie Privée* comes into full bloom; there, beyond argument, are manifested the creative power, the abundance of thought, and, above all else, the easy handling of technical resources. The first two are to be found in previous works, but not the self-confident method that knows how to make use of them with ease in order to vary the effects. The tale and the short story forced the writer to focus his efforts, to concentrate the interest in one episode. The novel, on the other hand, is a sequence of episodes that stretches out; it is a succession of scenes that makes it easier for time to produce incidents and to vary the angle from which we are shown the imaginary situation. The novel demands a more rigorously ordered composition.

The first technique that Balzac used, and continued to use constantly, was *contrast*. Most of the novels present a diptych: *La Maison du Chat-qui-pelote, Le Bal de Sceaux, Le Message, Un Drame au Bord de la Mer, Madame Firmiani, Adieu.* "These two parts," says the author of *Une Double Famille,* "will then form a single story that had produced two distinct actions." We see two portraits of the same character, two tableaux of his existence, *before* and *after* the event that divides it, contrasting the two parts and thus organizing the plan of the tale or the novel. In *La Maison du Chat-qui-pelote,* the tableau of the simple, serene life of Augustine Guillaume in her father's shop contrasts with that of her tortures after her marriage to the artist Théodore de Sommervieux.

This method gives the impression of arrangement adaptable to the dimensions of the largest novels. The very titles underline it. Just as *La Maison du Chat-qui-pelote* was originally called *Heur et Malheur* (Fortune and Misfortune), so we have *L'Histoire de la Grandeur et de la Décadence de César Birotteau, Mémoires de deux Jeunes Mariées, Splendeurs et Misères des Courtisanes, Illusions Perdues.* This taste for contrasts, opposition, and antitheses manifests itself not only in the plan of the works but in the descriptions, the portraits, the groupings of characters and the jealousies of clans. There are no end of examples. The whole of Balzac's work is shot through with plays of light that reflect, with echos that resound. In *Le Curé de Tours*, we have the added struggle of Vicar-General Troubert with the Listomère clan; in *Eugénie Grandet* we have the rivalries of the Grassin and the Cruchot families, coveting the hand of the rich heiress Eugénie, the former clan for a nephew, the latter for a son. This sort of competition is freely multiplied in *Le Cousin Pons* and *Le Père Goriot*. In *Un Grand Homme de Province à Paris*, the principal hero, Lucien de Rubempré, vacillates between two groups, the band of tarnished journalists who profane their calling in pursuit of gain or the pleasure of doing harm, and the Cénacle of d'Arthez, a friendly club of young writers, knights serving a very high ideal. The moral antagonism of these two contrary influences governs the fluctuations of the plot, as the heart of Lucien moves from one side or the other. The method broadens in *La Rabouilleuse*, where the action derives entirely from adverse characters: the two brothers, Joseph and Philippe Bridau; the two Rougets, father and son; the two half-pay officers, Maxence Gilet and Philippe Bridau, each one heading a group of friends.

Contrast is everywhere in *La Comédie Humaine*, but some works are not in opposition, but rather in the category of *rivalry*, a label that would classify *La Vieille Fille* and *Le Cabinet des Antiques*. Characters, portraits, situations, plots, the very localities where the action takes place, the houses and their inhabitants—among them all are corresponding similarities or dissimilarities subdivided in detail. By means of them there is established what might be called a dramatic movement in which the vital forces are as though polarized. This duality becomes organized into a sort of artistic unity. *L'Histoire de la Grandeur et de la Décadence de César Birotteau* abounds in these oppositions of characters, settings, and personages. The most powerful effects create the catastrophe. For example, when the perfumer, "that hero of commercial probity," solemnly restored to his former position of honor, returns to his former home, to his drawing room from which he had been ignominiously driven some years previously by his business failure, the same furnishings, the same women in the same ball dresses, the same eminent guests, the same music—the heroic movement from the finale of Beethoven's great symphony—cause "an enormous surprise," which lifts him to the heights of ineffable happiness; his sensation is so great that he drops dead. Happiness causes pain, life causes death.

Is not this law based on nature? "By an oddity that is explained by the proverb 'Extremes meet,' from the contrasts are born attraction"—a profound observation from which Balzac was able to derive full benefit. Thus it is that fellow feeling, sympathy, will be a bond between Minoret, a materialistic doctor and an atheist, and Father Chaperon, the parish priest of Nemours:

In order to be able to quarrel, two men must first understand one another. What pleasure is there in addressing sharp words to someone who does not feel their point? The doctor and the priest had too much good taste, they had frequented civilized company too long, not to practice its precepts; thus they could carry on that little war which is necessary to conversation. They hated each other's opinions, but they esteemed each other's character. If such contrasts, if such sympathies are not the elements of intimate life, would it not be necessary to despair of society, which, especially in France, demands antagonism of one sort or another? It is from shock of personalities that antipathies are born, not from the battle of ideas.

When formulating this principle of psychology in *Ursule Mirouët* (in 1841), the author was basing it on long experience, having applied it in the abstract to the behavior of numerous personages. One of his first novels, *Le Bal de Sceaux* (1829), had shown Emilie de Fontaine foolishly wrecking her marriage prospects because of her vain and frivolous character, which was incapable of understanding the nobility and "the firm character" of Viscount de Longueville.

In the play of opposition, the plan gains in variety; and the action, reduced to a symbol requiring explanation, to an idea needing demonstration, takes on a movement of shimmering oscillations. This is Balzac's way of revealing that in his vocabulary to describe is to comprehend. And here his poetic gift excels, as in *Jésus-Christ en Flandre*. One is tempted to say that the composition of this tale is glistening. It embraces two ideas: the lamentable state of the Church at the present time, the splendid state of the Church in the past. This contrast breaks up into smaller divisions by the scattering of images that illustrate the deformations and the defilements with which human passions have, in the course of centuries, disfigured the divine institution. The conclusion is, in effect, an appeal to turn again in the direction of the primitive ideal. This technique, animated by constantly alternating resonances, may be taken as a rather rudimentary sketch of the one that with more experienced handling sets face to face, in *La Cousine Bette*, actors embodying contrary vices and virtues. It would take too long to present their portraits here. Each of the virtues is represented by a different character, but the swarm of vices, like a covey of horrible birds, sweeps down on the central hero, the infamous Baron Hulot. There are the satellites of his moral hideousness —his frightful cousin Lisbeth; the ignoble Crevel; and his wife Valérie Marneffe, a depraved creature. Opposite them, the virtuous stand in contrast: Baroness Hulot, an angel of goodness; her daughter, the Countess of Steinbock, a proud and pure soul; her brother-in-law, the model of uprightness, Marshall Hulot. We cannot exhaust all the contrasts that branch out through the characters and the vicissitudes. Published in 1847 (one of the last three written by Balzac), the most voluminous, the most crowded, the most seething with characters, this novel is a vast synthesis of the dramatic techniques used by the writer. Now we can judge the primordial importance of the antithesis between individual passions and social rivalries. A permanent contrast whips up the waves of the Balzacian ocean. According to the hour and to the moment, a multitude of fierce or despairing figures move around, toss about, struggle with one another, or graciously tease. And our thoughts go to the retinue of Amphitrite, described in Fénelon's *Télémaque*, on the surface of the peaceful waters over which the chariot of the goddess skims, while Aeolus of the heavy eyebrows, uneasy and ardent, follows her, ready to unleash, with his threatening voice, the spirit of the black tempests and the mutinous winds.

Another element of Balzac's composition is *exposition*. This technique involves introducing the reader to the social environment in which the drama is to take place, presenting the actors and especially the central character and his companions. This role is entrusted at first to *description*. This means not only local color or the picturesque; more particularly, it means testimony on the epoch, a kind of social exploration, a document on the situation and on the nature of the people. It prepares the understanding by the recital of the range of colors that it projects into the field of vision. Because we have already studied the importance of this process, it will suffice to recall the house of the cloth merchant Guillaume, the mansion of Madame de Granville (*L'Interdiction*), the Vauquer boarding house (*Le Père Goriot*), the Claës house (*La Recherche de l'Absolu*), the office of Judge Popinot (*L'Interdiction*), which belong to *Les Scènes de la Vie Privée*. Throughout *La Comédie Humaine*, description will fulfill the same functions. The boudoir of Diane de Maufrigneuse and the Escrignon mansion (*Cabinet des Antiques*), the ancient home of Madame de la Chanterie (*L'Envers de l'Histoire Contemporaine*), the bachelor's quarters of Baron du Guénic, the city of Guérande—all are "portraits of olden times," the "images" of the "centuries" in which "the moral archeologist" hears the stones talking about the people who dwell there. To reach the very heart of the plot, we must know the antecedents of the characters, whence flow their rivalries, and then what events have aroused these rivalries and brought them to grips. The exposition becomes dramatic as it completes itself by a digression into the past: this is the "return backward," the flashback. It necessitates the depiction of the outward appearance of these personages, and now is the moment to present a full-length portrait.

Almost all the *Scènes de la Vie privée* make use of this kind of exposition. Let us take an example from *Une Double Famille*. This novelette begins with a description: the silent street, rue du Tourniquet Saint-Jean, near the city hall in Paris—the grimy old house, one window of which often frames the pretty face of a young embroidery worker, who quite often observes an unknown passer-by. An affair develops, children are born, events multiply around the couple. The lovers are shrouded in mystery, which excites our curiosity. At last it is necessary to rend the veil of anonymity. By a transitional phase, we are carried twelve years into the past. "It is necessary to forget the actors in it in order to undertand the interest that the introduction to this scene hides, to lend oneself to the tale of previ-

ous happenings. . . . Toward the end of 1806, a young lawyer. . . ." For several pages, all the detailed information about
the Advocate-General de Granville (Deputy Director of Public
Prosecutions) is made known to us in order to explain the
possibility of his adventure. He had the misfortune to be married to a bigoted woman totally ignorant of true Christian spirit.
She makes life so hateful for him that, although he is the
father of four children, he seeks the joys of domestic life with
Caroline Crochard, the embroideress.

Likewise in *César Birotteau*: "A rapid glance cast upon the
previous life" of his "domestic arrangements . . . will confirm
the ideas" that the initial scene of the novel "must suggest." A
long historical sketch on the mores of the Faubourg Saint-Germain in general and on the conjugal infidelities of the Duchess
of Langeais in particular and then a biographical account of
Montriveau are needed so that we may know about "the respective situations in which the two personages found themselves." In *Le Médecin de Campagne*: "the confession" of
Bénassis—"I was born in a small city of Languedoc . . ."—reveals the personality of the hero to us, toward the last third of
the novel. In *Illusions Perdues*: "It is all the more necessary here
to enter into some explanations concerning Angoulême, as they
will make comprehensible . . . Madame de Bargeton, one of the
most important personages of this story." We could continue to
multiply these phrases that announce the backward look. *L'Envers de l'Histoire Contemporaine* would supply several examples. It is one law of the disposition of events in the *plan* of the
Balzacian novels. They open with a description and often prepare the way for the exposition and the plot with a dialogue;
then, by means of a biographical account of the characters
already on the stage, the conflicts take on substance and become intelligible.

Time always takes its toll; everything that has ever lived—in
the world of ideas or in the world of facts, reality, or illusion—
belongs to it. It has been the actor, silent and hidden in the
shadow, himself invisible but not its effects on persons and on
things: the narrator's return into the past is intended to ac-
quaint us with these effects. In this relentless march, time ac-

complishes its work, humbling, leveling, destroying even without catastrophe to hasten destiny. Is it necessary for someone to intervene in the action to make it move forward? The novelist gives an order to time, and time, like a threatening old man, shakes off its lethargy. Formulas of this sort are not rare in *La Comédie Humaine*: "Five years passed without any unusual event disturbing the monotonous existence of Eugénie and her father. Always the same acts were constantly accomplished with the chronometric regularity of the old clock." Now its hands mark the hour of death: Eugénie Grandet is left alone with all the riches of the old miser. And then the action centers around her, in the persons of suitors who covet her hand in order to possess her fortune. This procedure had been previously used in *Les Scènes de la Vie Privée* and the *Contes Philosophiques* (*La Recherche de l'Absolu, Adieu*). It would go on being a dramatic auxiliary. When we peruse *La Comédie Humaine*, we often come upon these patches of shadow, we often go through periods of waiting wherein nothing visible manifests itself. Then suddenly the necessary incident looms up. Formulas like these are common: "Three months after these events. . . ." "Two years passed in this manner, with no other event. . . ." "Six months later. . . ."

In *Ursule Mirouët*, we find a typical example of the service that time renders to Balzac in advancing the drama. The incidents related in the exposition take a month; those of the action, seven years. Now, let it be said at once that each of these sections fills exactly the same number of pages. Later we shall explain the reasons for this disproportion. How many exploits accomplished in three years are related in a few lines! In the month of October, 1829, Savinien de Portenduère leaves his betrothed, Ursule, at Nemours, in order to complete his naval studies at Brest. Then he embarks as a midshipman to serve in the winning of Algiers. He distinguishes himself, wins the cross of the Legion of Honor, and returns covered with glory to his fiancée. The action of the novel starts with all this potential. But two years, full of secret joys, pass by with no happening other than the refusal of Madame de Portenduère to permit her son's marriage to Ursule Mirouët. In the month of December, 1834, Dr. Minoret, the guardian of the girl, departs this

life. Only after all this preparation does the definitive crisis of
the drama arise. After each of these stages, there is a gap that
calls on our imagination, a lack of clarity that must be com-
pensated by reveries. The reader is bidden by the author to fill
out the destinies on the basis of a few suggestions: the reader
thus participates in creating the story. The novelist compresses
the energy that makes the catastrophe explode. This result is
often considerable in *La Comédie Humaine*.

Instead of the overwhelming endings that we find in the
Contes of 1830, Balzac much prefers the long-drawn-out ending
in which time permits every latitude to the corrosion of existence, and allows passion to ravage an organism little by little,
but not the less surely. Of all the effects produced by this slow
abrasion, let us pause at a very characteristic one—two silhouettes of the same individual, one at the beginning, the other at
the end, of the novel. *Ursule Mirouët* starts with a portrait of
the massive Minoret-Levrault, the postmaster of Nemours.
This colossus stands before us. His high coloring is an indication of his boldness: he knows no other law than that of enriching himself by any means that the Code can not punish.
At the end of the novel, he is an old man, "white-haired, broken,
thin, in whom the old-timers of the town find no trace of the
happy imbecile you saw . . . at the beginning of the story."
He makes us think of an oak struck by lightning.

These contrasting portraits are the work of maleficent time:
Sprightly Emilie de Fontaine (*Le Bal de Sceaux*), disdainful as
the heron of the fable, resigns herself to marrying her seventy-
year-old uncle, Vice-Admiral de Kergarouët; at the end of the
novel, she appears tamed by her own arrogance. Vicar Birotteau,
with his florid complexion, happy to savor the material joys of
existence, contrasts with the parish priest Birotteau, gouty,
sunk into his armchair of sickness, waiting for death as for
deliverance.

Balzac widens the embrace of the exposition: he wants to
include all the causes and the smallest details that precipitate
the crisis. He gives his full attention to making intelligible the
generating cause of the essential drama and to rendering the
final catastrophe inevitable. Then he brings it to pass, having

released all the springs capable of accelerating it. This is called the art of *preparations*. After an accumulation of minute details, which sometimes seems to delay the march of events, fate, poised to deliver the mortal blow, rises up commanded by circumstances and summoned by the machinations of the characters. These doings make his intervention comprehensible and natural, by virtue of a logic that often draws its arguments from a metapsychics connected to psychophysiology.

Thus it is the writer imbues us with Romantic reality, brings to our intellectual and affective faculties the procedures of his mind and of his art. He triumphs if we ourselves are impressed by the stakes laid down on the table, if we are enthusiastic about the retort of this or that character, charged with menace and laden with consequences. We feel that the crisis has, so to speak, swelled the potential of emotion. A mere nothing may make it burst, and tension has reached its highest point. A word, an attitude, a gesture whose import we perhaps had not fully understood reappears for a moment, separates itself from the mass of previous actions, and strikes our understanding. There is no doubt whatsoever that Balzac borrowed the primary idea of these preparations from Walter Scott. But by his amazing artistry, he was capable of adjusting these complexities to an equilibrium that has a feeling of classicism, a classicism removed from contingencies, from the accidental, in order to move ahead rationally.

Let us finish verifying the cogency of these remarks by means of data from *Ursule Mirouët*. This novel is three things: a study of provincial morals and manners in the environments of the middle class and the nobility—a study of character: the man eager for profit and hungry for riches, Minoret-Levrault—an idyl that introduces a study of nascent love in a charming girl, Ursule Mirouët. The central plot involves an inheritance sordidly coveted by a host of relatives: three collateral heirs and their families weave schemes around the rich uncle; they wish to keep him from leaving his fortune to his ward Ursule. Minoret-Levrault is constantly maneuvering to get her married off to his son Désiré so that none of the inheritance will be lost. But two other candidates with no blood ties enter the lists.

To give body to the intrigues, Balzac makes use of his legal knowledge of inheritance cases: we must remember that he was once a notary's clerk. It is a notary, Dionis, a sharp-witted, false-hearted man, secretly associated with one of the heirs in the practice of usury, who gives the three heirs astute counsel for thwarting Dr. Minoret's plans. The doctor's chief clerk, Goupil, also has designs on the dowry of Ursule: he swears to make her "die of grief" if she does not marry him. Bribed by Minoret-Levrault, and under cover of anonymity, he torments the innocent child with a thousand infamies. This pack of petty bourgeois of Nemours, ambitious in a small and shabby way, hold the town by their infinitely complicated intermarriages as others held Issoudun in *La Rabouilleuse* (in part, also, a story of inheritance). Another very important element joins the already complicated exposition. One of the chapters of the original edition is entitled "Précis sur le Magnétisme." Dr. Minoret, until then a professed materialist, was converted after a case of second sight or prophetic vision, scientifically observed at the home of a colleague "in Paris, had demonstrated for him the existence of the soul and of the spiritual world." The influence of the intelligent and exceedingly virtuous priest Chaperon and the piety of Ursule bring the old atheist back to the faith and the practice of Catholicism. But the phenomena of magnetism will play an even more important part in the drama itself. This is the intrusion of supernatural dogma into the conduct of events. The exposition also allows us to be present at the beginning of an amorous intrigue without being able to divine the outcome, although we know that it will ruin the plans of the heirs. At the age of sixteen, Ursule falls in love with the Viscount Savinien de Portenduère, whose mother lives just across from Dr. Minoret. The two young people "have never said anything," but eyes have their own language and eloquence. Aristocratic prejudice, firm in the head and heart of Madame de Portenduère, "a Kergarouët," seems an insuperable obstacle. In addition, the viscount is temporarily shut up at Sainte Pélagie for debts occasioned by a few escapades. This situation gives the author a chance to tell us, by means of a flashback, the whole history of the Portenduère family. A miracle of paternal love: the doctor, although only an uncle, bears Ursule all the affection of a father. Miracle of the first love in the heart of a girl: her uncle leaves for Paris with Ursule, pays Savinien's debts, effects his release, and brings him back. The exposition is completed. "If the laws of the stage must be applied to the tale, the arrival of Savinien here ends the exposition by the introduction to Nemours of the only personage still mising among those who are to be brought face to face in this little drama."

It is now permissible for us to determine all the conditions that Balzac deems necessary to the structure of exposition. First he looks for *contrasts*. In his view, they form one of the essential realities of life and one of the artistic means most fertile in effects because it supplies a continual play of antagonisms in the drama. They abound in this particular mood. First of all is the plan of the novel presented in diptych, two parts, two tableaux: "The Heirs Alarmed," "The Minoret Estate." Each clan is opposed to the other—the clan of the doctor, his ward, and their friends, the priest and the police-court magistrate, joining battle with the clan of the heirs and their counselors, the notary and his chief clerk. In each group, internal opposition becomes manifest: the materialism of the doctor facing the deep faith of the priest, the democratic liberalism of Savinien de Portenduère facing the prejudice of his mother. Three candidates stand in opposition to Savinien. So much promises conflict. How many intrigues are started! The chapter titles in the original edition point up the announcement of the gathering storms:

1. The Heirs Alarmed; 2. The Rich Uncle; 3. The Friends of the Doctor; 4. Zélie [the postmaster's wife]; 5. Ursule; 6. Abstract on Magnetism; 7. The Double Conversion; 8. The Consultation [given by the notary and his chief clerk to the heirs]; 9. The First Confidence [of Ursule concerning her love for Savinien, given to the doctor, her guardian]; 10. The Portenduère Family; 11. Savinien Saved [from prison by Doctor Minoret].

The second technique that Balzac brings into play here is *description*: we already know all that he draws from it. It belongs first of all to the "laws of the modern poetics of local color." The writer pushes *the truth of realism*—his avowal is valuable—to the extreme limits of the conventions when, for example, it is a matter of repeating "the horrible insult larded with oaths" that escapes the lips of Postmaster Minoret-Levrault. The novel starts with a description of the little city of Nemours: Minoret-Levrault is dawdling on the bridge over the canal at the entrance to the town, out of patience from waiting for one of his coaches. It is a full-length portrait, the first of the gallery in which all the actors are presented to us one by one, group by group. We know them; they are painted with the peculiarities of their physiognomies, their dress, and their equipment, with the attitudes and the gestures that are most characteristic of the qualities and the vices of the soul, with their particular languages: the exterior is the sign of the interior, as truly for persons as for houses, other material objects, and Nature herself.

3   It is understood that this overload of facts requires numerous flashbacks. The novelist has to interpolate many monographs—do not forget the "Abstract on Magnetism"—to inform us about so many people, their antecedents, and their passions, to make his disposition of battle forces, if we may call them such, before unleashing the attack and the fray. If we consider that background is necessary to set forth happenings whose duration does not exceed a month, from mid-September to mid-October, 1829, we are no longer astonished that it—including expository flashbacks—requires more than half the volume, eleven chapters out of twenty-one, whereas the action of the "story proper" spreads out over eight years, from 1829 to 1837, and no more space. Let us examine by what method he makes the action move forward.

"The action began with the play of a mainspring so much used in the old as well as the new literature that no one could believe in its effects in 1829 if it were not a question of an old woman from Brittany, a Kergarouët, an émigrée!" This mainspring is misalliance. These are the terms with which Balzac initiates the conflict that brings to grips all the characters of the novel. A new intrigue mingles with the first or, rather, twines its tentacles around it—that is, the scenes, the incidents, the ups and downs that the love of Ursule and Savinien will cause. Far from dividing the interest, it makes it stronger. This question of marriage becomes the stake in the battle fought between the two lovers and their friends on the one side, and the heirs and their confederates on the other. If it miscarries, it means that the heirs triumph. It if succeeds, then the heirs lose the inheritance. The matrimonial intrigue, the love interest, becomes replaceable for the other intrigue.

The school terms that Voltaire used in speaking of the tragedy of Oedipus can be applied to *Ursule Mirouët*. This novel is "simple" because it "has only a single catastrophe" (the horrible defeat of the heirs); and it is "implex" because it has the amorous struggle "with the peripetia." These reversals of situation, these sudden changes, abound; one arises from the other; they are involved, in turn and simultaneously, in the action. Madame de Portenduère is uncompromising on the question of misalliance and bluntly tells her son so. Dr. Minoret, insulted by this disdain, tries to turn his niece away from her dream. The stronger the opposition grows, the more tenaciously Savinien holds to his project. Because the marriage is the key to the inheritance, new implications entwine themselves around it: Savinien counts three rivals for Ursule's hand. When one of them, Goupil, has given up of his own account, he rallies to the side of his competitor, for the sake of material profit. At last Madame de Portenduère gives her consent, but only after atrocious persecutions suffered by Ursule after the death of her uncle: the girl then reveals the nobility of her heart. The vicissitudes continue at a sharply accelerated cadence with the horrible swarming, crawling, and wriggling of viscous forms that the heirs, those evil creatures, take on in the shadow like snakes. As Joachim Merlant said so well: "They form sly, underhand alliances between them, they accept compromises, they betray each other, they hurl challenges at each other; it is a war that brings into play the most passionate, violent energies, exactly as a grandiose interest might if fought over by men of high lineage. Crime does not stop them; Minoret-Levrault, a sort of Hercules, led on by his viperine wife, steals the will that favors Ursule." Everything seems completely lost; then the whole thing rebounds.

Let us pause to draw some conclusions. Even if the art of composing plot is, of necessity, a lesser art, when we have reached this spot in the novel, we are forced to recognize that Balzac practices that art in a masterful fashion. We have already given the reasons: the movements of his plots develop out of the characters and enhance them; moreover, they arouse attention, curiosity, and emotion by the tragic situation in which he places the two lovers, especially the heroine. But the merit of a novel does not lie in its plot. That of *Une Ténébreuse Affaire* is admirably composed, but that of *Une Femme de Trente Ans* is merely a juxtaposition of episodes—and yet the face of this sorrowing woman takes on extraordinarily pathetic relief by the end of the novel. The same thing may be said of *Eugénie Grandet* or *Le Curé de Tours*. The quality of these masterpieces comes in part, however, from their very lack of plot. Balzac, with dramatic intensity, puts nakedly before our gaze souls tormented by a passion whose slightest changes and deviations are perceptible. In exploring the human heart, we discover involuntary complicities, activated by inevitable reflexes.

In the character of Grandet, the intelligence of his vice is thwarted by the intelligence of the heart that nascent love gives to his daughter. From the patient servitude imposed on her by the paternal yoke, from her sheep-like calmness, Eugénie reaches proud independence and lofty courage. With the energy she draws from her new feeling, she defies the tyranny of the miser and confronts him with a strength equal to his own. But that strength had always been drowsing in the blood transmitted to her by her father. From the same principle, two adverse passions have arisen. In *La Recherche de l'Absolu*, much the same thing can be said about Claës and his daughter Marguerite.

Many novels have only a weak plot: the mystical novels, *Louis Lambert*, *Séraphîta*, *Les Proscrits*; several didactic novels, *Le Médecin de Campagne*, *L'Envers de l'Histoire Contemporaine*, *Le Curé de Village*. In this latter the intrigue is perceived only in its consequences. The circumspection of the novelist concerning the affair of the two lovers produces delayed-action effects. Barely suspected from certain indications that we can divine only in the chiaroscuro of the allusions, the truth comes into broad daylight with the avowals of Véronique Graslin in her public confession. In *Le Cousin Pons*, the plot deriving from the planned marriage of Mademoiselle Camusot de Marville, which did not come off with Brunner but succeeded with Viscount Popinot, has slight interest; any other reason for a falling-out between the Camusot family and Pons would have done just as well. These examples permit us to declare that a plot is not to be considered the crucial point on which to appraise novelistic value. In any case, it is evident that the talent of Balzac, when he wishes, is not inferior in fertility or inventiveness. His flexibility adapted itself with ease and with success to the complications of *Ursule Mirouët*, while substituting for the drama of the inheritance a new interest, the success of love. He ties them together, joining them so strongly that attention shifts without producing any diminution of interest. *Béatrix, Illusions Perdues, Splendeurs et Misères des Courtisanes,* and above all *La Cousine Bette* also supply any number of similar examples.

The vicissitudes of *Ursule Mirouët* are closely tied together. Art calls on the least little detail whose vibrations can sometimes be felt in a character. Any complication arises from a movement of the conscience. Thus hostilities open against Minoret-Levrault, the stealer of the will: remorse poisons his conscience. All the incidents will be grafted onto this one, and from this invisible spring all the vicissitudes will spurt forth. But for this psychophysiological disturbance, the apparitions of Dr. Minoret would have found no likely grip on the plot, particularly because the guilty man endeavored to hide his moral uneasiness from everyone. In that way, the tragic depth of human conception asserts itself in the drama: the manner in which the external events act on the soul gives them a weight of eternity. "Human justice is the development of a divine thought that hovers over the worlds."

We are aware of the resources that the miraculous and the fantastic brought to Balzac; he accords them to the value of scientific Romanticism while preserving their mystical influence. What is to be regretted, from the purely artistic point of view, is that he is never able to do without those strange particulars as he evolves the character of a religious convert. He confounds grace and psychosis. Thus, he never gives us a true novel of conversion, although he tried often—and twice in *Ursule Mirouët;* in Dr. Minoret and again in Minoret-Levrault.

In *Illusions Perdues*, D'Arthez listens "religiously" while Lucien de Rubempré reads "for seven hours" the manuscript of his first novel, *L'Archet de Charles IX*. When he delivers an opinion on this work, his first remarks have to do with the form of the dialogues:

> If you do not want to ape Walter Scott, you must create your own personal style, and here you have imitated his. Like Scott, you begin with long conversations to pose your characters; when they have talked, you bring in description and start the action. This conflict, so necessary in any dramatic work, comes in last place. Just reverse the terms of the problem. Replace those diffuse chats, which are so magnificent in Scott but so colorless in your work, with descriptions for which our language is so well adapted. In your work, let the dialogue be the expected consequence that completes your preparatory steps. Start with action right from the beginning.

Here Balzac was acting as his own censor. In the person of his creation D'Arthez, he noted the evolution of the dialogue throughout his youthful novels, where this procedure is only an inconsistent game in *L'Héritière de Birague*. In *Argow* and *Wann-Chlore*, and later in *Le Corrupteur*, it becomes the lively translation of sentiments that influence the action. In *Les Chouans*, all the varied resources that dialogue can give are fully and richly realized to increase the reader's interest: light is cast upon the speakers' souls, whether principal or secondary characters. Dialogue distinguishes their status and their social condition, thanks to the propriety of their language and vocabularies; it sums up the situations and marks their progress; it creates an atmosphere; it colors the intrigue with an anguish that carries over into the action. "Words . . . are the germ or the fruit of deeds," as in Walter Scott's characters. They "magnify everything; the country, the scene." For example, the remarks of the two lovers, Montauran and Marie de Verneuil, cast on the environment, spiritual or physical, an air of mystery; they impart dramatic tremors. The dialogue becomes the woof of the exposition on which are worked the elements necessary for a knowledge of the historical events or the introduction of the actors.

By that time he wrote *Les Chouans*, the novelist was in possession of the right formula. Later he would perfect his technique. He would knit reality more tightly by putting on the lips of the speakers expressions indicative of their functions, their corporative environment: these are social peculiarities or personal quirks or sometimes characteristic words, as in the comedies of Molière. Some are to be found in *La Maison du Chat-qui-pelote* and *Une Double Famille*. Listen to Madame Guillaume in front of the canvas that Sommervieux is showing at the Salon; it represents the Cat and Racket: "That's all one gets at all these shows—headaches! Do you think it's amusing to see a painting of what we see every day in our streets?"

Another type of dialogue appears in *Le Curé de Tours*, that is, "a duel of words": *what is said* is the opposite of *what is thought*. "Under apparently insignificant phrases," the two antagonists, Baroness de Listomère and Vicar-General Troubert, are mutually hiding their thoughts. Balzac thought it necessary, in the edition of 1835, to write out these unexpressed implications: after each reply, he interpolates, in italics, the sense, the tenor, we might say, of these secret intentions. Who fails to see here the theater lending its stage technique to the novelist? We think we hear the tone of the retorts; we mentally see the gestures indicated by the author. This procedure operates to reveal the astuteness of feminine coquetries, with which the Duchess of Langeais, for example, is prodigal toward General de Montriveau. *Eugénie Grandet* (1833) and *Le Père Goriot* (1834) abound in character words. In *César Birotteau* (1837), the exposition opens with a comedy scene: Madame Birotteau awakens during the night and discovers that her husband has left the conjugal bed. A monologue ensues—Is it spoken aloud? Is it the interpretation of her mental state?—that informs us about the character of the husband, as judged by his wife. Then Constance Birotteau gets up, in a panic, and finds César, in his dressing gown, measuring the dimensions of his apartment, which he wants to enlarge, transform, and beautify, as he does his shop, for he has conceived some glittering projects for getting rich. All that is brought out in a long conversation between husband and wife. Thus, we come to know the character of each and their situation. This dialogue exposition takes not less than twelve pages. Thereafter, Balzac knew how to get the most astonishing effects from dialogue, how to adapt it to dramatic circumstances, and how with its help to create new ones and make comments on their consequences, with a light or serious touch, according to circumstances. We need but open any one of the novels to be convinced of this and to admire his virtuosity.

In an article in *La Revue Parisienne* (1840), he addresses a reproach to Eugène Sue for his clumsiness in this procedure. "Dialogue, let us proclaim it loudly, is the lowest of literary form, the least esteemed, and the easiest; but just see to what heights Walter Scott has raised it. He has made it a means for completing portraits." It was easy for Balzac to speak with self-confidence; we think that when he proffered this criticism, he was boasting a little about his own personal success in the art, which, we now know, he had achieved only after repeated trials. What versatility, what realism, in the tenor and the technique of the dialogues! Just reread *La Vieille Fille, La Rabouilleuse*, and some of the other novels. We can apply to *La Cousine Bette* the qualification that Balzac used in characterizing the genre of Walter Scott: a "drama in dialogue." We refrain from many remarks that might be useful. Some critics are too prompt to qualify many dialogues of *La Comédie Humaine* as conventional, inadmissible, or mechanically motivated by the characters—among others, André Gide, in *Pages de Journal* (1929–31), referring to *Eugénie Grandet*. They do not take into account all the genres—and we have paused to consider only the principal ones—that the genius of Balzac invented to make his work not only the mirror but (as we might say today) the televised reproduction of the daily scene of his time in all walks of society.

Beginning very early in his career, the technique of the theater influenced the Romantic art of Balzac. Traces can be found in the youthful novels; *Clothilde de Lusignan, Le Vicaire des Ardennes*, and *Argow-le-Pirate* contain numerous scenes in dialogue—subterfuges, reversals of situation, jokes, retorts, and words appropriate to the stage; sentimental duets between lovers; sudden intervention by the *deus ex machina*, precipitating the crisis and resolving the confusion—all procedures harrowed from the melodrama. They were to reappear in several *Scènes de la Vie privée* (1830): *La Vendetta, L'Elixir de Longue Vie*, and *La Grande Bretèche*, where many horrible crimes take place. *La Duchesse de Langeais* (1833) offers another typical—and regrettable—example of these melodramatic and too easy performances, when Montriveau, "like a tiger sure of his prey," threatens Antoinette de Langeais with the worst of tortures, having kidnapped her as she left a ball.

But Balzac also borrows from comedy. He overdoes the jargon peculiar to each class and each calling; he imitates too heavily the Teutonic accent of Baron Nucingen and Wilhelm Schmucke, a musician and great friend of Sylvain Pons. *La Maison Nucingen* from beginning to end consists of a conversation at a restaurant table between a caricaturist, Bixiou, and two journalists, Blondet and Finto. The humor, the scurvy tricks, the violent apostrophes of Bixiou against dishonest accumulation of capital, the keenness of the psychological remarks all make this work a sparkling sample of wit—Balzac's wit. *Les Comédiens sans le Savoir* is a revue written with infinite mischievousness and drollery: it might be called the marvelings of a man from the south, with a painter as his guide, on the Boulevard des Italiens. *La Cousine Bette*, by the limitless diversity of the individuals who fill the scene, presents all the characteristics of great drama: all the genres mingle here, including both the comic and the tragic. In this connection, let us mention the interview of Baron Hulot d'Ervy, Director General of the War Ministry, in the presence of the Minister, the Marshall Prince of Wissembourg, and his brother, Marshall Hulot, Count Forzheim, two celebrated wrecks left over from the Imperial Army, two comrades and friends. The Baron is to hear himself charged as a result of his malfeasances. The scene achieves an extraordinary grandeur, yet the strength of the emotion does not preclude familiar and very engaging details.

This grandeur is surpassed in the final scene of *Une Ténébreuse Affaire*, where we are offered the *dialogue animé*, animated by what I shall call the spirits of the place, by the trenchant passions that cut through the apparent control of the adversaries, by the importance of the interests at stake and the inimical personages, by the extraordinary ambience of sounds and movement that surround the protagonists and compete in forming and changing their sentiments. To bring together such a combination of circumstances is the sign of a genius. Our whole being—purely sensory faculties as well as the more noble parts of our souls—is stirred to the innermost core. Let us probe this situation more carefully.

The four cousins of Laurence de Cinq-Cygne (who was orphaned at the age of five)—the two Hauteserre brothers, with whom she was raised, and the two twin Simeuse brothers—have been condemned to death for plotting against Napoleon. Three of them are in love with this blond with deep blue eyes, the pretty and true thoroughbred. A soul of steel in a frail body, she is a fearless amazon, like Diana Vernon, the heroine of Scott's *Rob Roy*, of whom she is a sort of replica. In the forests of the department of Aube, Laurence had held in her own hands all the strands of conspiracy and insurrection until its discovery at the last moment by the police of Fouché. She hates, she scorns Napoleon; she has often dreamed of assassinating him herself, in imitation of the deed of Charlotte Corday, whose portrait she had hung in her drawing room to keep her resolution high. But she has resolved to win pardon for the four condemned by the emperor. Supplied by Talleyrand with diplomatic passports and accompanied by an old and chivalrous relative, the Marquis of Chargeboeuf, she has reached the outposts of the army in an old coach, having avoided the ambushes set up on her road by Fouché. It is the eve of the battle of Jena. Tossed on this ocean of a hundred and fifty thousand men, the girl is struck with astonishment by the display of military splendor. "The man who animated those masses assumed gigantic proportions in her imagination," the thought of a solemn meeting with "the man of destiny" frightens her, her arrogance vanishes, and she feels very small in the midst of this hurly-burly. As evening falls, this "daring barouche" astonishes the soldiers. A military policeman stops it; roughly he interrogates the two occupants: "Who are you? Where are you going? What do you want?" Laurence de Cinq-Cygne questions two officers, uniforms hidden by their cloth greatcoats, who are reconnoitering the terrain. "Where are we?" she asks, and one replies: "What is this young woman doing here?" The girl was soon to see that, unknowingly and rather impertinently, she had just spoken to the Emperor himself. Suddenly, a large escort sweeps about the barouche, uniforms covered with braid, horses prancing. Generals, marshalls, and officers "respected the carriage because it was *there*." "One of the two officers, the Emperor himself, dressed in his famous frock coat, was riding a white horse richly caparisoned. He was studying the Prussian army on the other side of the Saale with his field glasses. Laurence understood then why the barouche remained there" and why the general staff "spared it." The fires of the bivouac begin to burn through the darkness; arms glint in the firelight like little streaks of lightning. Thinking that the interview is at hand, Laurence clenches and unclenches her hands convulsively.

We are sorry to mutilate this magnificent section; it should be kept whole to preserve all its dramatic intensity. Each detail has its own tonality. The humble barouche, motionless as a rock in the rush of a torrent, becomes the symbol of the daring deployed by that "child," as she is soon to be called by the Caesar, the master of life and death. The dialogue moves here and there on the field, changing place with the speakers. Commands and orders resound in the air, which the tramping of the masses and the rolling of the caissons fill with fearsome muffled noise. What variety of sounds and tones! The descriptive passages, apparently tossed off in passing by the narrator, have their own language; they seem to be retorts to the words of the characters; they have their magic and magnetic word; they act on the mentality of the characters like direct discourse. Realism and poetry join and become as one. We look about us, mentally. Confronted by this immense spectacle, we feel a thousand sensations, as though the event were taking place before our very eyes; we seem to be present in flesh and blood. This scene and its dialogue let us live the famous victory better than any historical account. And we begin to regret sincerely that Balzac never realized the project that "plagued" him for so long after 1830: "To make a novel called *The Battle*, where on the first page we hear the cannon rumbling and on the last the cry of victory; and during the reading the reader thinks he is present at a real battle, as though seeing it from a mountain height, with all the accessories—uniforms, wounded, details. The eve of the battle and the day following: Napoleon dominating all that. The most poetic one would be Wagram"

(*Pensées, Sujets, Fragments*). The sketch in *Une Ténébreuse Affaire* assures us that Balzac's talent was not overbold. We understand why he wrote to Stendhal when *La Chartreuse de Parme* appeared, with its acount of the battle of Waterloo: "Yes, I was seized by an access of jealousy at that superb description of the battle that I was dreaming of for the *Scènes de la Vie Militaire*, the most difficult portion of my work; and that piece enraptured, chagrined, enchanted me and left me in despair."

Our demonstration of this animated dialogue should be terminated with a commentary on the one which took place between Napoleon and Laurence de Cinq-Cygne. Their meeting occurred in a "wretched thatched cottage" a few hours before the actual battle began, with the same characters on stage as in the preceding scene. This confrontation of the man "with the countenance of a Caesar, pale and terrible," and the frail suppliant kneeling to petition the ardently desired pardon is rousingly described. Between the two, each unconquerable in his own way, the staccato phrases of the replies spurt out from the very depths of their souls. The psychology of the two is revealed by lightning-like flashes. (I should like to reproduce all this dialogue.) Then the Emperor, taking Mademoiselle de Cinq-Cygne by the hand, leads her out onto the plateau where the armies about to engage in combat can be seen. "With his own personal eloquence, which turned cowards into heroes," he justifies his severity toward the four rebels, who, he had intimated, would be pardoned. "Remember, Mademoiselle, that men must die for the laws of their country as they die here for her glory."

Visualize that scene on the cinema screen. The inner visions follow each other more rapidly than the thought of the spectator can follow: each word sinks a little deeper into the feelings of the two protagonists, whose changes of attitude are carefully described. Reading, we notice a commentary following each reply—something that an actor would interpret by a gesture. This is real theater or, better, true cinema. Balzac idolized the memory of Napoleon, and all his admiration is apparent in the conclusion of the dialogue. There his phrase is worthy of the great war leader and profound philosopher. It confers high moral value on the drama; it attempts to legitimate many of the acts for which the sovereign had earlier been responsible. Merely from the point of view of technique, the scene is vibrant with life; it bears the imprint of the strength that Balzac considered the first requisite of any government, whether kingdom, empire, or republic. And from the direction we have approached it, it earns its author the title of excellent and powerful dramatist.

We should also comment on the role of the monologues, in which the characters betray the violence of their passions. In their disorder of mind and spirit, that violence of passion forces from the lips of Gobseck and Grandet an expression of the bitter, sensual pleasure provided by the sight of the gold they so covet and dearly love! Who is not familiar with the despairing moans, the curses, and then the blessings that mingle together in mad rage when the father, Goriot, on his deathbed, vainly awaits his two daughters to give them a last kiss? It is impossible to imagine more burning pathos, a more vehement image of desire.

Many other comments might be made concerning the thickening of the old lines in the portraits, appropriate to the optics of the theater. By contrast, what moving words of simplicity, grace, and suffering the Viscountess of Beauséant addresses to Rastignac at the moment she meets the guest at the last ball she is to give! All the important people of that world have come to feast on her martyrdom: her lover, Adjuda-Pinto, has broken off his affair with her a few hours previously, and all Paris is talking about it. At five o'clock in the morning, before getting into the carriage that is to carry her off to the castle in Normandy, that is to be the tomb of her destroyed happiness, she says farewell to the Duchess of Langeais and to Rastignac. She speaks like a humble woman, with no hint of artificiality. Balzac was able to find the words to express real grief, grief without artifice or pose. He showed that his art was capable of treating with exceeding delicacy the fleeting nuances of the feminine heart.

Is it not astonishing, then, that he was so very ill-starred in his attempts to be a dramatic author? From his youth, he was obsessed by the ambition of acquiring renown by means of comedies and dramas: let us remember his tragedy *Cromwell*

(1820). He was convinced that plays, "the income of which is enormous compared to what books bring in," would win him a fortune (letter to Madame Hanska, 1835). As a result—countless projects and comic sketches. Indeed, he was beset by them. Several were completed: *L'Ecole des Ménages* (1837), which was never accepted by any theater; *Vautrin* (1840), which was banned by the Minister of the Interior after its first performance; *Les Ressources de Quinola* (1842), which was not a success; *Pamela Giraud* (1843); *La Marâtre* (1848), which had only six performances; *Mercadet (le Faiseur)*, which was staged posthumously, after it had been revised. In the theater, the great novelist knew only failure. His imagination was too vast, unable to submit to the special technique of the stage. Abridgement, foreshortening, synthesis, brevity, simplification, all were contrary to his minutely analytical genius. His Romantic work is "an inexhaustible treasury of poignant situations, of deeply etched observations," but strangely enough, he was never able to turn them to account. They were a source of profit to others, however, for many of his novels have been adapted to the stage. Douchan Z. Milatchitch, in his thesis on *The Theater of H. de Balzac*, concludes that time was the factor that the brilliant novelist needed, but lacked, for success on the stage. He would have had to devote to the theater the same great effort that he lavished on the novel. Had he done so, he would have been able to transform the dramatic genre of his epoch. His attempts "portend masterpieces."

11 · Balzac's Style

EXTOLLED BY SOME, attacked by still more, Balzac's style raises a much-debated question. A brief glimpse of its complexity will lead the reader more deeply into it; a simple restatement of the basis of an arbitrary and overgeneralized opinion may incite everyone to undertake his own inquiry throughout the length of *La Comédie Humaine* in order to form a personal judgment. Such an examination would be more worthwhile than the repetition of a borrowed formula. I have too often heard this judgment pronounced with imperturable assurance: "Balzac is a bad writer; his style is lamentable." If I happen to ask the reason for such severity, I am cited, nine times out of ten, the response that Henriette de Mortsauf addresses to her over-urgent, overardent admirer Vandenesse: "Has not my confession shown you the *three* children whom I must not fail, on whom I must let my restoring dew fall and my soul shine without adulterating them the least bit? Do not sour a mother's milk!" For pathos, there is nothing better: that unwholesome flavor matters little to Jacques and Madeleine, who are over ten, and as for the third child, who is their father. . . . This conclusion, of itself, is too weak a support to sustain so weighty a judgment, a judgment that grows still heavier with all the weight of the forty volumes of *La Comédie Humaine* plus the *Miscellaneous Works* and the *Correspondance*. Such an opinion cannot end the debate, and I am about to bring forth the reasons adduced, the principal data produced in evidence, and the most important testimony.

Sainte-Beuve, in an article in *La Revue des Deux Mondes*, November 15, 1834, opined that "it is time to consider . . . the supreme novelist of the moment. . . . The author of *Louis Lambert* and *Eugénie Grandet* is no longer a talent whom it is possible to reject or to fail to recognize." The critic chooses the material for his examination from all the works appearing since *Le Dernier Chouan* (1829): *Physiologie du Mariage*, *La Peau de Chagrin*, *Les Scènes de la Vie privée*, *Les Contes Philosophiques*, *Le Médecin de Campagne*, and finally *La Recherche de L'Absolu*, which last novel lends its title to the article. Sainte-Beuve reproaches Balzac for not having "the pure, simple, clean and definitive pattern of the phrase; he retouches its outlines, smudging it, and he overloads; he has a vocabulary that is incoherent and exuberant, in which the words bubble and come up haphazardly, physiological phraseology, scientific terms, and all the risks of mixed colors." And mischievously he quotes a few samples. I select this one: "phrases cast forth by the capillary tubes of the great female conventicle" (*Le Curé de Tours*).

After the death of the novelist, a new, long, and definitive article appeared in *Le Constitutionnel* of September 2, 1850: Sainte-Beuve stated the law that governs the style of Balzac, contrasting it with that of the writers of the seventeenth and eighteenth centuries. The latter "wrote only with their heads, with the upper and completely intellectual part, with the essence of their being." As for Balzac, he throws his "person and his whole organism into his works, and they reveal his personality; he does not write them with pure thought alone, but with his blood and his muscles." This leaves nothing more to be said: the formula is striking and colorful. It has so profound a meaning that henceforward it will reign supreme. We shall see it repeated many times. Style becomes a matter of temperament and nature, and Balzac had "a rich, abundant, and opulent nature." Even today the most famous critics repeat this last qualifier; thanks to Sainte-Beuve, it has become a Homeric, a Balzacian epithet. That style feels the effects of all the humors that circulate in this "herculean," "luxuriant" organism. Nevertheless, "it is subtle, shrewd, flowing, picturesque . . . without any analogy whatsoever with tradition." It is quite often daring, complicated, overloaded, swollen with exaggerations, tangled, murky, trivial, and incorrect. Sainte-Beuve wonders "what effect a book by M. de Balzac would have on an honest mind educated by the reading of Nicole and Bourdaloue, that very serious and scrupulous style, *which goes far,* as La Bruyère used to say; such a mind would be dizzy for a month." The first quality of a writer is "taste before anything else." Samples taken from his works showed that Balzac was often lacking in it.

The second quality is measure: the artist "dominates and governs his work" and "remains superior to his creation." "Intoxicated" with his, the author of *La Comédie Humaine* lets himself be carried away by his own creations; he lapses into the illusive and the inordinate. His style then becomes "ticklish, touchy, softened, and nerveless"; it is a "style having delightful corruptions, quite Asiatic, as our teachers used to say, more broken up in spots and softer than the body of an ancient mime," from the grammatical point of view as well as the moral; the hostile critic underlines *il s'y en va de la vie* (an odd way to express the idea that "life is ebbing away" or "life is at stake") and some far-fetched expressions. Sainte-Beuve, in an appendix to his *Port-Royal* (1860), again spoke vigorously about "the lack of accuracy," the "amplification of the 'glance,'" the "false scientific airs" that affect the diction in Balzac, "the modern side of which is visible to the naked eye."

Although he was still more severe at other points, the critic had no suspicion that his perspicacity would serve to advance the memory of his victim; although the future would prove some of them erroneous, his judgments concerning style were to be used as a springboard by his successors. His remarks were so accurate that they compelled recognition. From them, without always mentioning Sainte-Beuve, later critics drew conclusions adapted to their own theories, literary or otherwise. Some penetrated more deeply into the understanding and the scope of his symbols. Since the time of Sainte-Beuve, clumsiness and maladroitness were admitted, accepted, no longer subject to questioning. Lack of taste, lack of measure, abuse of scientific, physiological, and technical terms—that is the list of defects. Balzac's style breaks with tradition because it springs out of the whole being, because the soul's states are reborn in it: thoughts, emotions, bents, passions, instincts. Balzac writes in his own

way; his way is utterly modern because, in his desire to reproduce the people of his century, he had to reproduce their
vocabulary; his palette adapts itself to the new aspects of morals
and manners. The framework of society, the manners, the needs,
the dress, even the utensils, were rapidly transformed after the
great revolution, as was scientific progress; the mentality of each
social class was affected by it. Being the first who tried to en-
compass this diversity, he had to invent an instrument having
flexibility equal to his minute analyses, metaphors so colored
as to render the least nuances of the external world, the relief of
salient features, and physiognomonic symbols. Let us leave
secondary critics to one side, and give our attention to the
masters.

In his *Nouveaux Essais de Critique et d'Histoire*, Taine
dwells at length on Balzac's style. This brilliant study first appeared in *Journal des Débats*, February, 1858; it will always
carry weight. Like Sainte-Beuve, Taine cites a number of examples of amphigoric, or rambling, style. This for example: "Caroline is a second edition of Nabuchodonosor; for some day, like
the royal chrysalis, she will pass from the furry state of the
animal to the ferocity of the imperial purple. That means that
a stupid woman can become ferocious. The daughters of
Gorgibus spoke in this manner." Along toward 1830, the new,
young literary school triumphed over those who held to the
classic spirit and tradition and to sobriety and orderliness. Taine,
after Sainte-Beuve, contrasts them with the tumultuous aspirations, the capricious sentiments, the varied curiosities of a vast
and very mixed public. Balzac's audience was not made up of
the habitués of the drawing rooms, those elegant, polite, and
discreet people. He addressed himself to the crowd, to the
motley crowd shot through with a thousand currents of ideas
and stirred up with unrestrained emotions. That noisy crowd,
shaken by so much revolution, takes an interest in scientific
ideas, takes a hand in politics and finance and business. A new
public needs a new language. And Taine's conclusion was that
"there are an infinite number of styles . . . as many as there are
centuries, nations, and great minds. . . . To claim the right to
judge all styles by a single rule is as outrageous as the aim of
fitting all minds into a single mold and of reconstructing all the

centuries on the same plan. . . . It is quite certain that this man, regardless of what has been said and what he has done, knew his language; indeed, he knew it better than any one, but he used it his own way."

Everyone knows what prodigious efforts Balzac expended to attain what he believed to be the perfection of style: Théophile Gautier and Desnoiresterres have told with what corrections, what interlineations, what erasures he covered his printers' proofs: a sheet "became a confusion of insertions, a labyrinth." It was cut up with brief vigorous dashes, riddled with added phrases, striped like a zebra, studded with marks and signs. According to Gautier, it looked like "the final display of a burst of fireworks as sketched by a child." Balzac kept on demanding new proofs: he revised them constantly, till he became the horror of the typographers—and of the publishers as well, because of the enormous expense of these revisions. It sometimes happened that, after these modifications, the fifth or sixth proof had not a word of the original text. *Pierrette*, claims Desnoiresterres, was not run off until the twenty-seventh proof. This habit of his often spoiled his style: sometimes the first draft was superior to the last. He was not always able to avoid, as La Fontaine recommended,

> a care too curious,
> And of vain ornaments the effort ambitious
>
> .   .   .
>
> An author spoils everything by wishing to do too well.

This sally of Stendhal is not exactly out of place: "I suppose he does his novels in two stages: first he writes them out soberly, and then he dresses them up in neological style with palpitations of the soul—'snow falls in my heart!' and other lovely things."

Since Taine, critics have done little more than repeat his opinions, some, like Faguet, to stress the defects, others, like Talmeyr, to extol the stylistic qualities, while still others praise and blame in the same paragraph. Brunetière underlines the compatibility with the epoch. Bellessort, with enthusiastic verve, praises the life, the color, the astonishingly rich vocabulary, which adapts itself to the most unexpected relationships between things and beings. After having demonstrated the power of this prodigious speech in the portrait of Cousin Pons, he comments on the expressions with an accuracy and success that win our approval and our admiration, and we freely second his conclusion: "We had nothing comparable in our literature." This criticism is no longer satisfied with mere general appraisals or trite comments: it probes its material, picks out its marvels one by one, happy choices of words by which twenty notions project on the character shafts of the most diverse colors. These beams pass through the character of Pons and let the causes of his mania, of his weakness—he is gluttonous—of his future misfortunes be perceived. Confronted with this result, it can no longer be thought that Balzac "lacks style." People wish to enjoy this verbal magic. There is hardly a smile when some incorrect expression or other trifle passes by, however unbearable to grammarians, they are wisps that the eye can no longer discern in the boiling torrent poured forth by an inspired genius sure of his effects.

It is all too easy to dwell on whatever is open to criticism in Balzac's work. No one denies that in his immense output there are passages to be condemned. To see only these, to dwell on them to the detriment of the many, many pages where his mastery of expression attains artistic perfection—is this not yielding to a temptation to disparage? Some critics failed in this way: Sainte-Beuve, Pontmartin, Caro, Lanson, Faguet, etc. Taine reestablished the artist's reputation. His intelligent initiative opened the way to more equitable inquiries. Paul Flat, in his *Seconds Essais sur Balzac*, shows how the learnings of the novelist, his visual gift, his power of observation and emotion, his scientific and philosophical curiosity, his swarms of acquaintances, his imagination sympathetic to all forms of sensual and moral life, his poetic intuitions—all served by an extraordinary verbal fecundity—gave Balzac the superiority of genius. When he was writing, the abundance of his points of view required a tenseness of effort that is felt in reading him. But this effort protected his writer's talent and kept it at the level of the most accomplished artists. When this effort led to nothing, the pen wandered, stumbled, dragged heavily: it makes one think of a man lost on marshy ground. For all its ingenuity, this psychological reason does not emerge from the speculative mysteries, and, making no positive contribution, it does not advance knowledge.

It is to be hoped that criticism will persevere in the channel in which Gilbert Mayer has directed it with his thorough study *La Qualification affective dans les romans d'Honoré de Balzac.* He shows that the writer was able to vary his effects by the use of epithets; Balzac tried to express infinite shades of meaning, and if necessary, he yoked words together in order to convey degrees of quality, to strengthen a fleeting hint. Thus he succeeded in making a tracing of reality, a transfer, and he never hesitated to make use of popular expressions. Deliberately, spontaneously, moved by the necessity imposed on him by his eagerness for truth, forced by yielding to the fate that poetical intuition imposes on his creations, he abandons purely literary language. "More anxious to create a world than to create a style," says Gilbert Mayer, "Balzac trusts to the real genius of the most everyday speech, which he knows to be capable of expressing even the loftiest ideas, of conveying all the emotions, as the present-day practice of life abundantly proves." Stendhal, George Sand, Mérimée are still very prudent in regard to the current idiom and continue to be users of the literary language. But Balzac knows only one language: from the current of life, he introduces it into the current of literature. It is precisely when he returns to the accepted, "literary" style, for his "bravura" passages, for his "speeches of the author," belabored, polished, "slicked up," that he expresses himself in a grandiloquent, inflated manner. This is artificial Balzac.

It is impossible to form a broad judgment without having explored the special speech attributed in *La Comédie Humaine* to the different social strata: high society, the middle classes, the masses, and, within each of them, the categories that compose it. In addition, it would be necessary to inspect the technical vocabularies: medicine, jurisprudence, church, navy, press, and the rest. The speech of the peasants (*Curé de Village, Les Paysans*), where the deforming pronunciation often sins by adopting tricks and conventions (the *n* that precedes the words beginning with a vowel used by old Mrs. Cibot in *Cousin Pons* and the strange lingua franca of Schmucke in *Cousin Pons* or of Kolb in *Illusions Perudes*). I accept as my own this opinion of Dagnaud: "There is not one Balzac style, but styles of Balzac. It is likely a priori that a scientific study of the facts would reveal a system of fundamental stylistic methods, but this system is susceptible to a host of individual adaptations." [1] We have had occasion to point them out in the course of this study: Balzac the landscape painter, Balzac the portrait artist, Balzac the painter of the jails, Balzac the dialoguist, admirable for his naturalness and for his pathos. The Balzac of grandiloquent nonsense affects only a very small part of *La Comédie Humaine*: it is ridiculous to exalt it to a commonplace. The idea that "Balzac writes badly" has had its day. That noxious formula fades deeper and deeper in the shadow in the face of the triumphant diversity of a style that can be firm or flexible, brutal or ingratiating, radiant or veiled in mystery, in its own good time, when it is necessary, and as it should be, according to people or to situations. It is a fascinating style. This diversity is a phenomenon unique in French literature; it takes its pattern from life itself, never unfolding smoothly, without bumps and jerks. This astonishing diversity of grandeur has never yet been excelled or even equaled.

This diversity is manifest in the *Contes Drolatiques*—an extraordinary success, but exceptional in modern literature. Taine considered its style "admirable and original, very much like the flesh tints of Jordaëns," a comparison that has been taken up and expanded by several critics. These dizains are not to be considered an archeological reconstitution, a scientific imitation of the language of the sixteenth century. Balzac has forged a speech of his own, drawing his inspiration from several centuries in the Middle Ages. He has preserved their vitality, strong savor, and boldness. Rabelais, whom he had read, bequeathed to him certain stylistic methods, such as verbal accumulation, sign of a very rich vocabulary. It is important to underline the relationship of this language to the native disposition of the storyteller:

1 I wish to thank Monsieur Dagnaud, assistant at the Faculté des Lettres in Paris, and Monsieur Gilbert Mayer, professor at the Faculté des Lettres of Rennes, for the readiness with which they have so kindly let me take advantage of their knowledge and their researches on the style and the language of Balzac.

an ardor for life, sensual exuberance of the instincts, unbridled desires for enjoyment. This overwhelming pours out in that varicolored language, "fleshly" and fleshy, lascivious and plump, an overflow of superabundant vitality. It has been called animal vitality; "the joyous boar" of which Théophile Gautier spoke has been evoked. And yet it has been possible to note in certain tales that Balzac had diffused through those debauches, those daring and lascivious paintings, those "hot jets of life," some hues of sentimental coloring, tinged with melancholy, with moral wisdom, in which are discernible certain qualities of style so striking in *La Comédie Humaine.*

Conclusion: Morality and Influence

"THE TIME FOR IMPARTIALITY has not yet arrived for me," wrote
Balzac in 1842, in the "Avant-Propos" to *La Comédie Humaine*.
He had often complained that his works were "little understood,
little appreciated." In France, yes, but not abroad, where his
talent received enthusiastic testimony of admiration, sometimes
"fabulous," said Sainte-Beuve truly. The details may be read
in a brochure by Marcel Bouteron, *Culte de Balzac*. In Italy,
Russia, Austria, Poland, Germany, and Hungary, the novelist,
often in person, was the object of very flattering, touching, and
fervent attention. These marks of veneration proved the profound influence exercised by his novels, not on the ideas only,
but on the mores that they penetrated: the doings and the
gestures of the characters were copied in order to experience their
feelings and sometimes to reenact their adventures. Moreover,
it must not be forgotten with what ardor the feminine French
public—grisettes, middle-class women, and great ladies—ap-
plauded *their* novelist: the thousands of letters he received from
them are not a myth. Balzac's immense success came to him
through the women: they found in him a confidant and a
consoler. He was reproached for this conquest, this ascendancy,
with a kind of vicious ill-temper, by such Catholic critics as
Pontmartin, Caro, and others, pen-pushers without intelligence,
and by the liberal Lerminier (and in our own day by André
Lebreton).

Balzac, sensitive to this reproach constantly hurled at him,
had answered it in 1842 in the "Avant-Propos." The ill-will was

directed at him because he had bared so many ignominies, so many worldly hypocrisies, secretly and vigorously maintained. His boldness angered those who found it advantageous to hide their vile actions under utilitarian conformity. He defended himself hotly and not without skill in his response to Hippolyte Castille, who admired his talent but was saddened to see so many corrupt types darken the Balzacian world. Balzac's argument might be summed up in this sentence: "Is it my fault if the representatives of vice abound on earth? Only the Sovereign Judge will strike the balance between the good and the bad, between the sheep and the goats." Balzac is moral because he makes his reader think.

If, in reading *La Comédie Humaine*, a young man finds little to blame in such men as Lousteau, Lucien de Rubempré, and some others, that young man stands condemned. Anyone who, instead of seeking his fortune as the rakes and the rascals do, does not prefer to play the part of the honest Birotteau, to resemble d'Espard, the hero of *L'Interdiction*, to act like *Le Médecin de Campagne*, to repent as Madame Graslin does, to be a worthy judge like Popinot, to work like David Séchard and D'Arthez, in short to model himself on the good and the virtuous persons sprinkled throughout *La Comédie Humaine* with greater profusion than we find in the real world, that man or woman is one on whom the most Catholic books, the most moral books, will not have the slightest effect.

Balzac was strong enough to speak the truth about morals and to attack the rich and the powerful. He has been reproached with allowing himself to be monopolized by the painting of moral ugliness. But opposite the sinister creatures, we can line up so many ideal figures transfigured by filial love, by conjugal devotion, by charity. To form an equitable judgment on the morality of *La Comédie Humaine* would require a mind capable of a synthesis embracing at one and the same time all the gigantic proportions of that epic work and transmuting into a few metaphysical principles the apperception of such a swarming mass of human beings, where some yield to the obscure complicities of so much animal force and others struggle to victory against unholy desires. In the past, there were cries against the evil sorcery of *La Fille aux Yeux d'Or*. Who would dare deny that fallen humanity, in our time, does not offer a replica of *La Gazette des Tribunaux?* Lucien de Rubempré is an early sample of the zazou style, the "zoot-suiter," the Teddy-boy. Who would deny that *L'Interdiction, La Messe de l'Athée, César Birotteau, Le Médecin de Campagne, Pierrette,* and *L'Envers de l'Histoire Contemporaine* lift up the best of our being, our soul, toward the heights of goodness, in a wholly spiritual atmosphere? There may be vulgarities, baseness, and trivialities in *La Comédie Humaine,* but there is no "vindication of evil" in it, whatever Count Armand de Pontmartin may have said. Like the spectacle we call life, it offers both good and evil. Everyone is free to choose his company. There comes a time in life when obligations mix you with good people and with evil. Virtue consists in maintaining one's will and one's judgment in what we believe to be the good: it is the struggle between the flesh and the spirit, sanctioned by Christ. We are addressing ourselves now to the cultivated minds for whom beauty does not exist without truth. (Balzac figures in the Catalogue of the Index: Honoré de Balzac, "omnes fabulae amatoriae." *Decrees of the Congregation of the Index,* September 16, 1841, January 28, 1842, June 20, 1864.) The falseness, the insipidity, the platitudes and dullness of convention are not a proper climate for determining opinion or esteem. An aesthetic worthy of the name cannot be founded on prejudices. We must rejoice that the hour for impartiality, so long awaited by Balzac, has struck. Around his work are gathering intelligent spirits, animated only by the desire to bring out all that those works hold of the human and the divine, of vital dynamism and artistic splendor.

The time is past when *La Comédie Humaine* was classed as a compilation of erotica. One of its merits is precisely that it offers us novels other than those of love, and before Balzac, love was the only passion that could be the soul of the novel. Balzac wanted to record all the passions, in all their varieties, as we have demonstrated. Thus, he provided as grazing land for the talent of his followers an immense and more nourishing range. Indeed, his literary influence began to be felt during his lifetime.

Balzac, the father of realism, had shown that the real has aesthetic and moral value. Those who came after him—Flaubert, Maupassant, the Goncourts, Daudet, Zola—while they preserved their own originality, continued to seek their subjects in the world around them, in their personal experiences. This influence had had wide extensions, invading the intellectual universe, as E. R. Curtius, in his *Balzac*, devoted an entire chapter to proving.

It is impossible to be ignorant of the fact that Balzacian erudition had as its pioneer Viscount Spoelberch de Lovenjoul, whose generous tenacity accumulated what might be called the Balzacian Archives; this is a treasury of documents that he donated to the Institut de France. His *Histoire des Oeuvres de Balzac* is an epitome of indispensable information, which no student of Balzac, no literary historian, can afford to neglect.

The cult of Balzac has found fervent adherents in the United States. They have devoted their efforts especially to the technical methods of the novelist, and to them we owe some valuable studies, which have done much to advance our knowledge of an art possessed of unsuspected resources.

To be complete, the influence of Balzac on the political and social ideas of the beginning of the twentieth century should not be forgotten. The continuer of Bonald and Joseph de Maistre—such is the aspect of Balzac that Paul Bourget emphasizes, while socialist writers draw from his works ferment for social renovation and progress.

Does not this clash of contradictory opinions show that *La Comédie Humaine* is above all that microcosm which reproduces in all its grandeur and its diversity the real and palpitating image of humanity? So it is that each of its readers is finally under the spell of Balzac's art, which is akin to magic: he is fascinated. And because Balzac transmutes miseries and joys— our own—into poetry, we not only admire the writer, but we give the man, in spite of his defects, our feelings of friendship and of gratitude.

A. *Etudes de Moeurs* (Studies of Morals and Manners)

I. SCÈNES DE LA VIE PRIVÉE
(SCENES FROM PRIVATE LIFE)

Action		First Publication
Before 1815	La Maison du Chat-qui-pelote (At the Sign of the Cat and Racket)	1830
1819	Le Bal de Sceaux (The Sceaux Ball)	1830
1825–33	Mémoires de deux Jeunes Mariées (Letters of Two Brides)	1841–42
1819	La Bourse (The Purse)	1832
1829	Modeste Mignon	1844
1822–38	Un Début dans la Vie (A Start in Life)	1842
1834–35	Albert Savarus	1842
1800–15	La Vendetta	1830
1806–33	Une Double Famille (A Second Home)	1830
1809	La Paix de Ménage (The Peace of a Home)	1830
1822–24	Madame Firmiani	1832
1822	Etude de Femme (A Study of Woman)	1830
1835–42	La Fausse Maîtresse (The Imaginary Mistress)	1841
1833–34	Une Fille d'Eve (A Daughter of Eve)	1830–39

1 Listed in the so-called traditional order, with the date of the plot's action and the date of publication. From the table drawn up by Ethel Preston, *Recherches sur la Technique de Balzac*, pp. 276–78, and from the table drawn up by Marcel Bouteron in his *Introduction à l'édition de la "Comédie Humaine,"* (La Pléiade, N.R.F., 1935) pp. xxiv–xxvi.

	Action		*First Publication*
1819	Le Message (The Message)		1832
1820	La Grenadière		1832
1822	La Femme abandonnée (The Deserted Woman)		1832
1836, 1824–30	Honorine		1843
1836–39	Béatrix		1839
1830, 1806	Gobseck		1830
1813–44	La Femme de Trente Ans (A Woman of Thirty)		1831–44
1819–20	Le Père Goriot (Old Goriot)		1834–35
1818–40	Le Colonel Chabert (Colonel Chabert)		1832
1821–31	La Messe de l'Athée (The Atheist's Mass)		1836
1821–27	Le Contrat de Mariage (A Marriage Settlement)		1835
1828	L'Interdiction (The Commission in Lunacy)		1836
1830, 1815–16	Autre Etude de Femme (Another Study of Woman)		1842

II.   SCÈNES DE LA VIE DE PROVINCE
        (SCENES FROM PROVINCIAL LIFE)

	Action		*First Publication*
1829–37	Ursule Mirouët		1841
1819–33	Eugénie Grandet		1833
	Les Célibataires: (The Celibates)		
1827–28	Vol. I.	Pierrette	1840
1826	Vol. II.	Le Curé de Tours (The Vicar of Tours)	1832
1792–1839	Vol. III.	La Rabouilleuse (A Bachelor's Establishment)	1841–42
	Les Parisiens en Province: (Parisians in the Country)		
1830–31	Vol. I.	L'Illustre Gaudissart (The Illustrious Gaudissart)	1833
1836–43	Vol. II.	La Muse du Département (The Muse of the Department)	1843
	Les Rivalités: (The Jealousies of a Country Town)		

Action			First Publication
1816	Vol. I.	La Vieille Fille (The Old Maid)	1837
1822–24	Vol. II.	Le Cabinet des Antiques (The Gallery of Antiquities)	1836–38, 1839
1819–23	Illusions Perdues: (Lost Illusions)		1837–39, 1843
	Vol. I.	Les deux Poètes (The Two Poets)	
	Vol. II.	Un grand Homme de Province à Paris (A Distinguished Provincial at Paris)	
	Vol. III.	Les Souffrances de l'Inventeur (The Sufferings of the Inventor)	

III. SCÈNES DE LA VIE PARISIENNE
(SCENES FROM PARISIAN LIFE)
Histoire des Treize:
(The Thirteen)

Action			First Publication
1819	Vol. I.	Ferragus	1833
1818–29	Vol. II.	La Duchesse de Langeais (The Duchess of Langeais)	1833–34
1815	Vol. III.	La Fille aux Yeux d'Or (The Girl with the Golden Eyes)	1834–35
1819–23	L'Histoire de la Grandeur et de la Décadence de César Birotteau (The Rise and Fall of César Birotteau)		1837
1836, 1826	La Maison Nucingen (The Firm of Nucingen)		1838
1824–30, 1845	Splendeurs et Misères des Courtisanes: (Scenes from a Courtesan's Life)		1839–47
	Vol. I.	Comment aiment les Filles (How Girls Love)	
	Vol. II.	A combien l'Amour revient aux Vieillards (What Love Costs Old Men)	
	Vol. III.	Où mènent les mauvais chemins (Where Evil Roads Lead)	
	Vol. IV.	La dernière incarnation de Vautrin (Vautrin's Last Avatar)	

Action		*First Publication*
1830–33	Les Secrets de la Princesse de Cadignan (The Secrets of a Princess)	1839
1822	Facino Cane	1836
1830, 1758	Sarrasine	1831
1832	Pierre Grassou	1840
	Les Parents Pauvres: (Poor Relations)	
1838–44	Vol. I. La Cousine Bette (Cousin Betty)	1846
1844–45	Vol. II. Le Cousin Pons (Cousin Pons)	1847
1840, 1833	Un Homme d'Affaires (A Man of Business)	1845
1830–37	Un Prince de la Bohême (A Prince of Bohemia)	1840
ca. 1844	Gaudissart II	1844
1824–30	Les Employés (The Government Clerks)	1837
1846	Les Comédiens sans le savoir (The Unconscious Humorists)	1846
1830–40	Les Petits Bourgeois (The Middle Classes)	posthumously
1809–36	L'Envers de l'Histoire Contemporaine (The Seamy Side of Contemporary History)	1842–46

IV.   SCÈNES DE LA VIE POLITIQUE (SCENES FROM POLITICAL LIFE)

1793	Un Episode sous la Terreur (An Episode under the Terror)	1830
1803–06, 1834	Une Ténébreuse Affaire (The Gondreville Mystery)	1841
1839	Le Député d'Arcis (The Deputy from Arcis)	1847
1836	Z. Marcas	1840

V.   SCÈNES DE LA VIE MILITAIRE (SCENES FROM MILITARY LIFE)

1799	Les Chouans (The Chouans)	1829
	Une Passion dans le Désert (A Passion in the Desert)	1830

VI.   SCÈNES DE LA VIE DE CAMPAGNE (SCENES FROM COUNTRY LIFE)

1823–26	Les Paysans (The Peasantry)	1844

Action		First Publication
1829	Le Médecin de Campagne (The Country Doctor)	1833
1829–43	Le Curé de Village (The Village Rector)	1838–39
1809–36	Le Lys dans la Vallée (The Lily of the Valley)	1835

B. *Etudes Philosophiques* (Philosophical Studies)

1830–31	La Peau de Chagrin (The Magic Skin)	1831
after 1426	Jésus-Christ en Flandre (Jesus Christ in Flanders)	1831
before 1822	Melmoth Réconcilié (Melmoth Absolved)	1835
1820	Massimilla Doni	1839
1612	Le Chef-d'Oeuvre Inconnu (The Unknown Masterpiece)	1831
1831–37	Gambara	1837
1812–24	La Recherche de l'Absolu (In Quest of the Absolute)	1834
1591–1617	L'Enfant Maudit (A Father's Curse)	1831–36
1812–19	Adieu (Farewell)	1830
1811	Les Marana	1832
1793	Le Réquisitionnaire (The Conscript)	1831
1808	El Verdugo	1830
1824	Un Drame au Bord de la Mer (A Seaside Tragedy)	1835
1479	Maître Cornélius (Master Cornelius)	1831
1799–1819	L'Auberge Rouge (The Red Inn)	1831
	Sur Catherine de Médicis: (About Catherine de Medicis)	
1560	Vol. I. Le Martyr Calviniste (The Calvinist Martyr)	1841
1573	Vol. II. Le Secret des Ruggieri (The Secret of the Ruggieri)	1836–37
1786	Vol. III. Les Deux Rêves (The Two Dreams)	1831
1500–1600	L'Elixir de Longue Vie (The Elixir of Life)	1830
1308	Les Proscrits (The Exiles)	1831

	First
Action	*Publication*
1812–24 Louis Lambert	1832–33
1799–1800 Séraphîta	1835

C. *Etudes Analytiques* (Analytical Studies)

1824–28	Physiologie du Mariage	1829
	(Physiology of Marriage)	
1830–45	Petites Misères de la Vie Conjugale	1830, 1840,
	(Petty Troubles of Married Life)	1845

I. EDITIONS

Oeuvres complètes (Complete Works). Illustrated edition, text revised and annotated by Marcel Bouteron and Henri Longnon. 40 vols. Paris: Conard, 1912–40.

La Comédie Humaine. Pléiade edition, 10 vols.; "Introduction," dealing with the history of the work, by Marcel Bouteron. Vol. XI, *Contes Drolatiques*; a Balzac chronology; Preface to the *Comédie Humaine*; *Oeuvres ébauchées* (Outlined Works), short accounts concerning each of the works included in the eleven vols.; important bibliography (pp. 981, 1,114, 1,822) by Roger Pierrot. *Index des personnes réelles et les allusions littéraires*; *Index des personnages fictifs de la Comédie Humaine* pp. 1,123–1,708, by Fernand Lotte. Paris: Gallimard, 1959.

Classiques Garnier: M. Allem, 13 vols. *Illusions perdues*, *Splendeurs et misères des courtisanes* by Antoine Adam. *Histoire des Treize*, *Vieille Fille*, *Père Goriot*, ed. by Pierre-Georges Castex. *Les Chouans*, *L'Envers de l'Histoire Contemporaine*, ed. by Maurice Regard.

Annotated collected editions: *La Comédie Humaine*, reviews by Albert Prioult (Hazan, 1947–53; 13 vols. published).

Oeuvres complètes illustrées (Complete Works, illustrated) Givors, 31 vols. Notes by Maurice Bardèche, and *Oeuvres complètes*, Club de l'Honnête Homme, illustrated documentary, in process, 15 vols. published. *L'Oeuvre de Balzac* (The Work of Balzac), *Formes et reflets*; each work prefaced by a contemporary writer; chronology of *La Comédie Humaine* by F. Lotte,

1950–53, 16 vols.; 2d ed., corrected, Club Français du Livre, 1953–55.

Correspondence: *Correspondance générale* (Michel Lévy, 1876, Vol. XXIV), detestable edition, not yet entirely supplanted. *Lettres à l'Etrangère*, 1833–47, annotated by Marcel Bouteron, 4 vols. published by C. Lévy; Vol. V in preparation, annotated by Roger Pierrot. Selections, Feb.–Sept., 1848, published in *Revue de Paris*, Nov., 1949, Aug., 1950 and 1952 by M. Bouteron. Sept.–Oct., 1954, Nov., 1956, Aug., 1957, Aug., 1959, by R. Pierrot. *Choix de Correspondance* (selections) by Ducourneau, Club Français du Livre, 1955, Vol. XVI.

Correspondance avec Zulma Carraud, ed. by M. Bouteron, 2d ed. rev., Gallimard, 1951.

Lettres à sa famille, published by W. S. Hastings, Albin Michel, 1950.

Cahiers balzaciens (Balzacian Notebooks), 1923–28, ed. by M. Bouteron, No. 1 with *Périolas*; No. 6, *Duchesse de Castries*; No. 8, *Dr. Nacquart*, Lapina.

Correspondance, collected, classified, and annotated by R. Pierrot (Garnier, Vol. I, Oct., 1960), bringing together all known letters of Balzac, except those to Madame Hanska and her family, and numerous letters addressed to Balzac.

II. GENERAL WORKS

Vicomte de Spoelberch de Lovenjoul, *Histoire des Oeuvres de Honoré de Balzac*, 3d ed., Calman-Lévy, 1888.

Fernand Lotte, *Dictionnaire biographique des personnages fictifs de la Comédie Humaine*, Corti, 1952, and *Dictionnaire des personnes anonymes*, Corti, 1956, Vol. XI, Pléiade.

E. Preston, *Technique, Retour systématique des personnages dans la Comédie Humaine*, Presses Françaises, 1926.

Marc Blanchard, *Témoignages et jugements sur Balzac* (Testimony and Opinions on Balzac), H. Champion, 1931.

P.-G. Castex, "Où en sont les études balzaciennes" (Present State of Balzac Studies), in *Information Littéraire*, Nov., Dec., 1955.

M. Bouteron, *Etudes balzaciennes*, Jouve, 1954.

F. Marceau, *Balzac et son monde* (Balzac and His World), Gallimard, 1955.

William H. Royce, A *Balzac Bibliography*, Chicago, 1929, 3 vols.

Philippe Bertault, *Introduction à Balzac*, Odilis, 1953, pp. 109–54.

Cf. the graph of critical opinions on Balzac up to 1953, including the immense production of the 1949–50 Centenary.[1]

III. BIOGRAPHY

André Billy, *Vie de Balzac* (Life of Balzac), 2 vols. illus., Flammarion, 2d ed., 1947.

L. J. Arrigon, *Les Débuts littéraires d'Honoré de Balzac*, Perrin, 1924. *Les Années romantiques de Balzac*, Perrin, 1927. *Balzac et la "Contessa,"* Portiques, undated.

Gabriel Hanotaux and Georges Vicaire, *La Jeunesse de Balzac, Imprimeur*, 1826–1838 (The Youth of Balzac, the Printer); *Balzac et Madame de Berny*, Ferroud, 1921.

G. Ruxton, *La Dilecta de Balzac* (Balzac's 'La Dilecta'), Plon-Nourrit, 1909.

René Bouvier and Edouard Maynial, *Les Comptes dramatiques de Balzac* (The Dramatic Accounts of Balzac), Sorlot, 1938.

Sophie de Korwin-Piotrowska, *Balzac et le Monde slave, Madame Hanska et l'Oeuvre balzacienne* (Balzac and the Slavic

---

1 It is necessary here to call attention to the Balzac Centenary, celebrated by two International Congresses of Literary History of France, one at Tours (May 28–31, 1949), the other in Paris, at the Sorbonne (Nov. 13–17, 1950), and by "Balzac Days" at the International Cultural Center of Royaumont (Nov. 18–19, 1952). This Centenary stimulated in the Balzacian universe a superabundance of learned research, historical works, new studies, works of criticism, expositions, congresses in the provinces and abroad, commemorations, and so on. Let us mention: *Balzac et la Touraine*, by H. Hennion (Gilbert Clarey). *Balzac, le Livre du Centenaire* (Balzac, the Book of the Centenary), with Introduction by Jacques R. Duron, (Flammarion, 1952). These two volumes, published under official auspices, reproduce the integral text of the speeches, communications, and lectures. The *Catalogues* of the Exposition at the Bibliothèque Nationale, at the Musée of Tours, at the bookstore of Paul Bérès. The collection of 1950–53, of the *Reviews*: Au Jardin de la France, Etudes balzaciennes, Courrier balzacien, Mercure de France, Revue d'Histoire Littéraire de la France, Revue des Sciences Humaines (Lille), Revue de Littérature Comparée. *Introduction à Balzac* by Philippe Bertault (Paris: Odilis, 1953) gives a glimpse of the two congresses and of the immense bibliographical production of the Centenary.

World; Madame Hanska and the Work of Balzac), Champion, 1933.

IV. CRITICISM

Literary genesis and creations, philosophy: In addition to Théophile Gautier, Sainte-Beuve, and Taine, already cited, we recommend:

Albert Prioult, *Balzac avant La Comédie Humaine* (Balzac Before the Human Comedy), Courville, 1936.

Maurice Bardèche, *Balzac romancier* (Balzac as Novelist), Plon, 1940.

Ph. Bertault, *Balzac et la Religion*, Boivin, 1942.

Bernard Guyon, *La Pensée politique et sociale de Balzac* (Balzac's Political and Social Thought), Colin, 1947; *La Création littéraire chez Balzac* (Literary Creation in Balzac), Colin, 195.

P.-G. Castex, *Le Conte fantastique en France de Nodier à Maupassant* (The Fantastic Tale in France), Corti, 1951.

H. Evans, *Louis Lambert et la philosophie de Balzac*, Corti, 1951.

Jean Pommier, *L'Invention et l'Ecriture dans "La Torpille" d'Honoré de Balzac* (Invention and Writing in "The Torpedo" of Balzac), Droz et Minard, Geneva, 1957.

E. Curtius (trans. Henri Jourdan), *Balzac*, Stock, 1943.

Ch. Bruneau, *Histoire de la Langue française* by F. Brunot, Vol. XII, Book V, Colin, 1948.

F. Baldensperger, *Orientations étrangères chez Balzac* (Foreign Orientations in Balzac), Champion, 1927.

Morceaux choisis d'Honoré de Balzac, with introduction and notes by Joachim Merlant, Didier, 1912. An excellent initiation.

Abraham, Pierre, 68
Abrantès, Duchess of, viii, 30, 37
Academy, the, see French Academy
Academy of Moral and Political Sciences, 96
Adieu, 38, 63, 158, 164
Agoult, Countess d', 30
Albert Savarus, 15, 36
Altzyler, Helen, 150n
Ancillon, Pastor, 86
Angers, David d', xiv
Annette et le Criminel, see *Argow-le-Pirate*
Apollonius of Tyana, 66
"Apostrophe, L'," 11
Apponyi, Countess, x
Argow-le-Pirate, 4, 21, 22, 60, 132, 146, 173, 175
Arrault, Albert, 15n, 37
Art de payer des dettes, L', 23n
Artois, Count of, 37
atheism, 20, 91
Atkinson, Norah, 126n
Auberge Rouge, L', 29, 33–34, 60, 63, 109
Aubrée, Etienne, 37
Autre Etude de Femme, 31, 33, 101, 150–51
"Avant-Propos" (to *La Comédie Humaine*), xiv, 82, 103–104, 120, 129–31 *passim*, 146, 191
Aventures administratives d'une idée heureuse, Les, 80

Baader, Franz von, 86, 130
Bacon, Francis, 86
Bagration, Princess, ix, 30
Bal de Sceaux, Le, 158, 160, 165
Ballanche, Pierre, 101, 102
Balssa, Louis, 5
Balthazar, 67
Balzac, Anne Charlotte Sallambier, vii, xv–xvi, 4, 6–8, 91
Balzac, Bernard François, 3–6, 91
Balzac, Henri, 6
Balzac, J. L. Guez de, 122
Balzac, Laure, vii, 4, 6, 9
Balzac, Laurence, 6
Balzac d'Entragues, 6
Bardèche, Maurice, 22, 134, 136
Barrès, Maurice, 118
Barrière, Marcel, 122
Baumann, Emile, 40, 118
Bazin, René, 118
Béatrix, xii, 17, 36, 41, 100, 104, 108, 153, 172
Beau Juif, Le, see *Clothilde de Lusignan*
Beaumarchais (Pierre Augustin Caron), 22
Bedel, Maurice, 13
Bella Imperia, La, ix
Bellesort, André, 32, 125, 186
Belloy, Auguste de, xi, 129
Béranger, Pierre de, 126
Bergson, Henri, 86n
Bernanos, Paul, 118

Valette, Hélène de, xii
Vautrin, xiii, 181
Vendetta, La, 175
Verdugo, El, 38, 63
Verkade, 78–79
Vernon, Félicien, 43, 44
Vicaire des Ardennes, Le, 21, 175
Vidocq, François, 37
Vie du Grand Monde, Une, 34
Vieille Fille, La, 15, 36, 100, 153, 159, 175
Viellerglé (pseudonym of Honoré de Balzac), 21
Viemars, Loëve, 60
Villeneuve-Bargement, Viscount of, 96
Villers, M. de, 37

Voleur, Le, xiii, 90
Voltaire, François de, 5, 19, 27, 91, 112, 142, 170
"Voyage de Paris à Java," 38

Wann-Chlore, see Jane la Pâle
Weelen, M. E., 37
Weill, Alexandre, 125–26
Werdet, x, xii, 90n

Zéro, see Jésus-Christ en Flandre
Z. Marcas, 9, 36
Zola, Emile, 32, 193